Principles, Definitions

E...

Draft Common Frame of Reference (DCFR)

Interim Outline Edition

Principles, Definitions and Model Rules of European Private Law

Draft Common Frame of Reference (DCFR)

Interim Outline Edition

Prepared by the

Study Group on a European Civil Code

and the

Research Group on EC Private Law (Acquis Group)

Based in part on a revised version of the Principles of
European Contract Law

Edited by

Christian von Bar, Eric Clive and Hans Schulte-Nölke

and

**Hugh Beale, Johnny Herre, Jérôme Huet,
Peter Schlechtriem†, Matthias Storme, Stephen Swann,
Paul Varul, Anna Veneziano and Fryderyk Zoll**

sellier.

**european law
publishers**

More texts by the Study Group and the Acquis Group are available at www.law-net.eu.

The print of this edition was supported by the Dieter Fuchs Stiftung in Dissen (Germany).

ISBN 978-3-86653-059-1

The Deutsche Nationalbibliothek lists this publication in the Deutsche Nationalbibliografie; detailed bibliographic data are available in the Internet at http://dnb.d-nb.de.

The Index was prepared by Rechtsanwältin Dr. Martina Schulz, Pohlheim.

Design: Sandra Sellier, Munich. Production: Karina Hack, Munich. Typesetting: fidus Publikations-Service GmbH, Augsburg. Printing and binding: Friedrich Pustet KG, Regensburg. Printed on acid-free, non-ageing paper. Printed in Germany.

Table of contents

Introduction

How the DCFR may be used as preparatory work for the CFR

Next steps

General

I. **DCFR and CFR distinguished.** In this volume the Study Group on a European Civil Code and the Research Group on Existing EC Private Law (the 'Acquis Group') present the first academic Draft of a Common Frame of Reference (DCFR). It contains Principles, Definitions and Model Rules of European Private Law in an interim outline edition. Among other goals its completion fulfils an obligation to the European Commission undertaken in 2005. The Commission's Research Directorate-General funded part of the work. One purpose of the text is to serve as a draft for drawing up a 'political' Common Frame of Reference (CFR) which was called for by the European Commission's 'Action Plan on A More Coherent European Contract Law' of January 2003.[1] As is explained more precisely below, the DCFR and the CFR must be clearly distinguished. The DCFR serves several other important purposes.

2. An interim outline edition of the DCFR. The DCFR is being published first in an interim outline edition. It is an interim edition because in the final edition this text will be completed with additional material in the form of model rules in Book IV on certain further specific contracts and the rights and obligations arising from them, and in Books VIII to X on selected matters of property law. It is an outline edition because this first edition appears without comments and notes. The European Commission received in December 2007 the material published here along with an explanatory and illustrative commentary on each model rule. The Commission has also received a substantial part of the extensive comparative legal material which has been gathered and digested in the past years. It was too early at present, however, for the entire work to be published in book form. The tight timeframe has not made it possible at this time to edit all the notes in a manner commensurate with the standards of an international scholarly publication.

3. The timing and nature of this edition. The timing and nature of this interim outline edition are essentially explained by the commitment in the contract with the Research Directorate-General to submit a first draft of the DCFR by the end of 2007. Many experts are aware of that commitment and there is already an appreciable interest in what the first draft will look like. Conferences and university courses are being planned in the expectation that it will be readily available. In the short period of time which remains until completion of the full edition (namely, until the end of 2008) that interest

---

[1]   COM (2003) final, OJ C 63/1 (referred to below as Action Plan).

can best be satisfied by the publication of an (inexpensive) paperback. The hope is that this publication will not only meet a need but also elicit responses and criticisms in time for them to be taken into account during the preparation of the full edition. Any contributions to the discussion should be made as soon as possible; the editorial deadline for the full edition will be the end of September 2008. The complete edition will be voluminous. It will invite study at one's desk at home or in the office, but will be too bulky to pack into luggage taken to meetings or conferences. That is another reason for publishing this edition in outline form, essentially Articles only.

4. An academic, not a politically authorised text. It must be stressed that this text originates in an initiative of European legal scholars. It amounts to the compression into rule form of decades of independent research and co-operation by academics with expertise in private law, comparative law and European Community law. The independence of the two Groups and of all the contributors has been maintained and respected unreservedly throughout. That in turn has made it possible to take on board many of the suggestions received in the course of meetings with stakeholders who indicated weaknesses in early working papers. The two Groups alone bear responsibility for the content of this draft. In particular, the draft does not contain a single rule or definition or principle which has been approved or mandated by a politically legitimated body at European or national level (save, of course, where it coincides with existing EU or national legislation). It may be that the DCFR at a later point in time will be carried over at least in part into a CFR, but that is a question for others to decide. This introduction merely sets out some considerations which might usefully be taken into account during the possible process of transformation.

5. About this introduction. This introduction explains the purposes pursued in preparing the DCFR and outlines its contents, underlying principles, coverage and structure. It elucidates the relationship between the DCFR and the publications which have already appeared or will appear in the course of the preparatory work. It sketches out how the DCFR might flow into the development of the CFR. Finally it looks towards the next steps. The introduction has been agreed with the Compilation and Redaction Team of both Groups.

The purposes of the DCFR

6. A possible model for a political CFR. As already indicated, this Draft is (among other things) a possible model for an actual or 'political' Common Frame of Reference (CFR). The DCFR presents a concrete text, hammered out in all its detail, to those who will be deciding whether or to what end or by what means there will be a CFR. At the time of writing it appears that none of these three questions is definitively resolved politically. Even if a CFR should emerge, it would not necessarily, of course, have the same coverage and contents as this DCFR. The question of which functions the DCFR can perform in the development of the CFR is considered under paragraphs 60-76 of this introduction.

7. Legal science, research and education. The DCFR ought not to be regarded merely as a building block of a possible Common Frame of Reference. The DCFR would stand on its own and retain its significance even if a CFR were not to emerge. The DCFR is an academic text. It sets out the results of a large European research project and invites evaluation from that perspective. The full breadth of that scholarly endeavour will be apparent when the final edition is published. Independent of the fate of the CFR, it is hoped that the DCFR will promote knowledge of private law in the jurisdictions of the European Union, and in particular will help to show how much national private laws resemble one another and have provided mutual stimulus for development and indeed how much those laws may be regarded as regional manifestations of an overall common European legacy. The function of the DCFR is thus detached from that of the CFR in that it serves to sharpen awareness of the existence of a European private law and also (via the comparative notes that will appear in the final edition) to demonstrate the relatively small number of cases in which the different legal systems produce substantially different answers to common problems. The DCFR may furnish the notion of a European private law with a new foundation which increases understanding for 'the others' and promotes collective deliberation on private law in Europe.

8. A possible source of inspiration. The drafters of the DCFR nurture the hope that it will be seen also outside the academic world as a text from which inspiration can be gained for suitable solutions for private law questions. Shortly after their publication the Principles of European Contract Law (PECL),[2] which the DCFR incorporates in a partly revised form (see paragraphs 50-54), received the attention of many higher courts in Europe and of numerous official bodies

---

[2] Ole Lando and Hugh Beale (eds.), Principles of European Contract Law Parts I and II. Prepared by the Commission on European Contract Law (The Hague 1999); Ole Lando, Eric Clive, André Prüm and Reinhard Zimmermann (eds.), Principles of European Contract Law Part III (The Hague, London and Boston 2003). Translations are available in French (Principes du droit européen du contract. Version française préparée par Georges Rouhette, avec le concours de Isabelle de Lamberterie, Denis Tallon et Claude Witz, Droit privé comparé et européen, vol. 2, Paris 2003); German (Grundregeln des Europäischen Vertragsrechts, Teile I und II, Kommission für Europäisches Vertragsrecht. Deutsche Ausgabe von Christian von Bar und Reinhard Zimmermann, München 2002; Grundregeln des Europäischen Vertragsrechts Teil III, Kommission für Europäisches Vertragsrecht. Deutsche Ausgabe von Christian von Bar und Reinhard Zimmermann, München 2005); Italian (Commissione per il Diritto Europeo dei Contratti. Principi di Diritto Europeo dei Contratti, Parte I & II, Edizione italiana a cura di Carlo Castronovo, Milano 2001; Commissione per il Diritto Europeo dei Contratti. Principi di Diritto Europeo dei Contratti, Parte III. Edizione italiana a cura di Carlo Castronovo, Milano 2005) and Spanish (Principios de Derecho Contractual Europeo, Partes I y II. Edición española a cargo de Pilar Barres Bennloch, José Miguel Embid Irujo, Fernando Martínes Sanz, Madrid 2003). Matthias Storme translated the articles of Parts I-III into Dutch (Tijdschrift voor privaatrecht 2005, 1181-1241); M.-A. Zachariasiewicz and J. Bełdowski translated the PECL articles of Parts I and II (Kwartalnik Prawa Prywatnego 3/2004, 814-881) and J. Bełdowski and A. Kozioł the articles of Part III (Kwartalnik Prawa Prywatnego 3/2006, 847-859) into the Polish language. For further translations (sometimes of the articles of Books I and II only) see http://frontpage.cbs.dk/law/commission_on_european_con tract_law/index.html.

charged with preparing the modernisation of the relevant national law of contract. It is possible that this development will continue in the context of the DCFR with repercussions for reform projects beyond as well as within the European Union. If the content of the DCFR convinces, it may contribute to a harmonious and informal Europeanisation of private law.

Contents of the DCFR

9. Principles, definitions and model rules. The DCFR contains 'principles, definitions and model rules'. The title of this book follows the scheme set out in the European Commission's communications (referred to below in para. 60) and in our contract with the Commission. The notion of 'definitions' is reasonably clear. The notions of 'principles' and 'model rules', however, appear to overlap and require some explanation.

10. Meaning of 'principles'. The European Commission's communications concerning the CFR do not elaborate on the concept of 'principles'. The word is susceptible to different interpretations. It is sometimes used, in the present context, as a synonym for rules which do not have the force of law. This is how it appears to be used, for example, in the 'Principles of European Contract Law' (PECL), which refer to themselves in Article 1:101(1) as 'Principles ... intended to be applied as general *rules* of contract law in the European Union' (italics added). The word appears to be used in a similar sense in the Unidroit Principles of International Commercial Contracts. In this sense the DCFR could be said to consist of principles and definitions. It is essentially of the same nature as those other instruments in relation to which the word 'principles' has become familiar. The word 'principles' might also be reserved for those rules which are of a more general nature, such as those on freedom of contract or good faith. In this sense the DCFR, in its present form and without more, could be said to consist already of principles, model rules and definitions.

11. **Underlying principles.** The word 'principles' surfaces occasionally in the Commission communications mentioned already, but with the prefix 'fundamental' attached. That suggests that it may have been meant to denote essentially abstract basic values. The model rules of course build on such underlying principles in any event, whether they are stated or not. It would be possible to include in the DCFR a separate part which states these basic values and suggests factors that the legislator should bear in mind when seeking to strike a balance between them. For example, this part could be formulated as recitals, i.e. an introductory list of reasons for the essential substance of the following text. To give some idea of what this might look like, at least in relation to contract law, some possible fundamental principles are outlined at paragraphs 22-36, but without any claim to comprehensiveness. If this idea is thought to be useful, a fuller version could be developed at a later stage. It must be conceded, however, that, taken in isolation, such fundamental principles do not advance matters much at a practical level because of their high level of abstraction. Abstract principles tend to contradict one another. They always have to be weighed up against one another more exactly because only then are optimal outcomes assured. That task, in turn, can only be accomplished with the help of well-formulated model rules. The fact that the word 'principles' might be construed quite naturally in this sense of 'fundamental principles' is a good reason for including 'model rules' in the title.

12. **Definitions.** 'Definitions' have the function of suggestions for the development of a uniform European legal terminology. DCFR I.–1:103(1) ('The definitions in Annex 1 apply for all the purposes of these rules unless otherwise provided or the context otherwise requires') expressly incorporates the list of terminology in Annex 1 as part of the DCFR. This drafting technique, by which the definitions are set out in an appendage to the main text, was chosen in order to keep the first chapter short and to enable the list of terminology to be extended at any time without great editorial labour. The substance is partly distilled from the *acquis*, but predominantly derived from the model rules of the DCFR. If the definitions are essential for the model rules, it is also true that the model rules are essential for the definitions. There would be little value in a set of

definitions which was internally incoherent. The definitions can be seen as components which can be used in the making of rules and sets of rules, but there is no point in having components which are incompatible with each other and cannot fit together. In contrast to a dictionary of terms assembled from disparate sources, the definitions in the Annex have been tested in the model rules and revised and refined as the model rules have developed. Ultimately, useful definitions cannot be composed without model rules and useful model rules can hardly be drafted without definitions.

13. **Model rules.** The greatest part of the DCFR consists of 'model rules'. The adjective 'model' indicates that the rules are not put forward as having any normative force but are soft law rules of the kind contained in the Principles of European Contract Law and similar publications. Whether particular rules might be used as a model for early legislation, for example, for the improvement of the internal coherence of the *acquis communautaire* (see further below, para. 61 ff) is for others to decide.

14. **Comments and notes.** In the full edition the model rules will be supplemented by comments and notes. The comments will elucidate each rule, will often illustrate its application by means of examples, and will outline the critical policy considerations at stake. The notes will reflect the legal position in the individual national legal systems and, so far as extant, the current Community law. How the notes were assembled is described in the section on the academic contributors and our funders.

Aims and underlying values

15. **Ongoing discussion on 'fundamental principles'.** As already explained in para. 11, it is still open whether the CFR should be introduced by some 'Fundamental Principles' which reflect its underlying values, to assist the reader to understand the CFR more fully and to give general guidance to those who are using the CFR when preparing legislation. Several projects within the Network entrusted with preparatory works by the European Commission are dealing

with the question of underlying values (see para. 77 below). It might therefore be useful at this point to sketch out some ideas on how the aims and underlying values of the DCFR, as it stands in this volume, could be expressed. The following remarks are based on an early draft presented to and discussed with a group of stakeholders in 2005[3] and on several discussions among the members of the Compilation and Redaction Team (CRT; see Academic contributors and funders below).

16. **A matter of political standpoint.** To some extent the 'fundamental principles' that underlie the DCFR are a matter of interpretation and debate. Although it is clear that the DCFR does not perceive private law and in particular contract law only as the balancing of private law relations between equally strong natural and legal persons, different readers may have different interpretations of the extent to which it suggests the correction of market failures or contains elements of 'social justice' and welfarism, re-distribution of wealth and other forms of social engineering. Thus this statement of fundamental principles can be no more than the considered view of those who have contributed to this Introduction, and it is not yet complete.

17. **Request for comments.** Readers are invited to comment on whether they think such a statement of fundamental principles would be useful and therefore should be completed and included in the final version of the DCFR to be presented in 2008.

18. **Function and purpose of 'fundamental principles'.** Private law and in particular contract law is one of those fields of law which are, or at least should be, based on and guided by deep-rooted underlying principles. Any statement of them must, in our view, give some

---

[3]   Workshop organised by the European Commission on 6 June 2005 at Brussels; a short summary of the results can be found in the volume Principles of the Existing EC Contract Law (Acquis Principles), Volume Contract I – Pre-contractual Obligations, Conclusion of Contract, Unfair Terms. Prepared by the Research Group on the Existing EC Private Law (Acquis Group) (Sellier 2007), p. XI-XIII.

practical guidance on how to read and to interpret the definitions and model rules contained in the CFR, and to reflect its theoretical underpinnings, including its underlying political, economic and social aims and values. These should be borne in mind by those using the CFR as a legislator's guide or tool-box.

19. **'Fundamental principles' expressed as aims.** There are different ways of expressing such 'fundamental principles'. Options would be, among many others, a normative style setting out rights of European citizens or an analytical explanation of the underlying values of the Model Rules and Definitions contained in the text. As the Europeanisation of private law is an ongoing development and as the CFR exercise may be seen as part of this process it may be useful here to describe 'Fundamental Principles' as some core aims European private law, in particular contract law, should have.

20. **Model of society and economic system.** The formulation of core aims and fundamental principles reveals the underlying model of society and of the economic system more directly than does the formulation of individual rules. It helps to clarify the position of the DCFR (and, eventually, the CFR) in the spectrum between free market and fair competition theories and more invasive approaches in favour of consumers, victims of discrimination, small and medium sized enterprises and the many other possibly weaker parties to contracts and members of society.

21. **Community law and Member States' laws as the measure.** As the DCFR is developed on the basis of comparative studies of Community law and the laws of the Member States, it has to reflect the underlying values to be found in the existing laws. These – or at any rate the balance struck between them – are not the same in each system. As far as there are differences between the underlying values in individual jurisdictions, or between the Member States' laws and EC law, the DCFR mediates between them and takes a balanced position.

22. Core aims of European private law. Any attempt to work on principles of private law will at least have to deal with the following core aims and the values expressed in them:

– Justice
– Freedom
– Protection of Human Rights
– Economic Welfare
– Solidarity and Social Responsibility.

In so far as it is the European Union which shapes private law, some specific aims may be added to that list, in particular:

– Promotion of the Internal Market
– Preservation of Cultural and Linguistic Plurality.

Moreover, if European private law is to be expressed in a set of Model Rules, some further, more 'formal' aims will have to be pursued:

– Rationality
– Legal Certainty
– Predictability
– Efficiency.

The words "at least" at the beginning of this paragraph are intended to indicate that there are other aims or principles which might be regarded as important, even if there might be argument as to whether they could be described as "core". For example, the protection of a person's reasonable reliance on another's conduct might be considered an important aim. An important underlying principle in some areas of the law might be that people are generally responsible for risks which they themselves create.

23. Balancing conflicting aims and values. It is characteristic for such fundamental aims that they conflict with each other. For example, on occasion, justice in a particular case may have to make way for legal certainty, as happens under the rules of prescription. Freedom, in particular freedom of contract, may be limited for the sake of human rights if, for instance, rules on non-discrimination apply. Therefore the aims can never be pursued in a pure and rigid way. The underlying values of a private law system can only be discerned and described by explaining how such fundamental aims are balanced in the individual model rules.

24. Justice. Every model rule in this DCFR pursues the aim of reaching a just and fair solution for the situation to be regulated. The DCFR is particularly concerned to promote what Aristotle termed 'corrective' justice. This notion is fundamental to contract, non-contractual liability for damage and unjustified enrichment. General clauses like good faith (see below, paragraph 33) also serve the overarching aim of justice. The DCFR is less concerned with issues of 'distributive justice', but sometimes distributive or 'welfarist' concerns may also be reflected in the DCFR, for instance when it is decided that a consumer should always have certain rights.

25. Freedom, in particular freedom of contract. Contract is the basic legal instrument which enables natural and legal persons to enjoy the freedom to regulate their relations with each other by agreement. As a rule, natural and legal persons are free both to decide whether or not to contract and to agree on the terms of their contract because in some situations, freedom of contract, without more, leads to justice. If, for instance, the parties to a contract are fully informed and in an equal bargaining position when concluding it, the content of their agreement can be presumed to be in their interest and thus just. Therefore a contract will be enforced or recognised by law if it is based on the parties' agreement and if there is no reason (such as an infringement of public policy) for the contract to be treated as invalid or set aside. But if one party to the contract is in a weaker position, it may not be just simply to enforce it. Thus a contract concluded as the result of mistake or fraud, or which involves unfair exploitation or discrimination, can be set aside by the aggrieved party. However, restrictions on freedom of contract, whether by way of mandatory rules, avoidance of unfair contract terms or in any other form, should be imposed only if they can be justified in relation to certain situations or types of contract.

26. Restrictions on freedom to contract. Thus in general persons should remain free to contract or to refuse to contract with anyone else. However, this freedom may be qualified where it might result in unacceptable discrimination, for example discrimination on the grounds of gender, race or religion.

27. Restrictions on freedom to determine contents of contract. Similarly, restrictions on the parties' freedom to fix the terms of their contract may be justified even outside the classic cases of procedural unfairness such as mistake, fraud, duress and the exploitation of a party's circumstances to obtain an excessive advantage. Grounds on which restrictions might be justified include inequality of information (about either the facts, such as the characteristics of the goods or services to be supplied, or the terms of the contract, or both); and lack of bargaining power. Such problems are most common when a consumer is dealing with a business, but can also occur in contracts between businesses, particularly when one party is a small business that lacks expertise.

28. Minimum intervention. Even when some intervention can be justified on one of the grounds just mentioned, thought must be given to the form of intervention. Is the problem one that can be solved adequately by requiring one party to provide the other with information before the contract is made, with perhaps a right in the other party to avoid the contract if the information was not given? Or will problems persist even if consumers (for example) are 'informed', possibly because they will not be able to make effective use of the information? In such a case a mandatory rule giving the consumer certain rights (for example, that the goods must be of a certain quality) may be justified. In general terms, the interference with freedom of contract should be the minimum that will solve the problem while providing the other party (e. g. the business seller) with sufficient guidance to be able to arrange its affairs efficiently. (Sometimes it may be easier to have a simple rule rather than a standard that varies according to the circumstances of each case.) Similarly with contract terms: it must be asked whether it is necessary to make a particular term mandatory or whether a flexible test such as 'fairness' would suffice to protect the weaker party. A fairness test may allow certain terms to be used providing these are clearly brought home to the consumer or other party before the contract is made. The fairness test thus interferes less with the parties' freedom of contract than making a particular term mandatory would do.

29. Economic welfare. All areas of the law covered by the DCFR
have the double aim of promoting general welfare by strengthening
market forces and at the same time allowing individuals to increase
their economic wealth. In many cases the DCFR is simply setting out
rules that reflect an efficient solution – what the parties might have
agreed but for the costs of trying to do so. This is most obviously true
for many of the rules of contract law: these are simply 'default rules'
to apply when the parties have not agreed anything on the point in
question. The rules should produce efficient outcomes since that is
presumably what the parties would have wanted. Many rules of the
law on non-contractual liability for damage and even of unjustified
enrichment law and the law on benevolent intervention in another's
affairs can be explained on the same basis; in any event, they should
be efficient. The rules in the DCFR are in general intended to be
such as will promote economic welfare; and this is a criterion against
which any legislative intervention should be checked.

30. Interventions to promote efficiency. Economic welfare may
sometimes be promoted by interference even when the parties have
reached an agreement, if there is reason to think that because of
some market failure (such as that caused by inequality of information) the agreement is less than fully efficient. Consumer protection
rules, for example, can be seen not only as protective for the benefit
of typically weaker parties but also as favourable for general welfare
because they may lead to more competition and thus to a better
functioning of markets. This holds true in particular for cases of the
type mentioned above, where consumers' lack of information about
either the characteristics of the goods sold or the terms being offered
leads to forms of market failure. Rules that, in relation to the making
of a contract of a particular type or in a particular situation, require
one party (typically a business) to provide the other (typically a
consumer) with specified information about its nature, terms and
effect, where such information is needed for a well-informed decision
and is not otherwise readily available to that other party, can be
justified as promoting efficiency in the relevant market. Indeed a
legislator should consider whether this is the justification for the
proposed intervention, or whether it is based on a welfarist notion
that consumers simply should have the right concerned. The answer

to that question may influence the choice of the extent and form of intervention.

31. Protection of human rights. Private law must contribute to the protection of human rights and human dignity. In contract law and in pre-contractual relations, for instance, the rules on non-discrimination serve this purpose. The rules on non-contractual liability for damage also have the function of protecting human rights.

32. Solidarity and social responsibility. Private law must also demand a minimum of solidarity among the members of society and allow for altruistic and social activities. Examples of this function of private law may be seen in the provisions on good faith or in the Book on Benevolent Intervention. In the future, specific rules on contracts of donation may be needed to strengthen this aim. Within the field of contractual relationships, many think that solidarity is a fundamental principle. Thus the obligation to co-operate might well be justified on this ground as well as on the ground of promoting economic welfare.

33. Good faith. Equally, some see the promotion of good faith in contractual and other relationships as a fundamental principle, an end in itself. Others (particularly, but not only, those from jurisdictions which give only very limited recognition to the principle of good faith) see it more as a legal technique for reaching fair and efficient results that might equally be reached by other, more fact-specific rules. Whatever the merits of this debate, the values that underlie the notion – for example, the promotion of honest market practice, so that one party should not depart from good commercial practice to take unfair advantage of the other – may be called fundamental. These values are enshrined in the DCFR and legislators should bear them in mind – just as they should bear in mind that not all legal systems in the EU apply a general requirement of good faith, so that European legislation may need to include express provisions on the issue (see below, para. 73).

34. Contracts harmful to third persons and society in general. A further ground on which a contract may be invalidated, even though freely agreed between two equal parties, is that it (or more often the performance of the obligation under it) would have a seriously harmful effect on third persons or society. Thus contracts which are illegal or contrary to public policy in this sense (within the framework of the EU a common example is contracts which infringe the competition articles of the Treaty) are invalid. The DCFR does not spell out when a contract is contrary to public policy in this sense, because that is a matter for law outside the scope of the DCFR – the law of competition or the criminal law of the Member State where the relevant performance should take place. However the fact that a contract might harm third persons or society is clearly a ground on which the legislator should consider invalidating it, and the DCFR contains rules to that effect.

35. EU-specific aims. The DCFR is to be interpreted and applied in a manner consistent with the aims and principles on which not only the laws of the Member States but also the European Union are based, including the aim of establishing an area of freedom, security and justice, and the creation of an open internal market with free and fair competition and free movement of goods, persons, services and capital between Member States, and the protection of consumers and of others in need of protection. Cultural and linguistic plurality of Europe must be taken into account and preserved.

36. Rationality, legal certainty, predictability, efficiency. The underlying material aims of private law can only be reached if the applicable rules are rational and provide a measure of legal certainty, predictability and efficiency. To this end, unnecessary burdens must be avoided and smooth legal transactions fostered. In some cases individual rights may also be cut off by rules on time limits or parties to a contract may be protected not because they are individually but just typically in need of protection.

The coverage of the DCFR

37. Wider coverage than PECL. The coverage of the PECL was already quite wide. They had rules not only on the formation, validity, interpretation and contents of contracts and, by analogy, other juridical acts, but also on the performance of obligations resulting from them and on the remedies for non-performance of such obligations. Indeed the later Chapters had many rules applying to private law rights and obligations in general – for example, rules on a plurality of parties, on the assignment of rights to performance, on set-off and on prescription. To this extent the Principles went well beyond the law on contracts as such. The DCFR continues this coverage but it goes further. It also covers (in Book IV) a series of model rules on so-called 'specific contracts' and the rights and obligations arising from them. For their field of application these latter rules expand and make more specific the general provisions (in Books I-III), deviate from them where the context so requires, or address matters not covered by them.

38. Non-contractual obligations. The DCFR also covers rights and obligations arising as the result of an unjustified enrichment, of damage caused to another and of benevolent intervention in another's affairs. It thus embraces non-contractual obligations to a far greater extent than the PECL.

39. Matters of movable property law. In its full and final edition the DCFR will also cover some matters of movable property law, such as transfer of ownership, proprietary security, and trust law.

40. Matters excluded. DCFR I. – 1:101(2) lists all matters which are excluded from its intended field of application.

41. Reasons for the approach adopted. The coverage of the DCFR is thus considerably broader than what the European Commission seems to have in mind for the coverage of the CFR (see para. 60 below). The 'academic' frame of reference is not subject to the constraints of the 'political' frame of reference. While the DCFR is linked to the CFR, it is conceived as an independent text. The research teams began in the tradition of the Commission on European Contract Law but with the aim of extending its coverage. When this work started there were no political discussions underway on the creation of a CFR of any kind, neither for contract law nor for any other part of the law. Our contract with the Research Directorate-General to receive funding under the sixth European Framework Programme on Research reflects this; it obliges us to address all the matters listed in paras. 37-39 above.

42. Contract law as part of private law. There are good reasons for not including *only* rules on general contract law in the DCFR. These general rules need to be tested to see whether or in what respect they have to be adjusted, amended and revised within the framework of the most important of the specific contracts. Nor can the DCFR contain only rules dealing with consumer contracts. The two Groups concur in the view that consumer law is not a self-standing area of private law. It consists of some deviations from the general principles of private law, but cannot be developed without them. And 'private law' for this purpose is not confined to the law on contract and contractual obligations. The correct dividing line between contract law (in this wide sense) and some other areas of law is in any event difficult to determine precisely.[4] This DCFR therefore approaches the whole of the law of obligations as an organic entity or unit. In the final edition, some areas of property law with regard to movable property will be dealt with for more or less identical reasons and because some aspects of property law are of great relevance to the good functioning of the internal market.

Structure and language of the DCFR model rules

43. Structure of the model rules. The structure of the model rules was discussed on many occasions by the Study Group and the joint Compilation and Redaction Team. It was accepted from an early

---

[4] See, in more detail, von Bar and Drobnig (eds.), The Interaction of Contract Law and Tort and Property Law in Europe (Munich 2004). This study was conducted on behalf of the European Commission.

stage that the whole text would be divided into Books and that each
Book would be subdivided into Chapters, Sections, Sub-sections
(where appropriate) and Articles. In addition the Book on specific
contracts and the rights and obligations arising from them was to be
divided, because of its size, into Parts, each dealing with a particular
type of contract (e. g. Book IV.A: Sale). All of this was relatively
uncontroversial.

44. Mode of numbering the model rules. The mode of numbering
the model rules corresponds in its basic approach to the technique
used in many of the newer European codifications. This too was
chosen in order to enable necessary changes to be made and missing
passages to be inserted into the DCFR later without more than minor
editorial labour. (In this edition places where additions are expected
are indicated by references such as '[in preparation]'). Books are
numbered by capitalised Roman numerals, i. e., Book I (General provisions), Book II (Contracts and other juridical acts), etc. Only one
Book (Book IV (Specific contracts and rights and obligations arising
from them)) is divided into Parts: Part A (Sale), Part B (Lease of
goods), etc. Chapters, sections (and also sub-sections) are numbered
using Arabic numerals, e. g. chapter 5, section 2, sub-section 4, etc.
Articles are then numbered sequentially within each Book (or Part)
using Arabic numerals. The first Arabic digit, preceding the colon, is
the number of the relevant chapter. The digit immediately following
the colon is the number of the relevant section of that chapter. The
remaining digits give the number of the Article within the section;
sub-sections do not affect the numbering. For example, III. – 3:509
(Effect on obligations under the contract) is the ninth Article in section 5 (Termination) of the third chapter (Remedies for non-performance) of the third book (Obligations and corresponding rights).
One cannot see from the numbering, however, that in that section it
is the first Article within sub-section 3 (Effects of termination).

45. Ten books. To a large extent the allocation of the subject matter to the different Books was also uncontroversial. It was readily
agreed that Book I should be a short and general guide for the reader
on how to use the whole text – dealing, for example, with its intended scope of application, how it should be interpreted and developed

and where to find definitions of key terms. The later Books, from Book IV on, also gave rise to little difficulty so far as structure was concerned. There was discussion about the best order, but eventually it was settled that this would be Specific contracts and rights and obligations arising from them (Book IV); Benevolent intervention in another's affairs (Book V); Non-contractual liability arising out of damage caused to another (Book VI); Unjustified enrichment (Book VII); Acquisition and loss of ownership in movables (Book VIII); Proprietary security rights in movable assets (Book IX) and Trusts (Book X). An important argument for putting the rules on specific contracts and their obligational effects in a Book of their own (subdivided into Parts) rather than in separate Books is that it would be easier in the future to add new Parts dealing with other specific contracts without affecting the numbering of later Books and their contents. As said before, this interim edition does not yet contain Books VIII-X and still has some lacunae in Book IV.

46. Books II and III. The difficult decisions concerned Books II and III. There was never much doubt that these Books should cover the material in the existing Principles of European Contract Law (PECL, see para. 8 above and paras. 50-54 below) – general rules on contracts and other juridical acts, and general rules on contractual and (often) other obligations – but there was considerable difficulty in deciding how this material should be divided up between and within them and what they should be called. It was only after decisions were taken by the Co-ordinating Group on how the key terms 'contract' and 'obligation' would be used in the model rules, and after a special Structure Group was set up, that the way forward became clear. Book II would deal with contracts and other juridical acts (how they are formed, how they are interpreted, when they are invalid, how their content is determined and so on) while Book III would deal with obligations within the scope of the DCFR – both contractual and non-contractual – and corresponding rights.

47. Juridical acts and obligations. A feature of this division of material is a clear distinction between a contract seen as a type of agreement – a type of juridical act – and the legal relationship, usually involving reciprocal sets of obligations and rights, which results from it. Book II deals with contracts as juridical acts; Book III deals with the obligations and rights resulting from contracts seen as juridical acts, as well as with non-contractual obligations and rights. To this extent a structural division which is only implicit in the PECL is made explicit.

48. Contractual and non-contractual obligations. A further problem was how best to deal with contractual and non-contractual obligations within Book III. One technique which was tried was to deal first with contractual obligations and then to have a separate part on non-contractual obligations. However, this proved cumbersome and unsatisfactory. It involved either unnecessary repetition or extensive and detailed cross-references to earlier Articles. Either way the text was unattractive and heavy for the reader to use. In the end it was found that the best technique was to frame the Articles in Book III so far as possible in general terms so that they could apply to both contractual and non-contractual obligations. Where a particular Article applied only to contractual obligations (which was the exception rather than the rule) this could be clearly stated. This approach was expressly approved by a meeting of the Co-ordinating Group at Lucerne in December 2006.

49. Language. The DCFR is being published first in English. This has been the working language for all the Groups responsible for formulating the model rules. However, for a substantial portion of the Books (or, in the case of Book IV, its Parts), teams have already composed a large number of translations into other languages. These will be published successively, first in the PEL series (see para. 55 below) and later separately for the DCFR. The Compilation and Redaction Team has tried to achieve not only a clear and coherent structure, but also a plain and clear wording. An attempt has been made to avoid technical terms from particular legal systems and to try to find, wherever possible, descriptive language which can be readily translated without carrying unwanted baggage with it. After all, one of the overarching goals of the DCFR is to improve the accessibility and intelligibility of private law in Europe.

How the DCFR relates to PECL, the SGECC PEL series, the Acquis and the Insurance Contract Group series

50. Based in part on the PECL. In Books II and III the DCFR contains many rules derived from the Principles of European Contract Law (PECL). These rules have been adopted with the express agreement of the Commission on European Contract Law, whose successor group is the Study Group. Tables of derivations and destinations help the reader to trace PECL articles within the DCFR. However, the PECL could not simply be incorporated as they stood. Deviations were unavoidable in part due to the different structure and the different coverage of the DCFR and in part because the scope of the PECL needed to be broadened so as to embrace matters of consumer protection.

51. Deviations from PECL. A primary purpose of the DCFR is to try to develop clear and consistent concepts and terminology. In pursuit of this aim the Study Group gave much consideration to the most appropriate way of using terms like 'contract' and 'obligation', taking into account not only national systems, but also prevailing usage in European and international instruments dealing with private law topics. One reason for many of the drafting changes from the PECL is the clearer distinction now drawn (as noted above) between a contract (seen as a type of agreement or juridical act) and the relationship (usually consisting of reciprocal rights and obligations) to which it gives rise. This has a number of consequences throughout the text.

52. Examples. For example, it is not the contract which is performed. A contract is concluded; obligations are performed. Similarly, a contract is not terminated. It is the contractual relationship, or particular rights and obligations arising from it, which will be terminated. The new focus on rights and obligations in Book III also made possible the consistent use of 'creditor' and 'debtor' rather than terms like 'aggrieved party' and 'other party', which were commonly used in the PECL. The decision to use 'obligation' consistently as the counterpart of a right to performance also meant some drafting changes. The PECL sometimes used 'duty' in this sense and sometimes 'obligation'. The need for clear concepts and terminology also meant more frequent references than in the PECL to juridical acts other than contracts. Examples of such juridical acts might be offers, acceptances, notices of termination, authorisations, guarantees, unilateral promises and so on. The PECL dealt with these by an Article (1:107) which applied the Principles to them 'with appropriate modifications'. However, what modifications would be appropriate was not always apparent. It was therefore decided to deal separately with other juridical acts.

53. Input from stakeholders. Other changes in PECL Articles resulted from the input from stakeholders to the workshops held by the European Commission on selected topics. For example, the rules on representation were changed in several significant respects for this reason, as were the rules on pre-contractual statements forming part of a contract, the rules on variation by a court of contractual rights and obligations on a change of circumstances and the rules on so-called 'implied terms' of a contract. Sometimes even the process of preparing for stakeholder meetings which were not, in the end, held led to proposals for changes in PECL which were eventually adopted. This was the case, for example, with the chapter on plurality of debtors and creditors, where academic criticism on one or two specific points also played a role.

54. Developments since the publication of the PECL. Finally, there were some specific Articles or groups of Articles which, in the light of recent developments or further work and thought, seemed to merit improvement. For example, the PECL rules on stipulations in favour of third parties, although a considerable achievement at the time, seemed in need of some expansion in the light of recent developments in national systems and international instruments. The detailed work which was done on the specific contracts in Book IV, and the rights and obligations resulting from them, sometimes suggested a need for some additions to, and changes in, the general rules in Books II and III. For example, it was found that it would be advantageous to have a general rule on 'mixed contracts' in Book II and a general rule on notifications of non-conformities in Book III. It was also found that the rules on 'cure' by a seller which were developed in

the Sale Part of Book IV could usefully be generalised and placed in
Book III. The work done on other later Books also sometimes fed
back into Books II and III. For example, the work done on unjustified
enrichment showed that rather more developed rules were needed
on the restitutionary effects of terminated contractual relationships,
while the work on the acquisition and loss of ownership in movables
(and also on proprietary security rights in movable assets) fed back
into the treatment of assignment in Book III. Although the general
approach was to follow the PECL as much as possible there were,
inevitably, a number of cases where it was found that small drafting
changes, or some slight restructuring of an Article or group of Articles, or some slightly sharper distinctions, could increase clarity or
consistency.

55. The PEL series. The Study Group began its labours in 1998.
From the outset it was envisaged that at the appropriate time its
results would be presented in an integrated complete edition, but it
was only gradually that its structure took shape (see paras. 43-48
above). As a first step the tasks in the component parts of the project
had to be organised and deliberated. The results are being published
in a separate series, the 'Principles of European Law' (PEL). To date
five volumes have appeared. They cover leases,[5] services,[6] commercial agency, franchise and distribution,[7] personal security contracts,[8]

---

[5]   Principles of European Law. Study Group on a European Civil Code.
      Lease of Goods (PEL LG). Prepared by Kåre Lilleholt, Anders Victo-
      rin†, Andreas Fötschl, Berte-Elen R. Konow, Andreas Meidell, Amund
      Bjøranger Tørum (Sellier, Bruylant, Staempfli, Oxford University Press
      2007).

[6]   Principles of European Law. Study Group on a European Civil Code.
      Service Contracts (PEL SC). Prepared by Maurits Barendrecht, Chris
      Jansen, Marco Loos, Andrea Pinna, Rui Cascão, Stéphanie van Gulijk
      (Sellier, Bruylant, Staempfli, Oxford University Press 2006).

[7]   Principles of European Law. Study Group on a European Civil Code.
      Commercial Agency, Franchise and Distribution Contracts (PEL
      CAFDC). Prepared by Martijn W. Hesselink, Jacobien W. Rutgers,
      Odavia Bueno Díaz, Manola Scotton, Muriel Veldmann (Sellier, Bruy-
      lant, Staempfli, Oxford University Press 2006).

and benevolent interventions in another's affairs.[9] Further books will follow, in 2008 on sales, unjustified enrichment law and the law regarding non-contractual liability arising out of damage caused to another, and in 2009 on mandate and loan contracts, contracts of donation and all the subjects related to property law. The volumes published within the PEL series contain additional material which will not be reproduced in the full DCFR, namely the comparative introductions to the various Books, Parts and Chapters, and the translations of the model rules published within the PEL series.

56. Deviations from the PEL series. In some cases, however, the model rules which the reader encounters in this DCFR deviate from their equivalent published in the PEL series. There are several reasons for such changes. First, in drafting a self-standing set of model rules for a given subject (such as e. g. service contracts) it proved necessary to have much more repetition of rules which were already part of the PECL. Such repetitions became superfluous in an integrated DCFR text which states these rules already at a more general level (i. e. in Books II and III). The DCFR is therefore considerably shorter than it would have been had all PEL model rules been included as they stood.

57. Improvements. The second reason for changing some already published PEL model rules is that in some cases the Compilation and Redaction Team saw room for improvement at the stage of revising and editing for DCFR purposes. After consulting the authors of the relevant PEL book, the CRT submitted the redrafted rules to the Study Group's Co-ordinating Committee for approval, amendment or rejection. Resulting changes are in part limited to mere drafting, but occasionally go to substance. They are a consequence of the

---

8   Principles of European Law. Study Group on a European Civil Code. Personal Security (PEL Pers.Sec.). Prepared by Ulrich Drobnig (Sellier, Bruylant, Staempfli, Oxford University Press 2007).

9   Principles of European Law. Study Group on a European Civil Code. Benevolent Intervention in Another's Affairs (PEL Ben.Int.). Prepared by Christian von Bar (Sellier, Bruylant, Staempfli, Oxford University Press 2006).

systematic revision of the model rules which commenced in 2006, the integration of ideas from others (including stakeholders) and the compilation of the list of terminology, which revealed some inconsistencies in the earlier texts. The DCFR in its full and final edition may reflect yet further refinements as compared with this interim outline edition.

58. The Acquis Principles (ACQP). The Research Group on the Existing EC Private Law, commonly called the Acquis Group, is also publishing its findings in a separate series.[10] The Acquis Principles are an attempt to present and structure the bulky and rather incoherent patchwork of EC private law in a way that should allow the current state of its development to be made clear and relevant legislation and case law to be found easily. This also permits identification of shared features, contradictions and gaps in the Acquis. Thus, the ACQP may have a function for themselves, namely as a source for the drafting, transposition and interpretation of EC law. Within the process of elaborating the DCFR, the Acquis Group and its output contribute to the task of ensuring that the existing EC law is appropriately reflected. The ACQP are consequently one of the sources from which the Compilation and Redaction Team has drawn.

59. Principles of European Insurance Contract Law. The CoPECL network of researchers established under the sixth framework programme for research (see below: academic contributors and funders) also includes the 'Project Group Restatement of European Insurance Contract Law (Insurance Group)'. That body is delivering its 'Principles of European Insurance Contract Law' to the European Commission contemporaneously with our submission of this provisional DCFR. It is not yet conclusively settled whether and, if so, how that text will be integrated into Book IV of the full DCFR. An appropriate slot for incorporation of that material has been reserved in case it is needed.

---

[10] See fn. 2 above; in preparation: Volume Contract II – Performance, Non-Performance, Remedies (Sellier 2008) and further volumes on specific contracts and extra-contractual matters.

How the DCFR may be used as preparatory work for the CFR

60. Announcements by the Commission. The European Commission's 'Action Plan on A More Coherent European Contract Law' of January 2003[11] called for comments on three proposed measures: increasing the coherence of the acquis communautaire, the promotion of the elaboration of EU-wide standard contract terms,[12] and further examination of whether there is a need for a measure that is not limited to particular sectors, such as an 'optional instrument.' Its principal proposal for improvement was to develop a Common Frame of Reference (CFR) which could then be used by the Commission in reviewing the existing acquis and drafting new legislation.[13] In October 2004 the Commission published a further paper, 'European Contract Law and the revision of the acquis: the way forward'.[14] This proposed that the CFR should provide 'fundamental principles, definitions and model rules' which could assist in the improvement of the existing acquis communautaire, and which might form the basis of an optional instrument if it were decided to create one. Model rules would form the bulk of the CFR,[15] its main purpose being to serve as a kind of legislators' guide or 'tool box'. Meanwhile a parallel review of eight consumer Directives[16] would be carried out. Members of the Acquis Group were involved in this review.[17] In 2007 the European Commission published a Green Pa-

---

[11] COM (2003) final, OJ C 63/1 (referred to here as Action Plan).

[12] This aspect of the plan is not being taken forward. See Commission of the European Communities. First Progress Report on The Common Frame of Reference, COM (2005), 456 final, p. 10.

[13] Action Plan para. 72.

[14] Communication from the Commission to the European Parliament and the Council, COM (2004) 651 final, 11 October 2004 (referred to as Way Forward).

[15] Way Forward para. 3.1.3, p. 11.

[16] Directives 85/577, 90/314, 93/13, 94/47, 97/7, 98/6; 98/27, 99/44. See Way Forward para. 2.1.1.

[17] See Schulte-Nölke/Twigg-Flesner/Ebers (eds), EC Consumer Law Compendium, Comparative Analysis, 2007, to be published in book form

per on the review of the consumer acquis.[18] This DCFR responds to these announcements by the Commission and contains proposals for the principles, definitions and model rules mentioned in them.

61. Purposes of the CFR. It remains to be seen what purposes the CFR may be called upon to serve. Some indication may be obtained from the expression 'principles, definitions and model rules' itself. Other indications can be obtained from the Commission's papers on this subject. These, and their implications for the coverage of the DCFR, will now be explored.

62. Green Paper on the Review of the Consumer Acquis. The Commission's Green Paper on the Review of the Consumer Acquis[19] asked questions at a number of different levels: for example, whether full harmonisation is desirable,[20] whether there should be a horizontal instrument,[21] and whether various additional matters should be dealt with by the Consumer Sales Directive.[22] It is possible that other Directives will also be revised, for example those relating to the provision of information to buyers of financial services. In the longer term, there may be proposals for further harmonisation measures in sectors where there still appears to be a need for consumer protection (e. g. contracts for services or personal security) or where the differences between the laws of the Member States appear to cause difficulties for the internal market (e. g. insurance or security over movable property).

63. Improving the existing and future acquis: model rules. The DCFR is intended to help in the process of improving the existing *acquis*

---

and in the meantime available at http://ec.europa.eu/consumers/cons_int/safe_shop/acquis/comp_analysis_en.pdf.

[18] Green Paper on the Review of the Consumer Acquis, COM(2006) 744 final of 8 February 2007 (http://ec.europa.eu/consumers/cons_int/safe_shop/acquis/green-paper_cons_acquis_en.pdf).

[19] See previous footnote.

[20] Question A3, p. 15.

[21] Question A2, p. 14.

[22] Directive 1999/44/EC. See questions H1-M3, pp. 24-32.

and in drafting any future EU legislation in the field of private law. By teasing out and stating clearly the principles that underlie the existing *acquis*, the DCFR can show how the existing Directives can be made more consistent and how various sectoral provisions might be given a wider application, so as to eliminate current gaps and overlaps – the 'horizontal approach' referred to in the Green Paper. The DCFR should also identify improvements in substance that might be considered. The research preparing the DCFR 'will aim to identify best solutions, taking into account national contract laws (both case law and established practice), the EC *acquis* and relevant international instruments, particularly the UN Convention on Contracts for the International Sale of Goods of 1980'.[23] The DCFR therefore provides recommendations, based on extensive comparative research and careful analysis, of what should be considered if legislators are minded to alter or add to EU legislation. This process of considering 'model rules' has begun even before the DCFR is complete. Many of the questions posed in the Green Paper draw on texts from the drafts which researchers presented to stakeholder workshops during 2006. However, the DCFR does not identify particular rules that are put forward as proposals for immediate legislation. Rather the aim is to provide rules from which the legislator may draw inspiration.

64. Improving the acquis: developing a coherent terminology. Directives frequently employ legal terminology and concepts which they do not define.[24] The classic example, seemingly referred to in the Commission's papers, is the *Simone Leitner* case,[25] but there are many

---

[23] Way Forward para. 3.1.3.

[24] In the CFR workshops on the consumer *acquis*, texts providing definitions of concepts used or pre-supposed in the EU acquis were referred to as 'directly relevant' material. See Second Progress Report on the Common Frame of Reference, COM (2007) 447 final, p. 2.

[25] Case C-168/00 Simone Leitner v TUI Deutschland [2002] ECR I-2631. The ECJ had to decide whether the damages to which a consumer was entitled under the provisions of the Package Travel Directive must include compensation for non-economic loss suffered when the holiday was not as promised. This head of damages is recognised by many na-

others. A CFR which provides definitions of these legal terms and concepts would be useful for questions of interpretation of this kind, particularly if it were adopted by the European institutions – for example, as a guide for legislative drafting.[26] It would be presumed that the word or concept contained in a Directive was used in the sense in which it is used in the CFR unless the Directive stated otherwise. National legislators seeking to implement the Directive, and national courts faced with interpreting the implementing legislation, would be able to consult the CFR to see what was meant. Moreover, if comparative notes on the Articles are included, as they will be in the final version of the DCFR, the notes will often provide useful background information on how national laws currently deal with the relevant questions.

65. No functional terminology list without rules. As said before, it is, however, impossible to draft a functional list of terminology without a set of model rules behind it, and vice versa. That in turn makes it desirable to consider a rather wide coverage of the CFR. For example, it would be very difficult to develop a list of key notions of the law on contract and contractual obligations (such as conduct, creditor, damage, indemnify, loss, intention, negligence etc.), without a sufficient awareness of the fact that many of these notions also play a role in the area of non-contractual obligations.

66. Improving the acquis: principles. It has already been noted that the word 'principles' may in the present context be synonymous with 'model rules', or those model rules which are of a more general nature, or may be understood in the sense of a statement of the values that underlie the rules of the CFR and general guidance to legislators

---

tional laws, but was not recognised by Austrian law. The ECJ held that 'damage' in the Directive must be given an autonomous, 'European' legal meaning – and in this context 'damage' is to be interpreted as including non-economic loss.

[26] In the absence of any formal arrangement, legislators could achieve much the same result for individual legislative measures by stating in the recitals that the measure should be interpreted in accordance with the CFR.

on the balance that may need to be struck between competing values. Paragraphs 15-36 above contain an indication of how such a statement might be developed if it is required.

67. Coverage of the CFR. The purposes to be served by the DCFR have a direct bearing on its coverage. As explained in paras. 37-42 above, the coverage of the DCFR goes well beyond the coverage of the CFR as contemplated by the Commission in its communications (whereas the European Parliament in earlier resolutions envisaged for the CFR more or less the same coverage as this DCFR[27]). Today, the coverage of the CFR still seems to be an open question. How far should it reach if it is to be effective as a legislators' guide or 'tool box'? How may this DCFR be used if it is decided that the coverage of the CFR will be narrower (or even much narrower) than the coverage of the DCFR? The following aspects would seem to be worthy of being taken into consideration when making the relevant political decisions.

68. Consumer law. It seems clear that the CFR must at any rate cover the fields of application of the existing Directives that are under review, and any others likely to be reviewed in the foreseeable future. Thus all consumer law should be included, and probably all contracts and contractual relationships that are the subject of existing Directives affecting questions of private law, since these may also be reviewed at some stage.

69. Revision of the acquis and further harmonisation measures. Secondly, the CFR should cover any field in which revision of the *acquis* or further harmonisation measures is being considered. This includes both areas currently under review (e. g. sales, and also leasing which is discussed in the Green Paper on revision of the consumer *acquis*[28]) and also areas where harmonisation is being considered, even if there are no immediate proposals for new legislation. Thus contracts for services should be covered, and also security over movable property,

---

[27] European Parliament, Resolution of 15 November 2001, OJ C 140E of 13 June 2002, p. 538.

[28] See footnote 19.

where divergences of laws cause serious problems. The same holds true for insurance contracts.[29]

70. Terms and concepts referred to in Directives. Thirdly, in order to provide the definitions that are wanted, the CFR must cover many terms and concepts that are referred to in Directives without being defined.[30] In practice this includes almost all of the general law on contract and contractual obligations. There are so few topics that are not at some point referred to in the *acquis*, or at least presupposed by it, that it is simpler to include all of this general law than to work out what few topics can be omitted. It is not only contract law terminology in the strict sense which is referred to, however, and certainly not just contract law which is presupposed in EU instruments. For example, consumer Directives frequently presuppose rules on unjustified enrichment law; and Directives on pre-contractual information refer to or presuppose rules that in many systems are classified as rules of non-contractual liability for damage, i. e. delict or tort. It is thus useful to provide definitions of terms and model rules in these fields – not because they are likely to be subjected to regulation or harmonisation by European legislation in the foreseeable future, but because existing European legislation already builds on assumptions that the laws of the Member States have relevant rules and provide appropriate remedies. Whether they do so in ways that fit well with the European legislation, actual or proposed, is another matter. It is for the European institutions to decide what might be needed or might be useful. What seems clear is that it is not easy to identify in advance topics which will never be wanted.

71. When in doubt, topics should be included. There are good arguments for the view that in case of doubt, topics should be included.

---

[29] See Way Forward para. 3.1.3 and Annex I.

[30] At the workshop on the possible structure of the CFR, 'there was an emerging consensus that the CFR should contain the topics directly related to the existing EU contract law acquis in combination with general contract law issues which are relevant for the acquis': Commission of the European Communities. Second Progress Report on the Common Frame of Reference, COM (2007) 447 final, pp. 8-9.

Excluding too many topics will result in the CFR being a fragmented patchwork, thus replicating a major fault in existing EU legislation on a larger scale. Nor can there be any harm in a broad CFR. It is not legislation, nor even a proposal for legislation. It merely provides language and definitions for use, when needed, in the closely targeted legislation that is, and will probably remain, characteristic of European Union private law.

72. Essential background information. There is a further way in which the CFR would be valuable as a legislators' guide, and it has been prepared with a view to that possible purpose. If EU legislation is to fit harmoniously with the laws of the Member States, and in particular if it is neither to leave unintended gaps nor to be more invasive than is necessary, the legislator needs to have accurate information about the different laws in the various Member States. The national notes to be included in the final version of the DCFR could be useful in this respect but would, of course, have to be frequently updated if this purpose is to be served on a continuing basis.

73. Good faith as an example. The principle of good faith can serve as an example. In many laws the principle is accepted as fundamental, but it is not accorded the same recognition in the laws of all the Member States – in particular, it is not recognised as a general rule of direct application in the Common Law jurisdictions. It is true that even the Common Law systems contain many particular rules that seem to be functionally equivalent to good faith, in the sense that they are aimed at preventing the parties from acting in ways that are incompatible with good faith, but there is no *general* rule. So the European legislator cannot assume that whatever requirements it chooses to impose on consumer contracts in order to protect consumers will always be supplemented by a general requirement that the parties act in good faith. If it wants a general requirement to apply in the particular context, even in the Common Law jurisdictions, the legislator will have to incorporate the requirement into the Directive in express words – as of course it did with the Directive on Unfair Terms in Consumer Contracts.[31] Alternatively, it will need to

---

[31] Council Directive 93/13/EEC, art. 3(1).

insert into the Directive specific provisions to achieve the results that in other jurisdictions would be reached by the application of the principle of good faith. In drafting or revising a Directive dealing with pre-contractual information, legislators will want to know what they need to deal with and what is already adequately covered, and covered in a reasonably harmonious way, by the law of all Member States. Thus general principles on mistake, fraud and provision of incorrect information form essential background to the consumer *acquis* on pre-contractual information. In this sense, even a 'legislators' guide' needs statements of the common principles found in the different laws, and a note of the variations. It needs information about what is in the existing laws and what can be omitted from the *acquis* because, in one form or another, all Member States already have it.

74. Presupposed rules of national law. The point is that a Directive normally presupposes the existence of certain rules in national law. For example, when a consumer exercises a right to withdraw from a contract, questions of liability in restitution are normally left to national law. It may be argued that information about the law that is presupposed is more than 'essential background'. The Commission's Second Progress Report describes it as 'directly relevant'.[32] Whatever the correct classification, this information is clearly important. Put simply, European legislators need to know what is a problem in terms of national laws and what is not. This is a further reason why the DCFR will have a wide coverage and why the final (and full) DCFR will contain extensive notes, comparing the definitions and rules stated to the various national laws.

75. DCFR not structured on an 'everything or nothing' basis. The DCFR is, so far as possible, structured in such a way that the political institutions, if they wish to proceed with an official Common Frame of Reference on the basis of some of its proposals, can sever certain parts of it and leave them to a later stage of deliberation or just to general discussion amongst academics. In other words, the DCFR is carefully not structured on an 'everything or nothing' basis; perhaps

---

[32] Loc. cit. (fn. 31 above) p. 2.

not every detail can be cherry-picked intact, but in any event larger areas could be taken up without any need to accept the entirety. For example, the reader will soon see that the provisions of Book III are directly applicable to contractual rights and obligations; it is simply that they also apply to non-contractual rights and obligations. Were the Commission to decide that the CFR should deal only with the former, it would be a quick and simple task to adjust the draft to apply only to contractual rights and obligations. We would not advise this, however, for reasons explained earlier. It would create the appearance of a gulf between contractual and other obligations that does not in fact exist in the laws of Member States, and it would put the coherence of the structure at risk.

76. The CFR as the basis for an optional instrument. What has been said so far about the purposes of the CFR relates to its function as a legislators' guide or toolbox. It is still unclear whether or not the CFR, or parts of it, might at a later stage be used as the basis for an optional instrument, i.e. as the basis for an additional set of legal rules which parties might choose to govern their mutual rights and obligations. In the view of the two Groups such an optional instrument would open attractive perspectives, not least for consumer transactions. A more detailed discussion of this issue, however, seems premature at this stage. It suffices to say that this DCFR is consciously drafted in a way that, given the political will, would allow progress to be made towards the creation of such an optional instrument.

Next steps

77. Review of the DCFR. In the time remaining until completion of the final edition of the DCFR the model rules published in this interim edition will be reviewed once more to check their correctness, acceptability and coherence. Criticism and comments are most welcome. Likewise, the impact of the work of the Evaluative Groups[33] which are integrated into the network of excellence has

---

[33] For more information see the homepage of the Network of Excellence: www.copecl.org.

yet to be assessed; their results are not yet available in published form and could therefore only be taken account of until now on the basis of their broad tenor. Part of this concomitant evaluation is an economic impact assessment, carried out by the Research Group on the Economic Assessment of Contract Law Rules, organised by the Tilburg Law and Economics Centre; an analysis of the philosophical underpinnings, undertaken by the Association Henri Capitant together with the Société de Législation Comparée and the Conseil Supérieur du Notariat; case assessments regarding the applicability of the principles made by the Common Core Group; and a case law database elaborated by a team of the University Paris-Sud.

78. Outstanding matters. Furthermore, some still outstanding matters need to be addressed. This relates not only to the missing Parts of Book IV and Books VIII-X, but also to the possible integration of new EC legislation (such as the new Services Directive[34] and the forthcoming Consumer Credit Directive[35]) into the DCFR.

79. Square brackets. The square brackets in II. – 9:404 (Meaning of "unfair" in contracts between a business and a consumer) are there because the Study Group and the Acquis Group were unable to reach agreement on whether the words in square brackets should or should not be included. The Acquis Group wished these words to be in the text. The Study Group considered that they should be excluded. The square brackets in III. – 5:108 (Assignability: effect of contractual prohibition) paragraph (5) indicate that there is an ongoing discussion about the scope of this paragraph which there has not been time to resolve.

80. Full and final DCFR. The full and final version of the DCFR is to be submitted to the European Commission at the end of December

---

[34] Directive 2006/123/EC of the European Parliament and of the Council of 12 December 2006 on services in the internal market.

[35] Political agreement on the new Consumer Credit Directive reached in Council on 21 May 2007; Common Position adopted on 20 September 2007; see further the Communication of the European Commission of 21 September 2007 COM (2007) 546 final.

2008. It will subsequently be reproduced in book form as a larger publication. We aim to publish at the same time a second edition of this volume, i. e. a second outline edition containing Articles only.

81. CFR. The creation of a CFR is a question for the European Institutions. If the current plan remains unchanged, the Commission, Council and Parliament will shortly form an opinion on fundamental questions concerning the CFR.

January 2008   *Christian von Bar,*
                                               Hugh Beale,
                                               Eric Clive,
                                               Hans Schulte-Nölke

Academic contributors and funders

The pan-European teams

As indicated already, this first edition of the DCFR is the result of more than 25 years' collaboration of jurists from all jurisdictions of the present Member States within the European Union. It began in 1982 with the constitution of the Commission on European Contract Law (CECL) and was furthered by the establishment of the Study Group in 1998 and the Acquis Group in 2002. From 2005 the Study Group, Acquis Group and Insurance Contract Group formed the so-called 'drafting teams' of the CoPECL network. The following DCFR is the result of the work of the Study Group, Acquis Group and CECL.

The Study Group on a European Civil Code

The Study Group has had the benefit of Working (or Research) Teams – groups of younger legal scholars under the supervision of a senior member of the Group (a Team Leader) – which undertook the basic comparative legal research, developed the drafts for discussion and assembled the extensive material required for the notes.

Furthermore, to each Working Team was allocated a consultative body – an Advisory Council. These bodies – deliberately kept small in the interests of efficiency – were formed from leading experts in the relevant field of law who are representative of the major European legal systems. The proposals drafted by the Working Teams and critically scrutinised and improved in a series of meetings by the respective Advisory Council were submitted for discussion on a revolving basis to the actual decision-making body of the Study Group on a European Civil Code, the Co-ordinating Group. Until June 2004 the Co-ordinating Group consisted of representatives from all the jurisdictions belonging to the EU immediately prior to its enlargement in Spring 2004 and in addition legal scholars from Estonia, Hungary, Norway, Poland, Slovenia and Switzerland. Representatives from the Czech Republic, Malta, Latvia, Lithuania and Slovakia joined us after the June 2004 meeting in Warsaw and representatives from Bulgaria and Romania after the December 2006 meeting in Lucerne. Besides its permanent members, other participants in the Co-ordinating Group with voting rights included all the Team Leaders and – when the relevant material was up for discussion – the members of the Advisory Council concerned. The results of the deliberations during the week-long sitting of the Co-ordinating Group were incorporated into the text of the Articles and the commentaries which returned to the agenda for the next meeting of the Co-ordinating Group (or the next but one depending on the work load of the Group and the Team affected). Each part of the project was the subject of debate on manifold occasions, some stretching over many years. Where a unanimous opinion could not be achieved, majority votes were taken.

Its Co-ordinating Group

The Study Group's Co-ordinating Group has (or had) the following members: Professor *Guido Alpa* (Genoa/Rome, until May 2005), Professor *Christian von Bar* (Osnabrück, chairman), Professor *Maurits Barendrecht* (Tilburg, until May 2005), Professor *Hugh Beale* (London/Warwick), Dr. *Mircea-Dan Bob* (Cluj, since June 2007), Professor *Michael Joachim Bonell* (Rome), Professor *Mifsud G. Bonnici* (Valetta, since December 2004), Professor *Carlo Castronovo* (Milan), Professor *Eric Clive* (Edinburgh), Professor *Eugenia Dacoronia* (Athens), Professor *Ulrich Drobnig* (Hamburg), Professor *Bénédicte Fauvarque-Cosson* (Paris), Professor *Marcel Fontaine* (Leuven, until December 2003), Professor *Andreas Furrer* (Lucerne, since December 2003), Professor *Júlio Manuel Vieira Gomes* (Oporto), Professor *Viggo Hagstrøm* (Oslo, since June 2002), Justitierådet Professor *Torgny Håstad* (Stockholm), Professor *Johnny Herre* (Stockholm), Professor *Martijn Hesselink* (Amsterdam), Professor *Ewoud Hondius* (Utrecht, until May 2005), Professor *Jérôme Huet* (Paris), Professor *Giovanni Iudica* (Milan, since June 2004), Dr. *Monika Jurčova* (Trnava, since June 2006), Professor *Konstantinos Kerameus* (Athens), Professor *Ole Lando* (Copenhagen), Professor *Kåre Lilleholt* (Bergen, since June 2003), Professor *Marco Loos* (Amsterdam); Professor *Brigitta Lurger* (Graz), Professor *Hector MacQueen* (Edinburgh), Professor *Ewan McKendrick* (Oxford), Professor *Valentinas Mikelenas* (Vilnius, since December 2004), Professor *Eoin O'Dell* (Dublin, until June 2006), Professor *Edgar du Perron* (Amsterdam), Professor *Denis Philippe* (Leuven, since June 2004), Professor *Jerzy Rajski* (Warsaw), Professor *Christina Ramberg* (Gothenburg), Judge Professor *Encarna Roca y Trias* (Madrid/Barcelona), Professor *Peter Schlechtriem†* (Freiburg i. Br.), Professor *Martin Schmidt-Kessel* (Osnabrück, since December 2004), Professor *Jorge Sinde Monteiro* (Coimbra, until December 2004), Professor *Lena Sisula-Tulokas* (Helsinki), Professor *Sophie Stijns* (Leuven), Professor *Matthias Storme* (Leuven), Dr. *Stephen Swann* (Osnabrück), Professor *Christian Takoff* (Sofia, since June 2007), Professor *Luboš Tichý* (Prague, since June 2005), Professor *Verica Trstenjak* (Maribor, until December 2006), Professor *Vibe Ulfbeck* (Copenhagen, since June 2006), Professor *Paul Varul* (Tartu, since June 2003), Professor *Lajos Vékás* (Budapest), Professor *Anna Veneziano* (Teramo).

The Study Group's Working Teams

Permanent working teams were and continue to be based in various European universities and research institutions. The teams' former and present 'junior members' conducted research into basically three main areas of private law: contract law, the law of extra-contractual obligations, and property law. They sometimes stayed for one or two years only, but often considerably longer in order additionally to pursue their own research projects. The meetings of the Co-ordi-nating Group and of numerous Advisory Councils were organised from Osnabrück, in conjunction with the relevant host, by *Ina El Kobbia*.

The members of the Working Teams were: *Begoña Alfonso de la Riva, Georgios Arnokouros*, Dr. *Erwin Beysen, Christopher Bisping, Ole Böger, Manuel Braga*, Dr. *Odavia Bueno Díaz*, Dr. *Sandie Calme*, Dr. *Rui Cascão, Cristiana Cicoria, Martine Costa, Inês Couto Guedes*, Dr. *John Dickie*, Dr. *Evlalia Eleftheriadou*, Dr. *Wolfgang Faber, Silvia Fedrizzi*, Dr. *Francesca Fiorentini*, Dr. *Andreas Fötschl, Laetitia Franck*, Dr. *Caterina Gozzi, Allessio Greco, Lodewijk Gualthérie van Weezel, Stéphanie van Gulijk, Judith Hauck*, Dr. *Lars Haverkamp, Annamaria Herpai*, Dr. *Viola Heutger*, Dr. *Matthias Hünert*, Professor *Chris Jansen*, Dr. *Christoph Jeloschek, Menelaos Karpathakis*, Dr. *Stefan Kettler, Ina El Kobbia*, Dr. *Berte-Elen R. Konow, Rosalie Koolhoven, Caroline Lebon, Jacek Lehmann, Martin Lilja, Roland Lohnert, Birte Lorenzen*, Dr. *María Án-geles, Martín Vida, Almudena de la Mata Muñoz, Pádraic McCannon*, Dr. *Mary-Rose McGuire, Paul McKane, José Carlos de Medeiros Nó-brega*, Dr. *Andreas Meidell, Philip Mielnicki, Anastasios Moraitis, Sandra Müller, Franz Nieper, Teresa Pereira*, Dr. *Andrea Pinna, Sandra Rohl-fing*, Dr. *Jacobien W. Rutgers, Johan Sandstedt, Marta dos Santos Silva*, Dr. *Mårten Schultz, Manola Scotton*†, *Frank Seidel, Susan Singleton*, Dr. *Hanna Sivesand*, Dr. *Malene Stein Poulsen, Dimitar Stoimenov*, Dr. *Stephen Swann, Ferenc Szilágyi*, Dr. *Amund Bjøranger Tørum, Muriel Veldman, Carles Vendrell Cervantes, Ernest Weiker, Aneta Wiewiorows-ka, Bastian Willers*.

The Study Group's Advisory Councils

The members of the Advisory Councils to the permanent working teams (who not infrequently served more than one team or per-formed other functions besides) were: Professor *John W. Blackie* (Strathclyde), Professor *Michael G. Bridge* (London), Professor *Angel*

Carrasco (Toledo), Professor *Carlo Castronovo* (Milan), Professor *Eric Clive* (Edinburgh), Professor *Pierre Crocq* (Paris); Professor *Eugenia Dacoronia* (Athens), Professor *Bénédicte Fauvarque-Cosson* (Paris), Professor *Jacques Ghestin* (Paris), Professor *Júlio Manuel Vieira Gomes* (Oporto), Professor *Helmut Grothe* (Berlin), Justitierådet Professor *Torgny Håstad* (Stockholm), Professor *Johnny Herre* (Stockholm), Professor *Jérôme Huet* (Paris), Professor *Giovanni Iudica* (Milan), Dr. *Monika Jurčova* (Trnava), Professor *Jan Kleineman* (Stockholm), Professor *Irene Kull* (Tartu), Professor *Denis Mazeaud* (Paris), Professor *Hector MacQueen* (Edinburgh), Professor *Ewan McKendrick* (Oxford), Professor *Graham Moffat* (Warwick), Professor *Andrea Nicolussi* (Milan), Professor *Eoin O'Dell* (Dublin), Professor *Guillermo Palao Moreno* (Valencia), Professor *Edgar du Perron* (Amsterdam), Professor *Maria A. L. Puelinckx-van Coene* (Antwerp), Professor *Philippe Rémy* (Poitiers), Professor *Peter Schlechtriem*† (Freiburg i. Br.), Professor *Martin Schmidt-Kessel* (Osnabrück), Dr. *Kristina Siig* (Arhus), Professor *Matthias Storme* (Leuven), Dr. *Stephen Swann* (Osnabrück), Professor *Stefano Troiano* (Verona), Professor *Antoni Vaquer Aloy* (Lleida), Professor *Anna Veneziano* (Rome), Professor *Alain Verbeke* (Leuven and Tilburg), Professor *Anders Victorin*† (Stockholm), Professor *Sarah Worthington* (London).

The Acquis Group

The Acquis Group texts result from a drafting process which involved individual Drafting Teams, the Redaction Committee, the Terminology Group, and the Plenary Meeting. The Drafting Teams produced a first draft of rules with comments for their topic or area on the basis of a survey of existing EC law. The drafts were then passed on to the Redaction Committee and to the Terminology Group which formulated proposals for making the various drafts by different teams dovetail with each other, also with a view towards harmonising the use of terminology and improving the language and consistency of drafts. All draft rules were debated several times at, and finally adopted by, Plenary Meetings of the Acquis Group, which convened twice a year. Several drafts which were adopted by Plenary Meetings (in particular those on pre-contractual information duties, unfair terms and withdrawal) were subsequently presented and discussed at CFR-Net Stakeholder Meetings. Their comments were considered within a second cycle of drafting and consolidation of the Acquis Principles.

The following members of the Acquis Group took part in the *Plenary Meetings:* Professor *Gianmaria Ajani* (Torino, speaker), Professor *Esther Arroyo i Amayuelas* (Barcelona), Professor *Carole Aubert de Vincelles* (Lyon), Dr. *Guillaume Busseuil* (Paris), Dr. *Simon Chardenoux* (Paris), Professor *Giuditta Cordero Moss* (Oslo), Professor *Gerhard Dannemann* (Berlin), Dr. *Martin Ebers* (Barcelona), Professor *Silvia Ferreri* (Torino), Professor *Lars Gorton* (Lund), Professor *Michele Graziadei* (Torino), Professor *Hans Christoph Grigoleit* (Regensburg), Professor *Luc Grynbaum* (Paris), Professor *Geraint Howells* (Lancaster), Professor *Tsvetana Kamenova* (Sofia), Professor *Konstantinos Kerameus* (Athens), Professor *Stefan Leible* (Bayreuth), Professor *Eva Lindell-Frantz* (Lund), Dr. hab. *Piotr Machnikowski* (Wrocław), Professor *Ulrich Magnus* (Hamburg), Professor *Peter Møgelvang-Hansen* (Copenhagen), Professor *Susana Navas Navarro* (Barcelona), Dr. *Paolisa Nebbia* (Oxford), Dr. *Barbara Pasa* (Torino), Professor *Thomas Pfeiffer* (Heidelberg), Professor *António Pinto Monteiro* (Coimbra), Professor *Jerzy Pisulinski* (Kraków), Professor *Elise Poillot* (Paris), Professor *Judith Rochfeld* (Paris), Professor *Ewa Rott-Pietrzyk* (Katowice), Professor *Søren Sandfeld Jakobsen* (Copenhagen), Professor *Hans Schulte-Nölke* (Bielefeld, co-ordinator), Professor *Reiner Schulze* (Münster), Professor *Carla Sieburgh* (Nijmegen), Dr. *Sophie Stalla-Bourdillon* (Florence), Professor *Matthias Storme* (Antwerp and Leuven), Dr. hab. *Maciej Szpunar* (Katowice), Professor *Evelyne Terryn* (Leuven), Dr. *Christian Twigg-Flesner* (Hull), Professor *Antoni Vaquer Aloy* (Lleida), Professor *Thomas Wilhelmsson* (Helsinki), Professor *Fryderyk Zoll* (Kraków).

The members of the *Redaction Committee* are, besides the speaker (*Gianmaria Ajani*) and the co-ordinator (*Hans Schulte-Nölke*) of the Acquis Group, *Gerhard Dannemann* (Chair), *Luc Grynbaum, Reiner Schulze, Matthias Storme, Christian Twigg-Flesner* and *Fryderyk Zoll*. The *Terminology Group* consists of *Gerhard Dannemann* (Chair), *Silvia Ferreri* and *Michele Graziadei*.

Members of the individual Acquis Group Drafting Teams are: 'Contract I' (originally organised in the subteams Definition of Consumer and Business, Form, Good Faith, Pre-contractual Information Duties, Formation, Withdrawal, Non-negotiated Terms): *Esther Arroyo i Amayuelas, Martin Ebers, Christoph Grigoleit, Peter Møgelvang-Hansen, Barbara Pasa, Thomas Pfeiffer, Hans Schulte-Nölke, Reiner Schulze, Evelyne Terryn, Christian Twigg-Flesner, Antoni Vaquer Aloy*; 'Contract II' (responsible for Performance, Non-Performance, Remedies): *Carole Aubert de Vincelles, Piotr Machnikowski, Ulrich Magnus, Jerzy Pisuliński, Judith Rochfeld, Reiner Schulze, Matthias Storme, Maciej Szpunar, Fryderyk Zoll*; 'E-Commerce': *Stefan Leible, Jerzy Pisulinski, Fryderyk Zoll*; 'Non-discrimination': *Stefan Leible, Susana Navas Navarro, Jerzy Pisulinski, Fryderyk Zoll*; 'Specific Performance': *Lars Gorton, Geraint Howells*.

The former Commission on European Contract Law

The members of the three consecutive commissions of the Commission on European Contract Law which met under the chairmanship of Professor *Ole Lando* (Copenhagen) from 1982 to 1999 were: Professor *Christian von Bar* (Osnabrück), Professor *Hugh Beale* (Warwick); Professor *Alberto Berchovitz* (Madrid), Professor *Brigitte Berlioz-Houin* (Paris), Professor *Massimo Bianca* (Rome), Professor *Michael Joachim Bonell* (Rome), Professor *Michael Bridge* (London), Professor *Carlo Castronovo* (Milan), Professor *Eric Clive* (Edinburgh), Professor *Isabel de Magalhães Collaço*† (Lisbon), Professor *Ulrich Drobnig* (Hamburg), Bâtonnier Dr. *André Elvinger* (Luxembourg), Maître *Marc Elvinger* (Luxembourg), Professor *Dimitri Evrigenis*† (Thessaloniki), Professor *Carlos Fereira di Almeida* (Lisbon), Professor Sir *Roy M. Goode* (Oxford), Professor *Arthur Hartkamp* (The Hague), Professor *Ewoud Hondius* (Utrecht), Professor *Guy Horsmans* (Louvain la Neuve), Professor *Roger Houin*† (Paris), Professor *Konstantinos Kerameus* (Athens), Professor *Bryan MacMahon* (Cork), Professor *Hector MacQueen* (Edinburgh), Professor *Willibald Posch* (Graz), Professor *André Prum* (Nancy), Professor *Jan Ramberg* (Stockholm), Professor *Georges Rouhette* (Clermont-Ferrand), Professor *Pablo Salvador Coderch* (Barcelona), Professor *Fernando Marti-*

nez Sanz (Castellon), Professor *Matthias E. Storme* (Leuven), Professor *Denis Tallon* (Paris), Dr. *Frans J. A. van der Velden* (Utrecht), Dr. *J. A. Wade* (The Hague), Professor *William A. Wilson*† (Edinburgh), Professor *Thomas Wilhelmsson* (Helsinki), Professor *Claude Witz* (Saarbrücken), Professor *Reinhard Zimmermann* (Regensburg).

The Compilation and Redaction Team

To co-ordinate between the Study and Acquis Groups, to integrate the PECL material revised for the purposes of the DCFR, and for revision and assimilation of the drafts from the sub-projects we established a "Compilation and Redaction Team" (CRT) at the beginning of 2006. The CRT members are (or were) Professors *Christian von Bar* (Osnabrück), *Hugh Beale* (London and Warwick), *Eric Clive* (Edinburgh), *Johnny Herre* (Stockholm), *Jérôme Huet* (Paris), *Peter Schlechtriem*† (Freiburg i.Br.), *Hans Schulte-Nölke* (Bielefeld), *Matthias Storme* (Leuven), *Stephen Swann* (Osnabrück), *Paul Varul* (Tartu), *Anna Veneziano* (Teramo) and *Fryderyk Zoll* (Cracow); it was chaired by *Eric Clive* and *Christian von Bar* (Osnabrück). Professor *Clive* carried the main drafting and editorial burden at the later (CRT) stages; he is also the main drafter of the list of terminology in Annex 1 of the DCFR. Professor Clive was assisted by *Ashley Theunissen* (Edinburgh), Professor von Bar by *Daniel Smith* (Osnabrück). Over the course of several years *Johan Sandstedt* (Bergen) took care of the Mastercopy of this DCFR and repeatedly brought it up to date.

Funding

The DCFR is the result of years of work by many pan-European teams of jurists. They have been financed from diverse sources which cannot all be named here.[1] Before we came together with other teams in

---

[1]   A complete survey of the sponsors of the Study Group on a European Civil Code will be found in the opening pages of the most recent volume of the Study Group on a European Civil Code's "Principles of

May 2005 to form the 'Network of Excellence'[2] under the European Commission's sixth framework programme for research, from which funds our research has since been supported, the members of the Study Group on a European Civil Code had the benefit of funding from national research councils. Among others the *Deutsche Forschungsgemeinschaft (DFG)* provided over several years the lion's share of the financing including the salaries of the Working Teams based in Germany and the direct travel costs for the meetings of the Co-ordinating Group and the numerous Advisory Councils. The work of the Dutch Working Teams was financed by the *Nederlandse Organisatie voor Wetenschappelijk Onderzoek (NWO)*. Further personnel costs were met by the Flemish *Fonds voor Wetenschappelijk Onderzoek-Vlaanderen (FWO)*, the Greek *Onassis-Foundation*, the Austrian *Fonds zur Förderung der wissenschaftlichen Forschung*, the Portuguese *Fundação Calouste Gulbenkian* and the *Norges forsknings-råd* (the Research Council of Norway). The Acquis Group received substantial support from its preceding Training and Mobility Networks on 'Common Principles of European Private Law' (1997-2002) under the fourth EU Research Framework Programme[3] and on 'Uniform Terminology for European Private Law' (2002-2006) under the fifth Research Framework Programme.[4] We are extremely indebted to all who in this way have made our work possible.

European Law (PEL)" series (as to which see para. 55 at p. 26 above). The sponsors of the Commission on European Contract Law are mentioned in the preface of both volumes of the Principles of European Contract Law (fn. 2 at p. 7 above).

2   'CoPECL: Common Principles of European Contract Law'.

3   TMR (Training and Mobility) Network 'Common Principles of European Private Law' of the Universities of Barcelona, Berlin (Humboldt), Lyon III, Münster (co-ordinator of the Network: Professor *Reiner Schulze*), Nijmegen, Oxford and Turin. funded under the 4th EU Research Framework Programme 1997-2002.

4   TMR (Training and Mobility) Network 'Uniform Terminology for European Private Law' of the Universities of Barcelona, Lyon III, Münster, Nijmegen, Oxford, Turin (co-ordinator of the Network: Professor *Gianmaria Ajani*), Warsaw, funded under the 5th EU Research Framework Programme 2002-2006.

Table of Destinations

An entry in this table indicates a model rule which addresses the same legal issue as that dealt with in the relevant article of the PECL. It does not imply that the corresponding model rule is in the same terms or to the same effect.

	PECL	DCFR Model Rules
Chapter I	1:101	
	(1)	I. – 1:101(1)
	(2)	–
	(3)	–
	(4)	–
	1:102	II. – 1:102(1)
	(1)	II. – 1:102(2)
	(2)	
	1:103	–
	1:104	–
	1:105	II. – 1:104(1), (2)
	1:106	I. – 1:102(1), (3), (4)
	1:107	–
	1:201	
	(1)	II. – 3:301(2); III. – 1:103(1)
	(2)	III. – 1:103(2)
	1:202	III. – 1:104
	1:301	
	(1)	I. – 1:103(1), Annex I: "Conduct"
	(2)	I. – 1:103(1), Annex I: "Court"
	(3)	–
	(4)	I. – 1:103(1), Annex I: "Non-performance"; III. – 1:101(3)
	(5)	–
	(6)	I. – 1:105

	PECL	DCFR Model Rules
	1:302	I. – 1:103(1), Annex 1: "Reasonable"
	1:303	
	(1)	II. – 1:106(2)
	(2)	II. – 1:106(3)
	(3)	II. – 1:106(4)
	(4)	III. – 3:106
	(5)	II. – 1:106(5)
	(6)	II. – 1:106(1)
	1:304	I. – 1:104, Annex 2
	1:305	II. – 1:105
Chapter 2	2:101	
	(1)	II. – 4:101
	(2)	II. – 1:107(1)
	2:102	II. – 4:102
	2:103	II. – 4:103
	2:104	
	(1)	II. – 9:103(1)
	(2)	II. – 9:103(3)(b)
	2:105	II. – 4:104
	2:106	II. – 4:105
	2:107	II. – 1:107(2)
	2:201	II. – 4:201
	2:202	II. – 4:202
	2:203	II. – 4:203
	2:204	II. – 4:204
	2:205	II. – 4:205
	2:206	II. – 4:206
	2:207	II. – 4:207
	2:208	II. – 4:208
	2:209	
	(1)	II. – 4:209(1)
	(2)	II. – 4:209(2)
	(3)	I. – 1:103(1), Annex 1: "Standard terms"
	2:210	II. – 4:210
	2:211	II. – 4:211
	2:301	II. – 3:301(1), (3), (4)
	2:302	II. – 3:302(1), (4)

	PECL	DCFR Model Rules
Chapter 3	3:101	
	(1)	II. – 6:101(1)
	(2)	–
	(3)	II. – 6:101(3)
	3:102	–
	3:201	
	(1)	II. – 6:103(2)
	(2)	II. – 6:104(2)
	(3)	II. – 6:103(3)
	3:202	II. – 6:105
	3:203	II. – 6:108
	3:204	
	(1)	II. – 6:107(1)
	(2)	II. – 6:107(2), (3)
	3:205	II. – 6:109
	3:206	II. – 6:104(3)
	3:207	II. – 6:111(1), (2)
	3:208	–
	3:209	II. – 6:112(1), (3), (4)
	3:301	II. – 6:106
	3:302	–
	3:303	–
	3:304	–
Chapter 4	4:101	II. – 7:101(2)
	4:102	II. – 7:102
	4:103	II. – 7:201
	4:104	II. – 7:202(1)
	4:105	II. – 7:203
	4:106	II. – 7:204
	4:107	II. – 7:205
	4:108	II. – 7:206
	4:109	II. – 7:207
	4:110	
	(1)	II. – 9:404 – II. – 9:406; II. – 9:408 – II. – 9:409
	(2)	II. – 9:407(2)
	4:111	II. – 7:208
	4:112	II. – 7:209

	PECL	DCFR Model Rules
	4:113	
	(1)	II. – 7:210
	(2)	–
	4:114	II. – 7:211
	4:115	II. – 7:212(2)
	4:116	II. – 7:213
	4:117	II. – 7:214
	4:118	II. – 7:215
	4:119	II. – 7:216
Chapter 5	5:101	II. – 8:101
	5:102	II. – 8:102(1)
	5:103	II. – 8:103
	5:104	II. – 8:104
	5:105	II. – 8:105
	5:106	II. – 8:106
	5:107	II. – 8:107
Chapter 6	6:101	II. – 9:102(1)–(4)
	6:102	II. – 9:101(2)
	6:103	II. – 9:201(1)
	6:104	II. – 9:104
	6:105	II. – 9:105
	6:106	II. – 9:106
	6:107	II. – 9:107
	6:108	II. – 9:108
	6:109	III. – 1:109(2)
	6:110	
	(1)	II. – 9:301(1)
	(2)	II. – 9:303(1)
	(3)	II. – 9:303(2), (3)
	6:111	III. – 1:110
Chapter 7	7:101	III. – 2:101(1),(2)
	7:102	III. – 2:102
	7:103	III. – 2:103
	7:104	III. – 2:104
	7:105	III. – 2:105
	7:106	III. – 2:107(1), (2)
	7:107	III. – 2:108
	7:108	III. – 2:109(1)–(3)

	PECL	DCFR Model Rules
	7:109	III. – 2:110
	7:110	III. – 2:111
	7:111	III. – 2:112(1)
	7:112	III. – 2:113(1)
Chapter 8	8:101	III. – 3:101
	8:102	III. – 3:102
	8:103	III. – 3:502(2)
	8:104	III. – 3:202; III. – 3:203
	8:105 (1) (2)	III. – 3:401(2) III. – 3:505
	8:106 (1) (2) (3)	III. – 3:103(1) III. – 3:103(2), (3) III. – 3:503; III. – 3:507(2)
	8:107	III. – 2:106
	8:108	III. – 3:104(1), (3), (5)
	8:109	III. – 3:105
Chapter 9	9:101	III. – 3:301
	9:102	III. – 3:302
	9:103	III. – 3:303
	9:201	III. – 3:401(1), (2), (4)
	9:301 (1) (2)	III. – 3:502(1) –
	9:302	III. – 3:506
	9:303 (1) (2) (3) (4)	III. – 3:507(1) III. – 3:508 III. – 3:508 III. – 3:104(4)
	9:304	III. – 3:504
	9:305	III. – 3:509
	9:306	III. – 3:510
	9:307 – 9:309	III. – 3:511 et seq.
	9:401	III. – 3:601
	9:501	III. – 3:701
	9:502	III. – 3:702

	PECL	DCFR Model Rules
	9:503	III. – 3:703
	9:504	III. – 3:704
	9:505	III. – 3:705
	9:506	III. – 3:706
	9:507	III. – 3:707
	9:508	III. – 3:708
	9:509	III. – 3:710
	9:510	III. – 3:711
Chapter 10	10:101	III. – 4:102
	10:102	III. – 4:103
	10:103	III. – 4:104
	10:104	III. – 4:105
	10:105	III. – 4:106
	10:106	III. – 4:107
	10:107	III. – 4:108
	10:108	
	(1)	III. – 4:109(1)
	(2)	–
	(3)	III. – 4:109(2)
	10:109	III. – 4:110
	10:110	III. – 4:111
	10:111	III. – 4:112
	10:201	III. – 4:202
	10:202	III. – 4:204
	10:203	III. – 4:205
	10:204	III. – 4:206
	10:205	III. – 4:207
Chapter 11	11:101	
	(1)	III. – 5:101(1)
	(2)	III. – 5:101(1)
	(3)	III. – 5:101(2)
	(4)	III. – 5:103(1)
	(5)	–
	11:102	
	(1)	III. – 5:105(1)
	(2)	III. – 5:106(1)
	11:103	III. – 5:107
	11:104	III. – 5:110
	11:201	III. – 5:115

	PECL	DCFR Model Rules
	11:202	III. – 5:114(1), (2)
	11:203	III. – 5:108(1), (3)
	11:204	III. – 5:112(2), (4), (6)
	11:301(1)	III. – 5:108(2), (4) – (6)
	11:302	III. – 5:109
	11:303	
	(1)	III. – 5:118(1); III. – 5:119(2)
	(2)	III. – 5:119(3), (4)
	(3)	III. – 5:119(1)
	(4)	III. – 5:118(1)
	11:304	III. – 5:118(2)
	11:305	–
	11:306	III. – 5:117
	11:307	III. – 5:116(1), (3)
	11:308	–
	11:401	
	(1)	III. – 5:120(1)
	(2)	III. – 5:114(3)
	(3)	III. – 5:108(3)
	(4)	III. – 5:108(3)
Chapter 12	12:101	III. – 5:201
	12:102	III. – 5:202
	12:201	III. – 5:301
Chapter 13	13:101	III. – 6:102
	13:102	III. – 6:103
	13:103	III. – 6:104
	13:104	III. – 6:105
	13:105	III. – 6:106
	13:106	III. – 6:107
	13:107	III. – 6:108
Chapter 14	14:101	III. – 7:101
	14:201	III. – 7:201
	14:202	III. – 7:202
	14:203	III. – 7:203
	14:301	III. – 7:301
	14:302	III. – 7:302
	14:303	III. – 7:303
	14:304	III. – 7:304

	PECL	DCFR Model Rules
	14:305	III. – 7:305
	14:306	III. – 7:306
	14:307	III. – 7:307
	14:401	III. – 7:401
	14:402	III. – 7:402
	14:501	III. – 7:501
	14:502	III. – 7:502
	14:503	III. – 7:503
	14:601	III. – 7:601
Chapter 15	15:101	II. – 7:301
	15:102	II. – 7:302
	15:103	–
	15:104	II. – 7:304
	15:105	II. – 7:305
Chapter 16	16:101	III. – 1:106(1)
	16:102	III. – 1:106(4)
	16:103	III. – 1:106(2), (3)
Chapter 17	17:101	III. – 3:709

Table of Derivations

An entry in this table indicates an article of the PECL which addresses the same legal issue as that dealt with in the relevant model rule. It does not imply that the article of the PECL is in the same terms or to the same effect.

	DCFR Model Rules	PECL
Book I	I. – 1:101	
	(1)	1:101(1)
	(2)	–
	(3)	–
	I. – 1:102	
	(1)	1:106(1), 1st sent.
	(2)	–
	(3)	1:106(1), 2nd sent.
	(4)	1:106(2), 1st sent.
	(5)	–
	I. – 1:103	
	(1) (with Annex 1)	1:301(1), (2), (4); 1:302; 2:209(3)
	(2)	–
	I. – 1:104 (with Annex 2)	1:304
	I. – 1:105	1:301(6)
	I. – 1:106	–
Book II	II. – 1:101	–
	II. – 1:102	
	(1)	1:102(1)
	(2)	1:102(2)
	(3)	–
	II. – 1:103	
	(1)	–
	(2)	2:107
	(3)	–
	II. – 1:104	
	(1)	1:105(1)

	DCFR Model Rules	PECL
Book II	(2)	1:105(2)
	(3)	–
	II. – 1:105	1:305
	II. – 1:106	
	(1)	1:303(6)
	(2)	1:303(1)
	(3)	1:303(2)
	(4)	1:303(3)
	(5)	1:303(5)
	(6)	–
	(7)	–
	II. – 1:107	
	(1)	2:101(2)
	(2)	–
	II. – 1:108	–
	II. – 1:109	–
	II. – 2:101	–
	II. – 2:102	–
	II. – 2:103	–
	II. – 2:104	–
	II. – 2:105	–
	II. – 3:101	–
	II. – 3:102	–
	II. – 3:103	–
	II. – 3:104	–
	II. – 3:105	–
	II. – 3:106	–
	II. – 3:107	–
	II. – 3:201	–
	II. – 3:301	
	(1)	2:301(1)
	(2)	1:201(1)
	(3)	2:301(2)
	(4)	2:301(3)
	II. – 3:302	
	(1)	2:302, 1st sent.
	(2)	–
	(3)	–
	(4)	2:302, 2nd sent.
	II. – 3:401	–

	DCFR Model Rules	PECL
Book II	II. – 4:101	2:101(1)
	II. – 4:102	2:102
	II. – 4:103	2:103
	II. – 4:104	2:105
	II. – 4:105	2:106
	II. – 4:201	2:201
	II. – 4:202	2:202
	II. – 4:203	2:203
	II. – 4:204	2:204
	II. – 4:205	2:205
	II. – 4:206	2:206
	II. – 4:207	2:207
	II. – 4:208	2:208
	II. – 4:209	2:209(1), (2)
	II. – 4:210	2:210
	II. – 4:211	2:211
	II. – 4:301	–
	II. – 4:302	–
	II. – 4:303	–
	II. – 5:101	–
	II. – 5:102	–
	II. – 5:103	–
	II. – 5:104	–
	II. – 5:105	–
	II. – 5:106	–
	II. – 5:201	–
	II. – 5:202	–
	II. – 6:101 (1) (2) (3)	 3:101(1) – 3:101(3)
	II. – 6:102	–
	II. – 6:103 (1) (2) (3)	 – 3:201(1) 3:201(3)
	II. – 6:104 (1)	 –

	DCFR Model Rules	PECL
Book II	(2)	3:201(2)
	(3)	3:206
	II. – 6:105	3:202
	II. – 6:106	3:301
	II. – 6:107	3:204
	II. – 6:108	3:203
	II. – 6:109	3:205
	II. – 6:110	–
	II. – 6:111	
	(1)	3:207(1)
	(2)	3:207(2)
	(3)	–
	II. – 6:112	
	(1)	3:209(1)
	(2)	–
	(3)	3:209(2)
	(4)	3:209(3)
	II. – 7:101	
	(1)	–
	(2)	4:101
	(3)	–
	II. – 7:102	4:102
	II. – 7:201	4:103
	II. – 7:202	4:104
	II. – 7:203	4:105
	II. – 7:204	4:106
	II. – 7:205	4:107
	II. – 7:206	4:108
	II. – 7:207	4:109
	II. – 7:208	4:111
	II. – 7:209	4:112
	II. – 7:210	4:113(1)
	II. – 7:211	4:114
	II. – 7:212	
	(1)	–
	(2)	4:115
	(3)	–
	II. – 7:213	4:116
	II. – 7:214	4:117

	DCFR Model Rules	PECL
Book II	II. – 7:215	4:118
	II. – 7:216	4:119
	II. – 7:301	15:101
	II. – 7:302	15:102
	II. – 7:303	15:104
	II. – 7:304	15:105
	II. – 8:101	5:101
	II. – 8:102	
	(1)	5:102
	(2)	–
	II. – 8:103	5:103
	II. – 8:104	5:104
	II. – 8:105	5:105
	II. – 8:106	5:106
	II. – 8:107	5:107
	II. – 8:201	–
	II. – 8:202	–
	II. – 9:101	
	(1)	–
	(2)	6:102
	(3)	–
	(4)	–
	II. – 9:102	
	(1)	6:101(1)
	(2)	6:101(2)
	(3)	6:101(3)
	(4)	6:101(3)
	(5)	–
	II. – 9:103	
	(1)	2:104(1)
	(2)	–
	(3)(a)	–
	(3)(b)	2:104(2)
	II. – 9:104	6:104
	II. – 9:105	6:105
	II. – 9:106	6:106
	II. – 9:107	6:107
	II. – 9:108	6:108

	DCFR Model Rules	PECL
Book II	II. – 9:201	
	(1)	6:103
	(2)	–
	II. – 9:301	
	(1)	6:110(1)
	(2)	–
	(3)	–
	II. – 9:302	–
	II. – 9:303	6:110(2), (3)
	II. – 9:401	–
	II. – 9:402	–
	II. – 9:403	–
	II. – 9:404	4:110(1)
	II. – 9:405	4:110(1)
	II. – 9:406	4:110(1)
	II. – 9:407	
	(1)	–
	(2)	4:110(2)
	II. – 9:408	
	(1)	4:110(1)
	(2)	–
	II. – 9:409	4:110(1)
	II. – 9:410	–
	II. – 9:411	–
Book III	III. – 1:101	
	(1)	–
	(2)	–
	(3)	1:301(4)
	(4)	–
	(5)	–
	III. – 1:102	–
	III. – 1:103	
	(1)	1:201(1)
	(2)	1:201(2)
	(3)	–
	III. – 1:104	1:202
	III. – 1:105	–
	III. – 1:106	
	(1)	16:101
	(2)	16:103(1)

	DCFR Model Rules	PECL
Book III	(3)	16:103(2)
	(4)	16:102
	(5)	–
	III. – 1:107	–
	III. – 1:108	–
	III. – 1:109	
	(1)	–
	(2)	6:109
	(3)	–
	III. – 1:110	6:111
	III. – 2:101	
	(1)	7:101(1)
	(2)	7:101(2), (3)
	(3)	–
	III. – 2:102	7:102
	III. – 2:103	7:103
	III. – 2:104	7:104
	III. – 2:105	7:105
	III. – 2:106	8:107
	III. – 2:107	
	(1)	7:106(1)
	(2)	7:106(2)
	(3)	–
	III. – 2:108	7:107
	III. – 2:109	
	(1)	7:108(1)
	(2)	7:108(2)
	(3)	7:108(3)
	(4)	–
	III. – 2:110	7:109
	III. – 2:111	7:110
	III. – 2:112	
	(1)	7:111
	(2)	–
	III. – 2:113	
	(1)	7:112
	(2)	–
	III. – 2:114	–
	III. – 3:101	8:101
	III. – 3:102	8:102

	DCFR Model Rules	PECL
Book III	III. – 3:103	
	(1)	8:106(1)
	(2)	8:106(2), 1st sent.
	(3)	8:106(2), 2nd sent.
	III. – 3:104	
	(1)	8:108(1)
	(2)	–
	(3)	8:108(2)
	(4)	9:303(4)
	(5)	8:108(3)
	III. – 3:105	8:109
	III. – 3:106	1:303(4)
	III. – 3:201	–
	III. – 3:202	8:104
	III. – 3:203	8:104
	III. – 3:204	–
	III. – 3:301	9:101
	III. – 3:302	9:102
	III. – 3:303	9:103
	III. – 3:401	
	(1)	9:201(1), 1st sent.
	(2)	8:105(1); 9:201(2)
	(3)	–
	(4)	9:201(1), 2nd sent.
	III. – 3:501	–
	III. – 3:502	
	(1)	9:301(1)
	(2)	8:103
	III. – 3:503	8:106(3)
	III. – 3:504	9:304
	III. – 3:505	8:105(2)
	III. – 3:506	9:302
	III. – 3:507	
	(1)	9:303(1)
	(2)	8:106(3)
	III. – 3:508	9:303(2)
	III. – 3:508	9:303(3)
	III. – 3:509	9:305
	III. – 3:510	9:306

	DCFR Model Rules	PECL
Book III	III. – 3:511	9:307
	III. – 3:511	9:308
	III. – 3:511	9:309
	III. – 3:512	–
	III. – 3:513	9:309
	III. – 3:514	–
	III. – 3:515	–
	III. – 3:601	9:401
	III. – 3:701	9:501
	III. – 3:702	9:502
	III. – 3:703	9:503
	III. – 3:704	9:504
	III. – 3:705	9:505
	III. – 3:706	9:506
	III. – 3:707	9:507
	III. – 3:708	9:508
	III. – 3:709	17:101
	III. – 3:710	9:509
	III. – 3:711	9:510
	III. – 4:101	–
	III. – 4:102	10:101
	III. – 4:103	10:102
	III. – 4:104	10:103
	III. – 4:105	10:104
	III. – 4:106	10:105
	III. – 4:107	10:106
	III. – 4:108	10:107
	III. – 4:109 (1) (2) (3)	 10:108(1) 10:108(3) –
	III. – 4:110	10:109
	III. – 4:111	10:110
	III. – 4:112	10:111
	III. – 4:201	–
	III. – 4:202	10:201
	III. – 4:203	–
	III. – 4:204	10:202

	DCFR Model Rules	PECL
Book III	III. – 4:205	10:203
	III. – 4:206	10:204
	III. – 4:207	10:205
	III. – 5:101	
	(1)	11:101(1), (2)
	(2)	11:101(3)
	III. – 5:102	–
	III. – 5:103	
	(1)	11:101(4)
	(2)	–
	III. – 5:104	–
	III. – 5:105	
	(1)	11:102(1)
	(2)	–
	III. – 5:106	
	(1)	11:102(2)
	(2)	–
	III. – 5:107	11:103
	III. – 5:108	
	(1)	11:203
	(2)	11:301(1)
	(3)	11:203
	(3)	11:401(3)
	(3)	11:401(4)
	(4)	11:301(1)
	(5)	11:301(1)
	(6)	11:301(2)
	III. – 5:109	11:302
	III. – 5:110	11:104
	III. – 5:111	–
	III. – 5:112	
	(1)	–
	(2)	11:204(a)
	(3)	–
	(4)	11:204(b)
	(5)	–
	(6)	11:204(c)
	(7)	–
	III. – 5:113	–

	DCFR Model Rules	PECL
Book III	III. – 5:114	
	(1)	11:202(1)
	(2)	11:202(2)
	(3)	11:401(2)
	III. – 5:115	11:201
	III. – 5:116	
	(1)	11:307(1)
	(2)	–
	(3)	11:307(2)
	III. – 5:117	11:306
	III. – 5:118	
	(1)	11:303(1), (4)
	(2)	11:304
	III. – 5:119	
	(1)	11:303(3)
	(2)	11:303(1)
	(3)	11:303(2)
	(4)	11:303(2)
	III. – 5:120	
	(1)	11:401(1)
	(2)	–
	III. – 5:201	12:101
	III. – 5:202	12:102
	III. – 5:301	12:201
	III. – 6:101	–
	III. – 6:102	13:101
	III. – 6:103	13:102
	III. – 6:104	13:103
	III. – 6:105	13:104
	III. – 6:106	13:105
	III. – 6:107	13:106
	III. – 6:108	13:107
	III. – 6:201	–
	III. – 7:101	14:101
	III. – 7:201	14:201
	III. – 7:202	14:202
	III. – 7:203	14:203
	III. – 7:301	14:301
	III. – 7:302	14:302

	DCFR Model Rules	PECL
Book III	III. – 7:303	14:303
	III. – 7:304	14:304
	III. – 7:305	14:305
	III. – 7:306	14:306
	III. – 7:307	14:307
	III. – 7:401	14:401
	III. – 7:402	14:402
	III. – 7:501	14:501
	III. – 7:502	14:502
	III. – 7:503	14:503
	III. – 7:601	14:601

Model Rules

Book I
General provisions

Book II
Contracts and other juridical acts

Chapter 3: Marketing and pre-contractual duties

Chapter 4: Formation

Chapter 9: Contents and effects of contracts

Book III
Obligations and corresponding rights

Chapter 1: General

Chapter 2: Performance

Chapter 5: Transfer of rights and obligations

Chapter 6: Set-off and merger

Chapter 7: Prescription

Book IV
Specific contracts and the rights and obligations arising from them

Part A. Sales

Chapter 1: Scope of application and general provisions

Chapter 2: Obligations of the seller

Chapter 3: Obligations of the buyer

Chapter 4: Remedies

Chapter 5: Passing of risk

Chapter 6: Consumer goods guarantees

Part B. Lease of goods

Chapter 1: Scope of application and general provisions

Chapter 2: Lease period

Chapter 3: Obligations of the lessor

Chapter 4: Remedies of the lessee

Part C. Services

Chapter 1: General provisions

Chapter 2: Rules applying to service contracts in general

Chapter 3: Construction

Chapter 4: Processing

Chapter 5: Storage

Chapter 6: Design

Chapter 7: Information and advice

Chapter 3: Performance by the representative

Chapter 4: Directions and changes

Chapter 5: Conflict of interest

Chapter 6: Termination by notice other than for non-performance

Chapter 7: Other provisions on termination

Part E. Commercial agency, franchise and distributorship

Chapter 1: General provisions

Chapter 2: Rules applying to all contracts within the scope of this part

Book V
Benevolent intervention in another's affairs

Book VI
Non-contractual liability arising out of damage caused to another

Chapter 1: Fundamental provisions

Chapter 2: Legally relevant damage

Book VII
Unjustified enrichment

Chapter 7: Relation to other legal rules

Book I
General provisions

I. – 1:101: Intended field of application

(1) These rules are intended to be used primarily in relation to contractual and non-contractual rights and obligations and related property matters.

(2) They are not intended to be used, or used without modification or supplementation, in relation to rights and obligations of a public law nature, or in relation to:

(a) the status or legal capacity of natural persons;

(b) wills and succession;

(c) family relationships, including matrimonial and similar relationships;

(d) bills of exchange, cheques and promissory notes and other negotiable instruments;

(e) employment relationships;

(f) the ownership of, or rights in security over, immovable property;

(g) the creation, capacity, internal organisation, regulation or dissolution of companies and other bodies corporate or unincorporated;

(h) matters relating primarily to procedure or enforcement.

(3) Further restrictions on intended fields of application are contained in later Books.

I. – 1:102: Interpretation and development

(1) These rules are to be interpreted and developed autonomously and in accordance with their objectives.

(2) They are to be read in the light of any applicable instruments guaranteeing human rights and fundamental freedoms and any applicable constitutional laws.

(3) In their interpretation and development regard should be had to the need to promote:

(a) uniformity of application;

(b) good faith and fair dealing; and

(c) legal certainty.

(4) Issues within the scope of the rules but not expressly settled by them are so far as possible to be settled in accordance with the principles underlying them.

(5) Where there is a general rule and a special rule applying to a particular situation within the scope of the general rule, the special rule prevails in any case of conflict.

I. – 1:103: Definitions

(1) The definitions in Annex 1 apply for all the purposes of these rules unless the context otherwise requires.

(2) Where a word is defined, other grammatical forms of the word have a corresponding meaning.

I. – 1:104: Computation of time

The provisions of Annex 2 apply in relation to the computation of time for any purpose under these rules.

I. – 1:105: Meaning of "in writing" and similar expressions

(1) For the purposes of these rules, a statement is "in writing" if it is in textual form, on paper or another durable medium and in directly legible characters.

(2) "Textual form" means a text which is expressed in alphabetical or other intelligible characters by means of any support which permits reading, recording of the information contained in the text and its reproduction in tangible form.

(3) "Durable medium" means any material on which information is stored so that it is accessible for future reference for a period of time adequate to the purposes of the information, and which allows the unchanged reproduction of this information.

I. – 1:106: Meaning of "signature" and similar expressions

(1) A reference to a person's signature includes a reference to that person's handwritten signature, electronic signature or advanced electronic signature, and references to anything being signed by a person are to be construed accordingly.

(2) A "handwritten signature" means the name of, or sign representing, a person written by that person's own hand for the purpose of authentication.

(3) An "electronic signature" means data in electronic form which are attached to or logically associated with other electronic data, and which serve as a method of authentication.

(4) An "advanced electronic signature" means an electronic signature which is:

(a) uniquely linked to the signatory;

(b) capable of identifying the signatory;

(c) created using means which can be maintained under the signatory's sole control; and

(d) linked to the data to which it relates in such a manner that any subsequent change of the data is detectable.

(5) In this Article, "electronic" means relating to technology with electrical, digital, magnetic, wireless, optical, electromagnetic, or similar capabilities.

Book II
Contracts and other juridical acts

Chapter 1:
General provisions

II. – 1:101: Definitions
(1) A contract is an agreement which gives rise to, or is intended to give rise to, a binding legal relationship or which has, or is intended to have, some other legal effect. It is a bilateral or multilateral juridical act.
(2) A juridical act is any statement or agreement or declaration of intention, whether express or implied from conduct, which has or is intended to have legal effect as such. It may be unilateral, bilateral or multilateral.

II. – 1:102: Party autonomy
(1) Parties are free to make a contract or other juridical act and to determine its contents, subject to the rules on good faith and fair dealing and any other applicable mandatory rules.
(2) Parties may exclude the application of any of the following rules relating to contracts or other juridical acts, or the rights and obligations arising from them, or derogate from or vary their effects, except as otherwise provided.
(3) A provision to the effect that parties may not exclude the application of a rule or derogate from or vary its effects does not prevent a party from waiving a right which has already arisen and of which that party is aware.

II. – 1:103: Binding effect
(1) A valid contract is binding on the parties.
(2) A valid unilateral promise or undertaking is binding on the person giving it if it is intended to be legally binding without acceptance.

(3) This Article does not prevent modification or termination of any result-ing right or obligation by agreement between the debtor and creditor or as provided by law.

II. – 1:104: Usages and practices

(1) The parties to a contract are bound by any usage to which they have agreed and by any practice they have established between themselves.
(2) The parties are bound by a usage which would be considered generally applicable by persons in the same situation as the parties, except where the application of such usage would be unreasonable.
(3) This Article applies to other juridical acts with any necessary adapta-tions.

II. – 1:105: Imputed knowledge etc.

If any person who with a party's assent was involved in making a contract or other juridical act or in exercising a right or performing an obligation under it:
(a) knew or foresaw a fact, or is treated as having knowledge or foresight of a fact; or
(b) acted intentionally or with any other relevant state of mind
this knowledge, foresight or state of mind is imputed to the party.

II. – 1:106: Notice

(1) This Article applies in relation to the giving of notice for any purpose under these rules. "Notice" includes the communication of a promise, offer, acceptance or other juridical act.
(2) The notice may be given by any means appropriate to the circumstan-ces.
(3) The notice becomes effective when it reaches the addressee, unless it provides for a delayed effect.
(4) The notice reaches the addressee:
    (a) when it is delivered to the addressee;
    (b) when it is delivered to the addressee's place of business, or, where there is no such place of business or the notice does not relate to a business matter, to the addressee's habitual residence;
    (c) in the case of a notice transmitted by electronic means, when it can be accessed by the addressee; or

(d) when it is otherwise made available to the addressee at such a place and in such a way that the addressee could reasonably be expected to obtain access to it without undue delay.

(5) The notice has no effect if a revocation of it reaches the addressee before or at the same time as the notice.

(6) Any reference in these rules to a notice given by or to a person includes a notice given by or to a representative of that person who has authority to give or receive it.

(7) In relations between a business and a consumer the parties may not, to the detriment of the consumer, exclude the rule in paragraph (4)(c) or derogate from or vary its effects.

II. – 1:107: Form

(1) A contract or other juridical act need not be concluded, made or evidenced in writing nor is it subject to any other requirement as to form.

(2) Particular rules may require writing or some other formality.

II. – 1:108: Mixed contracts

(1) For the purposes of this Article a mixed contract is a contract which contains:
   (a) parts falling within two or more of the categories of contracts regulated specifically in these rules; or
   (b) a part falling within one such category and another part falling within the category of contracts governed only by the rules applicable to contracts generally.

(2) Where a contract is a mixed contract then, unless this is contrary to the nature and purpose of the contract, the rules applicable to each relevant category apply, with any appropriate adaptations, to the corresponding part of the contract and the rights and obligations arising from it.

(3) Paragraph (2) does not apply where:
   (a) a rule provides that a mixed contract is to be regarded as falling primarily within one category; or
   (b) in a case not covered by the preceding sub-paragraph, one part of a mixed contract is in fact so predominant that it would be unreasonable not to regard the contract as falling primarily within one category.

(4) In cases covered by paragraph (3) the rules applicable to the category into which the contract primarily falls (the primary category) apply to the contract and the rights and obligations arising from it. However, rules applicable to any elements of the contract falling within another category apply with any appropriate adaptations so far as is necessary to regulate those elements and provided that they do not conflict with the rules applicable to the primary category.

(5) Nothing in this Article prevents the application of any mandatory rules.

II. – 1:109: Partial invalidity or ineffectiveness
Where only part of a contract or other juridical act is invalid or ineffective, the remaining part continues in effect if it can reasonably be maintained without the invalid or ineffective part.

Chapter 2:
Non-discrimination

II. – 2:101: Right not to be discriminated against
A person has a right not to be discriminated against on the grounds of sex or ethnic or racial origin in relation to a contract or other juridical act the object of which is to provide access to, or supply, goods or services which are available to the public.

II. – 2:102: Meaning of discrimination
(1) "Discrimination" means any conduct whereby, or situation where, on grounds such as those mentioned in the preceding Article:
   (a) one person is treated less favourably than another person is, has been or would be treated in a comparable situation; or
   (b) an apparently neutral provision, criterion or practice would place one group of persons at a particular disadvantage when compared to a different group of persons.
(2) Discrimination also includes harassment on grounds such as those mentioned in the preceding Article. "Harassment" means unwanted conduct (including conduct of a sexual nature) which violates a per-

son's dignity, particularly when such conduct creates an intimidating, hostile, degrading, humiliating or offensive environment, or which aims to do so.

(3) Any instruction to discriminate also amounts to discrimination.

II. – 2:103: Exception

Unequal treatment which is justified by a legitimate aim does not amount to discrimination if the means used to achieve that aim are appropriate and necessary.

II. – 2:104: Remedies

(1) If a person is discriminated against contrary to II. – 2:101 (Right not to be discriminated against) then, without prejudice to any remedy which may be available under Book VI (Non-contractual liability for damage caused to another), the remedies for non-performance of an obligation under Book III, Chapter 3 (including damages for economic and non-economic loss) are available.

(2) Any remedy granted must be proportionate to the injury or anticipated injury; the dissuasive effect of remedies may be taken into account.

II. – 2:105: Burden of proof

(1) If a person who considers himself or herself discriminated against on one of the grounds mentioned in II. – 2:101 (Right not to be discriminated against) establishes, before a court or another competent authority, facts from which it may be presumed that there has been such discrimination, it falls on the other party to prove that there has been no such discrimination.

(2) Paragraph (1) does not apply to proceedings in which it is for the court or another competent authority to investigate the facts of the case.

Chapter 3:
Marketing and pre-contractual duties
Section 1:
Information duties

II. – 3:101: Duty to disclose information about goods and services

(1) Before the conclusion of a contract for the supply of goods or services by a business to another person, the business has a duty to disclose to the other person such information concerning the goods or services to be supplied as the other person can reasonably expect, taking into account the standards of quality and performance which would be normal under the circumstances.

(2) In assessing what information the other party can reasonably expect to be disclosed, the test to be applied, if the other party is also a business, is whether the failure to provide the information would deviate from good commercial practice.

II. – 3:102: Specific duties for businesses marketing goods or services to consumers

(1) Where a business is marketing goods or services to a consumer, the business must, so far as is practicable having regard to all the circumstances and the limitations of the communication medium employed, provide such material information as the average consumer needs in the given context to take an informed decision on whether to conclude a contract.

(2) Where a business uses a commercial communication which gives the impression to consumers that it contains all the relevant information necessary to make a decision about concluding a contract, it must in fact contain all the relevant information. Where it is not already apparent from the context of the commercial communication, the information to be provided comprises:

    (a) the main characteristics of the goods or services, the identity and address, if relevant, of the business, the price, and any available right of withdrawal;

    (b) peculiarities related to payment, delivery, performance and complaint handling, if they depart from the requirements of professional diligence.

II. – 3:103: Duty to provide information when concluding contract with a consumer who is at a particular disadvantage

(1) In the case of transactions that place the consumer at a significant informational disadvantage because of the technical medium used for contracting, the physical distance between business and consumer, or the nature of the transaction, the business must, as appropriate in the circumstances, provide clear information about the main characteristics of the goods or services, the price including delivery charges, taxes and other costs, the address and identity of the business with which the consumer is transacting, the terms of the contract, the rights and obligations of both contracting parties, and any available right of withdrawal or redress procedures. This information must be provided a reasonable time before the conclusion of the contract. The information on the right of withdrawal must, as appropriate in the circumstances, also be adequate in the sense of II. – 5:104 (Adequate notification of the right to withdraw).

(2) Where more specific information duties are provided for specific situations, these take precedence over the general information duties under paragraph (1).

II. – 3:104: Information duties in direct and immediate distance communication

(1) When initiating direct and immediate distance communication with a consumer, a business must provide at the outset explicit information on its identity and the commercial purpose of the contact.

(2) Direct and immediate distance communication includes telephone and electronic means such as voice over internet protocol and internet related chat.

(3) The business bears the burden of proof that the consumer has received the information required under paragraph (1).

II. – 3:105: Formation by electronic means

(1) If a contract is to be concluded by electronic means and without individual communication, a business must provide information about the following matters before the other party makes or accepts an offer:
   (a) the technical steps which must be followed in order to conclude the contract;

   (b) whether or not a contract document will be filed by the business and whether it will be accessible;

   (c) the technical means for identifying and correcting input errors before the other party makes or accepts an offer;

   (d) the languages offered for the conclusion of the contract;

   (e) any contract terms used.

(2) The contract terms referred to in paragraph (1)(e) must be available in textual form.

II. – 3:106: Clarity and form of information

(1) A duty to provide information imposed on a business under this Chapter is not fulfilled unless the information is clear and precise, and expressed in plain and intelligible language.

(2) Rules for specific contracts may require information to be provided on a durable medium or in another particular form.

(3) In the case of contracts between a business and a consumer concluded at a distance, information about the main characteristics of the goods or services, the price including delivery charges, taxes and other costs, the address and identity of the business with which the consumer is transacting, the terms of the contract, the rights and obligations of both contracting parties, and any available redress procedures, as may be appropriate in the particular case, need to be confirmed in textual form on a durable medium at the time of conclusion of the contract. The information on the right of withdrawal must also be adequate in the sense of II. – 5:104 (Adequate notification of the right to withdraw).

(4) Failure to observe a particular form will have the same consequences as breach of information duties.

II. – 3:107: Remedies for breach of information duties

(1) If a business is required under II. – 3:103 (Duty to provide information when concluding contract with a consumer who is at a particular disadvantage) to provide information to a consumer before the conclusion of a contract from which the consumer has the right to withdraw, the withdrawal period does not commence until all this information has been provided. Regardless of this, the right of withdrawal lapses after one year from the time of the conclusion of the contract.

(2) Whether or not a contract is concluded, a business which has failed to comply with any duty imposed by the preceding Articles of this Section is liable for any loss caused to the other party to the transaction by such failure.

(3) If a business has failed to comply with any duty imposed by the preceding Articles of this Section and a contract has been concluded, the business has such obligations under the contract as the other party has reasonably expected as a consequence of the absence or incorrectness of the information. Remedies provided under Book III, Chapter 3 apply to non-performance of these obligations.

(4) The remedies provided under this Article are without prejudice to any remedy which may be available under II. – 7:201 (Mistake).

(5) In relations between a business and a consumer the parties may not, to the detriment of the consumer, exclude the application of this Article or derogate from or vary its effects.

Section 2:
Duty to prevent input errors

II. – 3:201: Correction of input errors

(1) A business which intends to conclude a contract by making available electronic means without individual communication for concluding it, must make available to the other party appropriate, effective and accessible technical means for identifying and correcting input errors before the other party makes or accepts an offer.

(2) Where a person concludes a contract in error because of a failure by a business to comply with the duty under paragraph (1) the business is liable for any loss caused to that person by such failure. This is without prejudice to any remedy which may be available under II. – 7:201 (Mistake).

(3) In relations between a business and a consumer the parties may not, to the detriment of the consumer, exclude the application of this Article or derogate from or vary its effects.

Section 3:
Negotiation and confidentiality duties

II. – 3:301: Negotiations contrary to good faith and fair dealing
(1) A person is free to negotiate and is not liable for failure to reach an agreement.
(2) A person who is engaged in negotiations has a duty to negotiate in accordance with good faith and fair dealing. This duty may not be excluded or limited by contract.
(3) A person who has negotiated or broken off negotiations contrary to good faith and fair dealing is liable for any loss caused to the other party to the negotiations.
(4) It is contrary to good faith and fair dealing, in particular, for a person to enter into or continue negotiations with no real intention of reaching an agreement with the other party.

II. – 3:302: Breach of confidentiality
(1) If confidential information is given by one party in the course of negotiations, the other party is under a duty not to disclose that information or use it for that party's own purposes whether or not a contract is subsequently concluded.
(2) In this Article, "confidential information" means information which, either from its nature or the circumstances in which it was obtained, the party receiving the information knows or could reasonably be expected to know is confidential to the other party.
(3) A party who reasonably anticipates a breach of the duty may obtain a court order prohibiting it.
(4) A party who is in breach of the duty is liable to pay damages to the other party for any loss caused by the breach and may be ordered to pay over to the other party any benefit obtained by the breach.

Section 4:
Unsolicited goods or services

II. – 3:401 No obligation arising from failure to respond
(1) If a business delivers unsolicited goods to, or performs unsolicited services for, a consumer:
  (a) no contract arises from the consumer's failure to respond or from any other action or inaction by the consumer in relation to the goods and services; and
  (b) no non-contractual obligation arises from the consumer's acquisition, retention, rejection or use of the goods or receipt of benefit from the services.
(2) Sub-paragraph (b) of the preceding paragraph does not apply if the goods or services were supplied:
  (a) by way of benevolent intervention in another's affairs; or
  (b) in error or in such other circumstances that there is a right to reversal of an unjustified enrichment.
(3) This Article is subject to the rules on delivery of excess quantity under a contract for the sale of goods.

Chapter 4:
Formation
Section 1:
General provisions

II. – 4:101: Requirements for the conclusion of a contract
A contract is concluded, without any further requirement, if the parties:
(a) intend to enter into a binding legal relationship or bring about some other legal effect; and
(b) reach a sufficient agreement.

II. – 4:102: How intention is determined
The intention of a party to enter into a binding legal relationship or bring about some other legal effect is to be determined from the party's statements or conduct as they were reasonably understood by the other party.

II. – 4:103: Sufficient agreement

(1) Agreement is sufficient if:
- (a) the terms of the contract have been sufficiently defined by the parties for the contract to be given effect; or
- (b) the terms of the contract, or the rights and obligations of the parties under it, can be otherwise sufficiently determined for the contract to be given effect.

(2) If one of the parties refuses to conclude a contract unless the parties have agreed on some specific matter, there is no contract unless agreement on that matter has been reached.

II. – 4:104: Merger clause

(1) If a contract document contains an individually negotiated clause stating that the document embodies all the terms of the contract (a merger clause), any prior statements, undertakings or agreements which are not embodied in the document do not form part of the contract.

(2) If the merger clause is not individually negotiated it establishes only a presumption that the parties intended that their prior statements, undertakings or agreements were not to form part of the contract. This rule may not be excluded or restricted.

(3) The parties' prior statements may be used to interpret the contract. This rule may not be excluded or restricted except by an individually negotiated clause.

(4) A party may by statements or conduct be precluded from asserting a merger clause to the extent that the other party has reasonably relied on such statements or conduct.

II. – 4:105: Modification in certain form only

(1) A term in a contract requiring any agreement to modify its terms, or to terminate the relationship resulting from it, to be in a certain form establishes only a presumption that any such agreement is not intended to be legally binding unless it is in that form.

(2) A party may by statements or conduct be precluded from asserting such a term to the extent that the other party has reasonably relied on such statements or conduct.

Section 2:
Offer and acceptance

II. – 4:201: Offer

(1) A proposal amounts to an offer if:
  (a) it is intended to result in a contract if the other party accepts it; and
  (b) it contains sufficiently definite terms to form a contract.
(2) An offer may be made to one or more specific persons or to the public.
(3) A proposal to supply goods or services at stated prices made by a business in a public advertisement or a catalogue, or by a display of goods, is treated, unless the circumstances indicate otherwise, as an offer to sell or supply at that price until the stock of goods, or the business's capacity to supply the service, is exhausted.

II. – 4:202: Revocation of offer

(1) An offer may be revoked if the revocation reaches the offeree before the offeree has dispatched an acceptance or, in cases of acceptance by conduct, before the contract has been concluded.
(2) An offer made to the public can be revoked by the same means as were used to make the offer.
(3) However, a revocation of an offer is ineffective if:
  (a) the offer indicates that it is irrevocable;
  (b) the offer states a fixed time for its acceptance; or
  (c) it was reasonable for the offeree to rely on the offer as being irrevocable and the offeree has acted in reliance on the offer.

II. – 4:203: Rejection of offer

When a rejection of an offer reaches the offeror, the offer lapses.

II. – 4:204: Acceptance

(1) Any form of statement or conduct by the offeree is an acceptance if it indicates assent to the offer.
(2) Silence or inactivity does not in itself amount to acceptance.

II. – 4:205: Time of conclusion of the contract

(1) If an acceptance has been dispatched by the offeree the contract is concluded when the acceptance reaches the offeror.

(2) In the case of acceptance by conduct, the contract is concluded when notice of the conduct reaches the offeror.

(3) If by virtue of the offer, of practices which the parties have established between themselves, or of a usage, the offeree may accept the offer by doing an act without notice to the offeror, the contract is concluded when the offeree begins to do the act.

II. – 4:206: Time limit for acceptance

(1) An acceptance of an offer is effective only if it reaches the offeror within the time fixed by the offeror.

(2) If no time has been fixed by the offeror the acceptance is effective only if it reaches the offeror within a reasonable time.

(3) Where an offer may be accepted by performing an act without notice to the offeror, the acceptance is effective only if the act is performed within the time for acceptance fixed by the offeror or, if no such time is fixed, within a reasonable time.

II. – 4:207: Late acceptance

(1) A late acceptance is nonetheless effective as an acceptance if without undue delay the offeror informs the offeree that it is treated as an effective acceptance.

(2) If a letter or other communication containing a late acceptance shows that it has been dispatched in such circumstances that if its transmission had been normal it would have reached the offeror in due time, the late acceptance is effective as an acceptance unless, without undue delay, the offeror informs the offeree that the offer is considered to have lapsed.

II. – 4:208: Modified acceptance

(1) A reply by the offeree which states or implies additional or different terms which materially alter the terms of the offer is a rejection and a new offer.

(2) A reply which gives a definite assent to an offer operates as an acceptance even if it states or implies additional or different terms, provided

these do not materially alter the terms of the offer. The additional or different terms then become part of the contract.

(3) However, such a reply is treated as a rejection of the offer if:
- (a) the offer expressly limits acceptance to the terms of the offer;
- (b) the offeror objects to the additional or different terms without undue delay; or
- (c) the offeree makes the acceptance conditional upon the offeror's assent to the additional or different terms, and the assent does not reach the offeree within a reasonable time.

II. – 4:209: Conflicting standard terms

(1) If the parties have reached agreement except that the offer and acceptance refer to conflicting standard terms, a contract is nonetheless formed. The standard terms form part of the contract to the extent that they are common in substance.

(2) However, no contract is formed if one party:
- (a) has indicated in advance, explicitly, and not by way of standard terms, an intention not to be bound by a contract on the basis of paragraph (1); or
- (b) without undue delay, informs the other party of such an intention.

II. – 4:210: Formal confirmation of contract between businesses

If businesses have concluded a contract but have not embodied it in a final document, and one without undue delay sends the other a notice in textual form on a durable medium which purports to be a confirmation of the contract but which contains additional or different terms, such terms become part of the contract unless:

(a) the terms materially alter the terms of the contract; or

(b) the addressee objects to them without undue delay.

II. – 4:211: Contracts not concluded through offer and acceptance

The rules in this Section apply with appropriate adaptations even though the process of conclusion of a contract cannot be analysed into offer and acceptance.

Section 3:
Other juridical acts

II. – 4:301: Requirements for a unilateral juridical act
The requirements for a unilateral juridical act are:
(a) that the party doing the act intends to be legally bound or to achieve
    the relevant legal effect;
(b) that the act is sufficiently certain; and
(c) that notice of the act reaches the person to whom it is addressed or, if
    the act is addressed to the public, the act is made public by advertise-
    ment, public notice or otherwise.

II. – 4:302: How intention is determined
The intention of a party to be legally bound or to achieve the relevant legal
effect is to be determined from the party's statements or conduct as they
were reasonably understood by the person to whom the act is addressed.

II. – 4:303: Right or benefit may be rejected
Where a unilateral juridical act confers a right or benefit on the person to
whom it is addressed, that person may reject it by notice to the maker of the
act, provided that is done without undue delay and before the right or
benefit has been expressly or impliedly accepted. On such rejection, the
right or benefit is treated as never having accrued.

Chapter 5:
Right of withdrawal
Section 1:
Exercise and effects

II. – 5:101: Scope and mandatory nature
(1) The provisions in this Section apply where under any rule in Section 2
    or Book IV a party has a right to withdraw from a contract within a
    certain period.
(2) The parties may not, to the detriment of the entitled party, exclude the
    application of the rules in this Chapter or derogate from or vary their
    effects.

II. – 5:102: Exercise of right to withdraw
A right to withdraw is exercised by notice to the other party. No reasons need to be given. Returning the subject matter of the contract is considered a notice of withdrawal unless the circumstances indicate otherwise.

II. – 5:103: Withdrawal period
(1) A right to withdraw may be exercised at any time before the end of the withdrawal period, even if that period has not begun.
(2) Unless provided otherwise, the withdrawal period begins at the latest of the following times;
    (a) the time of conclusion of the contract;
    (b) the time when the entitled party receives from the other party adequate notification of the right to withdraw; or
    (c) if the subject-matter of the contract is the delivery of goods, the time when the goods are received.
(3) The withdrawal period ends fourteen days after it has begun, but no later than one year after the time of conclusion of the contract.
(4) A notice of withdrawal is timely if dispatched before the end of this period.

II. – 5:104: Adequate notification of the right to withdraw
An adequate notification of the right to withdraw requires that the right is appropriately brought to the entitled party's attention, and that the notification provides, in textual form on a durable medium and in clear and comprehensible language, information about how the right may be exercised, the withdrawal period, and the name and address of the person to whom the withdrawal is to be communicated.

II. – 5:105: Effects of withdrawal
(1) Withdrawal terminates the contractual relationship and the obligations of both parties under the contract.
(2) The restitutionary effects of such termination are governed by the rules in Book III, Chapter 3, Section 5, Sub-section 4 (Restitution) as modified by this Article, unless the contract provides otherwise in favour of the withdrawing party. Any payment made by the withdrawing party must be returned without undue delay, and in any case not later than thirty days after the withdrawal becomes effective.

(3) The withdrawing party is not liable to pay:
  (a) for any diminution in the value of anything received under the contract caused by inspection and testing;
  (b) for any destruction or loss of, or damage to, anything received under the contract, provided the withdrawing party used reasonable care to prevent such destruction, loss or damage.

(4) The withdrawing party is liable for any diminution in value caused by normal use, unless that party had not received adequate notice of the right of withdrawal.

(5) Except as provided in this Article, the withdrawing party does not incur any liability through the exercise of the right of withdrawal.

II. – 5:106: Linked contracts

(1) If a consumer exercises a right of withdrawal from a contract for the supply of goods or services by a business, the effects of withdrawal extend to any linked contract.

(2) Where a contract is partially or exclusively financed by a credit contract, they form linked contracts, in particular:
  (a) if the business supplying goods or services finances the consumer's performance;
  (b) if a third party which finances the consumer's performance uses the services of the business for preparing or concluding the credit contract;
  (c) if the credit contract refers to specific goods or services to be financed with this credit, and if this link between both contracts was suggested by the supplier of goods or services, or by the supplier of credit; or
  (d) if there is a similar economic link.

(3) The provisions of II. – 5:105 (Effects of withdrawal) apply accordingly to the linked contract.

(4) Paragraph (1) does not apply to credit contracts financing the contracts mentioned in paragraph (2)(f) of the following Article.

Section 2:
Particular rights of withdrawal

II. – 5:201: Contracts negotiated away from business premises

(1) A consumer is entitled to withdraw from a contract under which a business supplies goods or services, including financial services, to the consumer, or is granted a personal security by the consumer, if the consumer's offer or acceptance was expressed away from the business premises.

(2) Paragraph (1) does not apply to:
   (a) a contract concluded by means of an automatic vending machine or automated commercial premises;
   (b) a contract concluded with telecommunications operators through the use of public payphones;
   (c) a contract for the construction and sale of immovable property or relating to other immovable property rights, except for rental;
   (d) a contract for the supply of foodstuffs, beverages or other goods intended for everyday consumption supplied to the home, residence or workplace of the consumer by regular roundsmen;
   (e) a contract concluded by means of distance communication, but outside of an organised distance sales or service-provision scheme run by the supplier;
   (f) a contract for the supply of goods or services whose price depends on fluctuations in the financial market outside the supplier's control, which may occur during the withdrawal period;
   (g) a contract concluded at an auction;
   (h) travel and baggage insurance policies or similar short-term insurance policies of less than one month's duration.

(3) If the business has exclusively used means of distance communication for concluding the contract, paragraph (1) also does not apply if the contract is for:
   (a) the supply of accommodation, transport, catering or leisure services, where the business undertakes, when the contract is concluded, to supply these services on a specific date or within a specific period;
   (b) the supply of services other than financial services if performance has begun, at the consumer's express and informed request, before

the end of the withdrawal period referred to in II. – 5:103 (Withdrawal period) paragraph (1);

(c) the supply of goods made to the consumer's specifications or clearly personalised or which, by reason of their nature, cannot be returned or are liable to deteriorate or expire rapidly;

(d) the supply of audio or video recordings or computer software
  (i) which were unsealed by the consumer, or
  (ii) which can be downloaded or reproduced for permanent use, in case of supply by electronic means;

(e) the supply of newspapers, periodicals and magazines;

(f) gaming and lottery services.

(4) With regard to financial services, paragraph (1) also does not apply to contracts that have been fully performed by both parties, at the consumer's express request, before the consumer exercises his or her right of withdrawal.

II. – 5:202: Timeshare contracts

(1) A consumer who acquires a right to use immovable property under a timeshare contract with a business is entitled to withdraw from the contract.

(2) Where a consumer exercises the right of withdrawal under paragraph (1), the contract may require the consumer to reimburse those expenses which:

(a) have been incurred as a result of the conclusion of and withdrawal from the contract;

(b) correspond to legal formalities which must be completed before the end of the period referred to in II. – 5:103 (Withdrawal period) paragraph (1);

(c) are reasonable and appropriate;

(d) are expressly mentioned in the contract; and

(e) are in conformity with any applicable rules on such expenses.

The consumer is not obliged to reimburse any expenses when exercising the right of withdrawal in the situation covered by II. – 3:107 (Remedies for breach of information duties) paragraph (1).

(3) The business must not demand or accept any advance payment by the consumer during the period in which the latter may exercise the right of withdrawal.

Chapter 6:
Representation

II. – 6:101: Scope
(1) This Chapter applies to the external relationships created by acts of representation – that is to say, the relationships between:
 (a) the principal and the third party; and
 (b) the representative and the third party.
(2) It applies also to situations where a person purports to be a representative without actually being a representative.
(3) It does not apply to the internal relationship between the representative and the principal.

II. – 6:102: Definitions
(1) A "representative" is a person who has authority to affect the legal position of another person (the principal) in relation to a third party by acting on behalf of the principal.
(2) The "authority" of a representative is the power to affect the principal's legal position.
(3) The "authorisation" of the representative is the granting or maintaining of the authority.
(4) "Acting without authority" includes acting beyond the scope of the authority granted.
(5) A "third party", in this Chapter, includes the representative who, when acting for the principal, also acts in a personal capacity as the other party to the transaction.

II. – 6:103: Authorisation
(1) The authority of a representative may be granted by the principal or by the law.
(2) The principal's authorisation may be express or implied.
(3) If a person causes a third party reasonably and in good faith to believe that the person has authorised a representative to perform certain acts, the person is treated as a principal who has so authorised the apparent representative.

II. – 6:104: Scope of authority

(1) The scope of the representative's authority is determined by the grant.
(2) The representative has authority to perform all incidental acts necessary to achieve the purposes for which the authority was granted.
(3) A representative has authority to delegate authority to another person (the delegate) to do acts on behalf of the principal which it is not reasonable to expect the representative to do personally. The rules of this Chapter apply to acts done by the delegate.

II. – 6:105: When representative's act affects principal's legal position

When the representative acts:

(a) in the name of a principal or otherwise in such a way as to indicate to the third party an intention to affect the legal position of a principal; and
(b) within the scope of the representative's authority,

the act affects the legal position of the principal in relation to the third party as if it had been done by the principal. It does not as such give rise to any legal relation between the representative and the third party.

II. – 6:106: Representative acting in own name

When the representative, despite having authority, does an act in the representative's own name or otherwise in such a way as not to indicate to the third party an intention to affect the legal position of a principal, the act affects the legal position of the representative in relation to the third party as if done by the representative in a personal capacity. It does not as such affect the legal position of the principal in relation to the third party unless this is specifically provided for by any rule of law.

II. – 6:107: Person purporting to act as representative but not having authority

(1) When a person acts in the name of a principal or otherwise in such a way as to indicate to the third party an intention to affect the legal position of a principal but acts without authority, the act does not affect the legal position of the purported principal or, save as provided in paragraph (2), give rise to legal relations between the unauthorised person and the third party.

(2) Failing ratification by the purported principal, the person is liable to pay the third party such damages as will place the third party in the same position as if the person had acted with authority.

(3) Paragraph (2) does not apply if the third party knew or could reasonably be expected to have known of the lack of authority.

II. – 6:108: Unidentified principal

If a representative acts for a principal whose identity is to be revealed later, but fails to reveal that identity within a reasonable time after a request by the third party, the representative is treated as having acted in a personal capacity.

II. – 6:109: Conflict of interest

(1) If an act done by a representative involves the representative in a conflict of interest of which the third party knew or could reasonably be expected to have known, the principal may avoid the act according to the provisions of II. – 7:209 (Notice of avoidance) to II. – 7:213 (Partial avoidance).

(2) There is presumed to be a conflict of interest where:
   (a) the representative also acted as representative for the third party; or
   (b) the transaction was with the representative in a personal capacity.

(3) However, the principal may not avoid the act:
   (a) if the representative acted with the principal's prior consent;
   (b) if the representative had disclosed the conflict of interest to the principal and the principal did not object within a reasonable time; or
   (c) if the principal otherwise knew, or could reasonably be expected to have known, of the representative's involvement in the conflict of interest and did not object within a reasonable time.

II. – 6:110: Several representatives

Where several representatives have authority to act for the same principal, each of them may act separately.

II. – 6:111: Ratification

(1) Where a person purports to act as a representative but acts without authority, the purported principal may ratify the act.

(2) Upon ratification, the act is considered as having been done with authority, without prejudice to the rights of other persons.

(3) The third party who knows that an act was done without authority may by notice to the purported principal specify a reasonable period of time for ratification. If the act is not ratified within that period ratification is no longer possible.

II. – 6:112: Effect of ending or restriction of authorisation

(1) The authority of a representative continues in relation to a third party who knew of the authority notwithstanding the ending or restriction of the representative's authorisation until the third party knows or can reasonably be expected to know of the ending or restriction.

(2) Where the principal is under an obligation to the third party not to end or restrict the representative's authorisation, the authority of a representative continues notwithstanding an ending or restriction of the authorisation even if the third party knows of the ending or restriction.

(3) The third party can reasonably be expected to know of the ending or restriction if, in particular, it has been communicated or publicised in the same way as the granting of the authority was originally communicated or publicised.

(4) Notwithstanding the ending of authorisation, the representative continues to have authority for a reasonable time to perform those acts which are necessary to protect the interests of the principal or the principal's successors.

Chapter 7:
Grounds of invalidity
Section 1:
General provisions

II. – 7:101: Scope

(1) This Chapter deals with the effects of:
   (a) mistake, fraud, threats, or unfair exploitation; and
   (b) infringement of fundamental principles or mandatory rules.

(2) It does not deal with lack of capacity.

(3) It applies in relation to contracts and, with any necessary adaptations, other juridical acts.

II. – 7:102: Initial impossibility

A contract is not invalid, in whole or in part, merely because at the time it is concluded performance of any obligation assumed is impossible, or because a party is not entitled to dispose of any assets to which the contract relates.

Section 2:
Vitiated consent or intention

II. – 7:201: Mistake

(1) A party may avoid a contract for mistake of fact or law existing when the contract was concluded if:
  (a) the party, but for the mistake, would not have concluded the contract or would have done so only on fundamentally different terms and the other party knew or could reasonably be expected to have known this; and
  (b) the other party:
    (i) caused the mistake;
    (ii) caused the contract to be concluded in mistake by leaving the mistaken party in error, contrary to good faith and fair dealing, when the other party knew or could reasonably be expected to have known of the mistake;
    (iii) caused the contract to be concluded in mistake by failing to comply with a pre-contractual information duty or a duty to make available a means of correcting input errors; or
    (iv) made the same mistake.
(2) However a party may not avoid the contract for mistake if:
  (a) the mistake was inexcusable in the circumstances; or
  (b) the risk of the mistake was assumed, or in the circumstances should be borne, by that party.

II. – 7:202: Inaccuracy in communication may be treated as mistake

An inaccuracy in the expression or transmission of a statement is treated as a mistake of the person who made or sent the statement.

II. – 7:203: Adaptation of contract in case of mistake

(1) If a party is entitled to avoid the contract for mistake but the other party performs, or indicates a willingness to perform, the obligations under the contract as it was understood by the party entitled to avoid it, the contract is treated as having been concluded as that party understood it. This applies only if the other party performs, or indicates a willingness to perform, without undue delay after being informed of the manner in which the party entitled to avoid it understood the contract and before that party acts in reliance on any notice of avoidance.

(2) After such performance or indication the right to avoid is lost and any earlier notice of avoidance is ineffective.

(3) Where both parties have made the same mistake, the court may at the request of either party bring the contract into accordance with what might reasonably have been agreed had the mistake not occurred.

II. – 7:204: Liability for loss caused by reliance on incorrect information

(1) A party who has concluded a contract in reasonable reliance on incorrect information given by the other party in the course of negotiations has a right to damages for loss suffered as a result if the provider of the information:

    (a) believed the information to be incorrect or had no reasonable grounds for believing it to be correct; and

    (b) knew or could reasonably be expected to have known that the recipient would rely on the information in deciding whether or not to conclude the contract on the agreed terms.

(2) This Article applies even if there is no right to avoid the contract.

II. – 7:205: Fraud

(1) A party may avoid a contract when the other party has induced the conclusion of the contract by fraudulent misrepresentation, whether by words or conduct, or fraudulent non-disclosure of any information which good faith and fair dealing, or any pre-contractual information duty, required that party to disclose.

(2) A misrepresentation is fraudulent if it is made with knowledge or belief that the representation is false and is intended to induce the recipient to make a mistake. A non-disclosure is fraudulent if it is intended to

induce the person from whom the information is withheld to make a mistake.
(3) In determining whether good faith and fair dealing required a party to disclose particular information, regard should be had to all the circumstances, including:
  (a) whether the party had special expertise;
  (b) the cost to the party of acquiring the relevant information;
  (c) whether the other party could reasonably acquire the information by other means; and
  (d) the apparent importance of the information to the other party.

II. – 7:206: Coercion or threats
(1) A party may avoid a contract when the other party has induced the conclusion of the contract by coercion or by the threat of an imminent and serious harm which it is wrongful to inflict, or wrongful to use as a means to obtain the conclusion of the contract.
(2) A threat is not regarded as inducing the contract if in the circumstances the threatened party had a reasonable alternative.

II. – 7:207: Unfair exploitation
(1) A party may avoid a contract if, at the time of the conclusion of the contract:
  (a) the party was dependent on or had a relationship of trust with the other party, was in economic distress or had urgent needs, was improvident, ignorant, inexperienced or lacking in bargaining skill; and
  (b) the other party knew or could reasonably be expected to have known this and, given the circumstances and purpose of the contract, exploited the first party's situation by taking an excessive benefit or grossly unfair advantage.
(2) Upon the request of the party entitled to avoidance, a court may if it is appropriate adapt the contract in order to bring it into accordance with what might have been agreed had the requirements of good faith and fair dealing been observed.
(3) A court may similarly adapt the contract upon the request of a party receiving notice of avoidance for unfair exploitation, provided that this party informs the party who gave the notice without undue delay after receiving it and before that party has acted in reliance on it.

II. – 7:208: Third persons

(1) Where a third person for whose acts a party is responsible or who with a party's assent is involved in the making of a contract:

    (a) causes a mistake, or knows of or could reasonably be expected to know of a mistake; or

    (b) is guilty of fraud, coercion, threats or unfair exploitation, remedies under this Section are available as if the behaviour or knowledge had been that of the party.

(2) Where a third person for whose acts a party is not responsible and who does not have the party's assent to be involved in the making of a contract is guilty of fraud, coercion, threats or unfair exploitation, remedies under this Section are available if the party knew or could reasonably be expected to have known of the relevant facts, or at the time of avoidance has not acted in reliance on the contract.

II. – 7:209: Notice of avoidance

Avoidance under this Section is effected by notice to the other party.

II. – 7:210: Time

A notice of avoidance under this Section is ineffective unless given within a reasonable time, with due regard to the circumstances, after the avoiding party knew or could reasonably be expected to have known of the relevant facts or became capable of acting freely.

II. – 7:211: Confirmation

If a party who is entitled to avoid a contract under this Section confirms it, expressly or impliedly, after the period of time for giving notice of avoidance has begun to run, avoidance is excluded.

II. – 7:212: Effects of avoidance

(1) A contract which may be avoided under this Section is valid until avoided but, once avoided, is retrospectively invalid from the beginning.

(2) The question whether either party has a right to the return of whatever has been transferred or supplied under a contract which has been avoided under this Section, or a monetary equivalent, is regulated by the rules on unjustified enrichment.

(3) The effect of avoidance under this Section on the ownership of property which has been transferred under the avoided contract is governed by the rules on the transfer of property.

II. – 7:213: Partial avoidance

If a ground of avoidance under this Section affects only particular terms of a contract, the effect of an avoidance is limited to those terms unless, giving due consideration to all the circumstances of the case, it is unreasonable to uphold the remaining contract.

II. – 7:214: Damages for loss

(1) A party who has the right to avoid a contract under this Section (or who had such a right before it was lost by the effect of time limits or confirmation) is entitled, whether or not the contract is avoided, to damages from the other party for any loss suffered as a result of the mistake, fraud, coercion, threats or unfair exploitation, provided that the other party knew or could reasonably be expected to have known of the ground for avoidance.

(2) The damages recoverable are such as to place the aggrieved party as nearly as possible in the position in which that party would have been if the contract had not been concluded, with the further limitation that, if the party does not avoid the contract, the damages are not to exceed the loss caused by the mistake, fraud, coercion, threats or unfair exploitation.

(3) In other respects the rules on damages for non-performance of a contractual obligation apply with any appropriate adaptation.

II. – 7:215: Exclusion or restriction of remedies

(1) Remedies for fraud, coercion, threats and unfair exploitation cannot be excluded or restricted.

(2) Remedies for mistake may be excluded or restricted unless the exclusion or restriction is contrary to good faith and fair dealing.

II. – 7:216: Overlapping remedies

A party who is entitled to a remedy under this Section in circumstances which afford that party a remedy for non-performance may pursue either remedy.

Section 3:
Infringement of fundamental principles or mandatory rules

II. – 7:301: Contracts infringing fundamental principles
A contract is void to the extent that:
(a) it infringes a principle recognised as fundamental in the laws of the Member States of the European Union; and
(b) nullity is required to give effect to that principle.

II. – 7:302: Contracts infringing mandatory rules
(1) Where a contract is not void under the preceding Article but infringes a mandatory rule of law, the effects of that infringement on the validity of the contract are the effects, if any, expressly prescribed by that mandatory rule.
(2) Where the mandatory rule does not expressly prescribe the effects of an infringement on the validity of a contract, a court may:
    (a) declare the contract to be valid;
    (b) avoid the contract, with retrospective effect, in whole or in part; or
    (c) modify the contract or its effects.
(3) A decision reached under paragraph (2) should be an appropriate and proportional response to the infringement, having regard to all relevant circumstances, including:
    (a) the purpose of the rule which has been infringed;
    (b) the category of persons for whose protection the rule exists;
    (c) any sanction that may be imposed under the rule infringed;
    (d) the seriousness of the infringement;
    (e) whether the infringement was intentional; and
    (f) the closeness of the relationship between the infringement and the contract.

II. – 7:303: Effects of nullity or avoidance
(1) The question whether either party has a right to the return of whatever has been transferred or supplied under a contract, or part of a contract, which is void or has been avoided under this Section, or a monetary equivalent, is regulated by the rules on unjustified enrichment.

(2) The effect of nullity or avoidance under this Section on the ownership of property which has been transferred under the void or avoided contract, or part of a contract, is governed by the rules on the transfer of property.

(3) This Article is subject to the powers of the court to modify the contract or its effects.

II. – 7:304: Damages for loss

(1) A party to a contract which is void or avoided, in whole or in part, under this Section is entitled to damages from the other party for any loss suffered as a result of the invalidity, provided that the first party did not know and could not reasonably be expected to have known, and the other party knew or could reasonably be expected to have known, of the infringement.

(2) The damages recoverable are such as to place the aggrieved party as nearly as possible in the position in which that party would have been if the contract had not been concluded or the infringing term had not been included.

Chapter 8:
Interpretation
Section 1:
Interpretation of contracts

II. – 8:101: General rules

(1) A contract is to be interpreted according to the common intention of the parties even if this differs from the literal meaning of the words.

(2) If one party intended the contract, or a term or expression used in it, to have a particular meaning, and at the time of the conclusion of the contract the other party was aware, or could reasonably be expected to have been aware, of the first party's intention, the contract is to be interpreted in the way intended by the first party.

(3) The contract is, however, to be interpreted according to the meaning which a reasonable person would give to it:
   (a) if an intention cannot be established under the preceding paragraphs; or

    (b) if the question arises with a person, not being a party to the contract or a person who by law has no better rights than such a party, who has reasonably and in good faith relied on the contract's apparent meaning.

II. – 8:102: Relevant matters

(1) In interpreting the contract, regard may be had, in particular, to:
    (a) the circumstances in which it was concluded, including the preliminary negotiations;
    (b) the conduct of the parties, even subsequent to the conclusion of the contract;
    (c) the interpretation which has already been given by the parties to terms or expressions which are the same as, or similar to, those used in the contract and the practices they have established between themselves;
    (d) the meaning commonly given to such terms or expressions in the branch of activity concerned and the interpretation such terms or expressions may already have received;
    (e) the nature and purpose of the contract;
    (f) usages; and
    (g) good faith and fair dealing.
(2) In a question with a person, not being a party to the contract or a person such as an assignee who by law has no better rights than such a party, who has reasonably and in good faith relied on the contract's apparent meaning, regard may be had to the circumstances mentioned in sub-paragraphs (a) to (c) above only to the extent that those circumstances were known to, or could reasonably be expected to have been known to, that person.

II. – 8:103: Interpretation against party supplying term

Where there is doubt about the meaning of a contract term not individually negotiated, an interpretation of the term against the party who supplied it is to be preferred.

II. – 8:104: Preference for negotiated terms

Terms which have been individually negotiated take preference over those which have not.

II. – 8:105: Reference to contract as a whole
Terms and expressions are to be interpreted in the light of the whole contract in which they appear.

II. – 8:106: Preference for interpretation which gives terms effect
An interpretation which renders the terms of the contract lawful, or effective, is to be preferred to one which would not.

II. – 8:107: Linguistic discrepancies
Where a contract document is in two or more language versions none of which is stated to be authoritative, there is, in case of discrepancy between the versions, a preference for the interpretation according to the version in which the contract was originally drawn up.

Section 2:
Interpretation of other juridical acts

II. – 8:201: General rules
(1) A unilateral juridical act is to be interpreted in the way in which it could reasonably be expected to be understood by the person to whom it is addressed.
(2) If the person making the juridical act intended the act, or a term or expression used in it, to have a particular meaning, and at the time of the act the person to whom it was addressed was aware, or could reasonably be expected to have been aware, of the first person's intention, the act is to be interpreted in the way intended by the first person.
(3) The act is, however, to be interpreted according to the meaning which a reasonable person would give to it:
    (a) if neither paragraph (1) nor paragraph (2) applies; or
    (b) if the question arises with a person, not being the addressee or a person who by law has no better rights than the addressee, who has reasonably and in good faith relied on the contract's apparent meaning.

II. – 8:202: Application of other rules by analogy
The provisions of Section 1, apart from its first Article, apply with appropriate adaptations to the interpretation of a juridical act other than a contract.

Chapter 9:
Contents and effects of contracts
Section 1:
Contents

II. – 9:101: Terms of a contract

(1) The terms of a contract may be derived from the express or tacit agreement of the parties, from rules of law or from practices established between the parties or usages.

(2) Where it is necessary to provide for a matter which the parties have not foreseen or provided for, a court may imply an additional term, having regard in particular to:

(a) the nature and purpose of the contract;

(b) the circumstances in which the contract was concluded; and

(c) the requirements of good faith and fair dealing.

(3) Any term implied under paragraph (2) should, where possible, be such as to give effect to what the parties, had they provided for the matter, would probably have agreed.

(4) Paragraph (2) does not apply if the parties have deliberately left a matter unprovided for, accepting the consequences of so doing.

II. – 9:102: Certain pre-contractual statements regarded as contract terms

(1) A statement made by one party before a contract is concluded is regarded as a term of the contract if the other party reasonably understood it as being made on the basis that it would form part of the contract terms if a contract were concluded. In assessing whether the other party was reasonable in understanding the statement in that way account may be taken of:

(a) the apparent importance of the statement to the other party;

(b) whether the party was making the statement in the course of business; and

(c) the relative expertise of the parties.

(2) If one of the parties to a contract is a business and before the contract is concluded makes a statement, either to the other party or publicly, about the specific characteristics of what is to be supplied by that

business under the contract, the statement is regarded as a term of the contract unless:

    (a) the other party was aware when the contract was concluded, or could reasonably be expected to have been so aware, that the statement was incorrect or could not otherwise be relied on as such a term; or

    (b) the other party's decision to conclude the contract was not influenced by the statement.

(3) For the purposes of paragraph (2), a statement made by a person engaged in advertising or marketing on behalf of the business is treated as being made by the business.

(4) Where the other party is a consumer then, for the purposes of paragraph (2), a public statement made by or on behalf of a producer or other person in earlier links of the business chain between the producer and the consumer is treated as being made by the business unless the business, at the time of conclusion of the contract, did not know and could not reasonably be expected to have known of it.

(5) In the circumstances covered by paragraph (4) a business which at the time of conclusion of the contract did not know and could not reasonably be expected to have known that the statement was incorrect has a right to be indemnified by the person making the statement for any liability incurred as a result of that paragraph.

II. – 9:103: Terms not individually negotiated

(1) Terms supplied by one party and not individually negotiated may be invoked against the other party only if the other party was aware of them, or if the party supplying the terms took reasonable steps to draw the other party's attention to them, before or when the contract was concluded.

(2) If a contract is to be concluded by electronic means, the party supplying any terms which have not been individually negotiated may invoke them against the other party only if they are made available to the other party in textual form.

(3) For the purposes of this Article:

    (a) "not individually negotiated" has the meaning given by II. – 9:403 (Meaning of "not individually negotiated"); and

(b) terms are not sufficiently brought to the other party's attention by a mere reference to them in a contract document, even if that party signs the document.

II. – 9:104: Determination of price

Where the amount of the price payable under a contract cannot be determined from the terms agreed by the parties, from any other applicable rule of law or from usages or practices, the price payable is the price normally charged in comparable circumstances at the time of the conclusion of the contract or, if no such price is available, a reasonable price.

II. – 9:105: Unilateral determination by a party

Where the price or any other contractual term is to be determined by one party and that party's determination is grossly unreasonable then, notwithstanding any provision in the contract to the contrary, a reasonable price or other term is substituted.

II. – 9:106: Determination by a third person

(1) Where a third person is to determine the price or any other contractual term and cannot or will not do so, a court may, unless this is inconsistent with the terms of the contract, appoint another person to determine it.

(2) If a price or other term determined by a third person is grossly unreasonable, a reasonable price or term is substituted.

II. – 9:107: Reference to a non-existent factor

Where the price or any other contractual term is to be determined by reference to a factor which does not exist or has ceased to exist or to be accessible, the nearest equivalent factor is substituted unless this would be unreasonable in the circumstances, in which case a reasonable price or other term is substituted.

II. – 9:108: Quality

Where the quality of anything to be supplied or provided under the contract cannot be determined from the terms agreed by the parties, from any other applicable rule of law or from usages or practices, the quality required is the quality which the recipient could reasonably expect in the circumstances.

Section 2:
Simulation

II. – 9:201: Effect of simulation

(1) When the parties have concluded a contract or an apparent contract and have deliberately done so in such a way that it has an apparent effect different from the effect which the parties intend it to have, the parties' true intention prevails.

(2) However, the apparent effect prevails in relation to a person, not being a party to the contract or apparent contract or a person who by law has no better rights than such a party, who has reasonably and in good faith relied on the apparent effect.

Section 3:
Effect of stipulation in favour of a third party

II. – 9:301: Basic rules

(1) The parties to a contract may, by the contract, confer a right or other benefit on a third party. The third party need not be in existence or identified at the time the contract is concluded.

(2) The nature and content of the third party's right or benefit are determined by the contract and are subject to any conditions or other limitations under the contract.

(3) The benefit conferred may take the form of an exclusion or limitation of the third party's liability to one of the contracting parties.

II. – 9:302: Rights, remedies and defences

Where one of the contracting parties is bound to render a performance to the third party under the contract, then, in the absence of provision to the contrary in the contract:

(a) the third party has the same rights to performance and remedies for non-performance as if the contracting party was bound to render the performance under a binding unilateral promise in favour of the third party; and

(b) the contracting party may assert against the third party all defences which the contracting party could assert against the other party to the contract.

II. – 9:303: Rejection or revocation of benefit

(1) The third party may reject the right or benefit by notice to either of the contracting parties, if that is done without undue delay after being notified of the right or benefit and before it has been expressly or impliedly accepted. On such rejection, the right or benefit is treated as never having accrued to the third party.

(2) The contracting parties may remove or modify the contractual term conferring the right or benefit if this is done before either of them has given the third party notice that the right or benefit has been conferred. The contract determines whether and by whom and in what circumstances the right or benefit can be revoked or modified after that time.

(3) Even if the right or benefit conferred is by virtue of the contract revocable or subject to modification, the right to revoke or modify is lost if the parties have, or the party having the right to revoke or modify has, led the third party to believe that it is not revocable or subject to modification and if the third party has reasonably acted in reliance on it.

Section 4:
Unfair terms

II. – 9:401: Mandatory nature of following provisions

The parties may not exclude the application of the provisions in this Section or derogate from or vary their effects.

II. – 9:402: Duty of transparency in terms not individually negotiated

(1) Terms which have not been individually negotiated must be drafted and communicated in plain, intelligible language.

(2) In a contract between a business and a consumer a term which has been supplied by the business in breach of the duty of transparency imposed by paragraph (1) may on that ground alone be considered unfair.

II. – 9:403: Meaning of "not individually negotiated"

(1) A term supplied by one party is not individually negotiated if the other party has not been able to influence its content, in particular because it has been drafted in advance, whether or not as part of standard terms.

(2) If one party supplies a selection of terms to the other party, a term will not be regarded as individually negotiated merely because the other party chooses that term from that selection.

(3) The party supplying a standard term bears the burden of proving that it has been individually negotiated.

(4) In a contract between a business and a consumer, the business bears the burden of proving that a term supplied by the business, whether or not as part of standard terms, has been individually negotiated.

(5) In contracts between a business and a consumer, terms drafted by a third person are considered to have been supplied by the business, unless the consumer introduced them to the contract.

II. – 9:404: Meaning of "unfair" in contracts between a business and a consumer

In a contract between a business and a consumer, a term [which has not been individually negotiated] is unfair for the purposes of this Section if it is supplied by the business and if it significantly disadvantages the consumer, contrary to good faith and fair dealing.

II. – 9:405: Meaning of "unfair" in contracts between non-business parties

In a contract between parties neither of whom is a business, a term is unfair for the purposes of this Section only if it is a term forming part of standard terms supplied by one party and significantly disadvantages the other party, contrary to good faith and fair dealing.

II. – 9:406: Meaning of "unfair" in contracts between businesses

A term in a contract between businesses is unfair for the purposes of this Section only if it is a term forming part of standard terms supplied by one party and of such a nature that its use grossly deviates from good commercial practice, contrary to good faith and fair dealing.

II. – 9:407: Exclusions from unfairness test

(1) Contract terms are not subjected to an unfairness test under this Section if they are based on:

    (a) provisions of the applicable law;

    (b) international conventions to which the Member States are parties, or to which the European Union is a party; or

    (c) these rules.

(2) For contract terms which are drafted in plain and intelligible language, the unfairness test extends neither to the definition of the main subject matter of the contract, nor to the adequacy of the price to be paid.

II. – 9:408: Factors to be taken into account in assessing unfairness

(1) When assessing the unfairness of a contractual term for the purposes of this Section, regard is to be had to the duty of transparency under II. – 9:402 (Duty of transparency in terms not individually negotiated), to the nature of the goods or services to be provided under the contract, to the circumstances prevailing during the conclusion of the contract, to the other terms of the contract and to the terms of any other contract on which the contract depends.

(2) For the purposes of II. – 9:404 (Meaning of "unfair" in contracts between a business and a consumer) the circumstances prevailing during the conclusion of the contract include the extent to which the consumer was given a real opportunity to become acquainted with the term before the conclusion of the contract.

II. – 9:409: Effects of unfair terms

(1) A term which is unfair under this Section is not binding on the party who did not supply it.

(2) If the contract can reasonably be maintained without the unfair term, the other terms remain binding on the parties.

II. – 9:410: Exclusive jurisdiction clauses

(1) A term in a contract between a business and a consumer is unfair for the purposes of this Section if it is supplied by the business and if it confers exclusive jurisdiction for all disputes arising under the contract on the court for the place where the business is domiciled.

(2) Paragraph (1) does not apply if the chosen court is also the court for the place where the consumer is domiciled.

II. – 9:411: Terms which are presumed to be unfair in contracts between a business and a consumer

(1) A term in a contract between a business and a consumer is presumed to be unfair for the purposes of this Section if it is supplied by the business and if it:

(a) excludes or limits the liability of a business for death or personal injury caused to a consumer through an act or omission of that business;

(b) inappropriately excludes or limits the remedies, including any right to set-off, available to the consumer against the business or a third party for non-performance by the business of obligations under the contract;

(c) makes binding on a consumer an obligation which is subject to a condition the fulfilment of which depends solely on the intention of the business;

(d) permits a business to keep money paid by a consumer if the latter decides not to conclude the contract, or perform obligations under it, without providing for the consumer to receive compensation of an equivalent amount from the business in the reverse situation;

(e) requires a consumer who fails to perform his or her obligations to pay a disproportionately high amount of damages;

(f) entitles a business to withdraw from or terminate the contractual relationship on a discretionary basis without giving the same right to the consumer, or entitles a business to keep money paid for services not yet supplied in the case where the business withdraws from or terminates the contractual relationship;

(g) enables a business to terminate a contractual relationship of indeterminate duration without reasonable notice, except where there are serious grounds for doing so; this does not affect terms in financial services contracts where there is a valid reason, provided that the supplier is required to inform the other contracting party or parties thereof immediately;

(h) automatically extends a contract of fixed duration unless the consumer indicates otherwise, in cases where such terms provide for an unreasonably early deadline;

(i) enables a business to alter the terms of the contract unilaterally without a valid reason which is specified in the contract; this does not affect terms under which a supplier of financial services reserves the right to change the rate of interest to be paid by, or to, the consumer, or the amount of other charges for financial services without notice where there is a valid reason, provided that the supplier is required to inform the consumer at the earliest opportunity and that the consumer is free to terminate the contractual relationship with immediate effect; neither does it affect terms under which a business reserves the right to alter unilaterally the conditions of a contract of indeterminate duration, provided that the business is required to inform the consumer with reasonable notice, and that the consumer is free to terminate the contractual relationship;

(j) enables a business to alter unilaterally without a valid reason any characteristics of the goods or services to be provided;

(k) provides that the price of goods is to be determined at the time of delivery, or allows a business to increase the price without giving the consumer the right to withdraw if the increased price is too high in relation to the price agreed at the conclusion of the contract; this does not affect price-indexation clauses, where lawful, provided that the method by which prices vary is explicitly described;

(l) gives a business the right to determine whether the goods or services supplied are in conformity with the contract, or gives the business the exclusive right to interpret any term of the contract;

(m) limits the obligation of a business to respect commitments undertaken by its agents, or makes its commitments subject to compliance with a particular formality;

(n) obliges a consumer to fulfil all his or her obligations where the business fails to fulfil its own;

(o) allows a business to transfer its rights and obligations under the contract without the consumer's consent, if this could reduce the guarantees available to the consumer;

(p) excludes or restricts a consumer's right to take legal action or to exercise any other remedy, in particular by referring the consumer to arbitration proceedings which are not covered by legal provisions, by unduly restricting the evidence available to the consumer, or by shifting a burden of proof on to the consumer.

(2) Subparagraphs (g), (i) and (k) do not apply to:

    (a) transactions in transferable securities, financial instruments and other products or services where the price is linked to fluctuations in a stock exchange quotation or index or a financial market rate beyond the control of the business;

    (b) contracts for the purchase or sale of foreign currency, traveller's cheques or international money orders denominated in foreign currency.

Book III
Obligations and corresponding rights

Chapter 1:
General

III. – 1:101: Definitions
(1) An obligation is a duty to perform which one party to a legal relationship, the debtor, owes to another party, the creditor.
(2) Performance of an obligation is the doing by the debtor of what is to be done under the obligation or the not doing by the debtor of what is not to be done.
(3) Non-performance of an obligation is any failure to perform the obligation, whether or not excused, and includes delayed performance and any other performance which is not in accordance with the terms regulating the obligation.
(4) An obligation is reciprocal in relation to another obligation if:
   (a) performance of the obligation is due in exchange for performance of the other obligation;
   (b) it is an obligation to facilitate or accept performance of the other obligation; or
   (c) it is so clearly connected to the other obligation or its subject matter that performance of the one can reasonably be regarded as dependent on performance of the other.
(5) The terms regulating an obligation may be derived from a contract or other juridical act, the law or a legally binding usage or practice, or a court order; and similarly for the terms regulating a right.

III. – 1:102: Scope of Book
This Book applies to obligations within the scope of these rules, whether they are contractual or not, and to corresponding rights to performance.

III. – 1:103: Good faith and fair dealing

(1) A person has a duty to act in accordance with good faith and fair dealing in performing an obligation, in exercising a right to performance, in pursuing or defending a remedy for non-performance, or in exercising a right to terminate an obligation or contractual relationship.

(2) The duty may not be excluded or limited by contract.

(3) Breach of the duty does not give rise directly to the remedies for non-performance of an obligation but may preclude the person in breach from exercising or relying on a right, remedy or defence which that person would otherwise have.

III. – 1:104: Co-operation

The debtor and creditor are obliged to co-operate with each other when and to the extent that this can reasonably be expected for the performance of the debtor's obligation.

III. – 1:105: Non-discrimination

Chapter 2 (Non-discrimination) of Book II applies with appropriate adaptations to:

(a) the performance of any obligation to provide access to, or supply, goods, services or other benefits which are available to members of the public;

(b) the exercise of a right to performance of any such obligation or the pursuing or defending of any remedy for non-performance of any such obligation; and

(c) the exercise of a right to terminate any such obligation.

III. – 1:106: Conditional rights and obligations

(1) The terms regulating a right or obligation may provide that it is conditional upon the occurrence of an uncertain future event, so that it takes effect only if the event occurs (suspensive condition) or comes to an end if the event occurs (resolutive condition).

(2) Upon fulfilment of a suspensive condition, the relevant right or obligation takes effect.

(3) Upon fulfilment of a resolutive condition, the relevant right or obligation comes to an end.

(4) When a party, contrary to the duty of good faith and fair dealing or the obligation to co-operate, interferes with a condition so as to bring

about its fulfilment or non-fulfilment to that party's advantage, the other party may treat the condition as not having been fulfilled or as having been fulfilled as the case may be.

(5) When a contractual obligation comes to an end on the fulfilment of a resolutive condition any restitutionary effects are regulated by the rules in Chapter 3, Section 5, Sub-section 4 (Restitution) with appropriate adaptations.

III. – 1:107: Time-limited rights and obligations

(1) The terms regulating a right or obligation may provide that it is to take effect from or end at a specified time, after a specified period of time or on the occurrence of an event which is certain to occur.

(2) It will take effect or come to an end at the time or on the event without further steps having to be taken .

(3) When a contractual obligation comes to an end under this Article any restitutionary effects are regulated by the rules in Chapter 3, Section 5, Sub-section 4 (Restitution) with appropriate adaptations.

III. – 1:108: Variation or termination by agreement

(1) A right, obligation or contractual relationship may be varied or terminated by agreement at any time.

(2) Where the parties do not regulate the effects of termination, then:
   (a) it has prospective effect only and does not affect any right to damages, or a stipulated payment, for non-performance of any obligation performance of which was due before termination;
   (b) it does not affect any provision for the settlement of disputes or any other provision which is to operate even after termination; and
   (c) in the case of a contractual obligation or relationship any restitutionary effects are regulated by the rules in Chapter 3, Section 5, Sub-section 4 (Restitution) with appropriate adaptations.

III. – 1:109: Variation or termination by notice

(1) A right, obligation or contractual relationship may be varied or terminated by notice by either party where this is provided for by the terms regulating it.

(2) Where, in a case involving continuous or periodic performance of a contractual obligation, the terms of the contract do not say when the contractual relationship is to end or say that it will never end, it may be

terminated by either party by giving a reasonable period of notice. If the performance or counter-performance is to be made at regular intervals the reasonable period of notice is not less than the interval between performances or, if longer, between counter-performances.

(3) Where the parties do not regulate the effects of termination, then:

   (a) it has prospective effect only and does not affect any right to damages, or a stipulated payment, for non-performance of any obligation performance of which was due before termination;

   (b) it does not affect any provision for the settlement of disputes or any other provision which is to operate even after termination; and

   (c) in the case of a contractual obligation or relationship any restitutionary effects are regulated by the rules in Chapter 3, Section 5, Sub-section 4 (Restitution) with appropriate adaptations.

III. – 1:110: Variation or termination by court on a change of circumstances

(1) An obligation must be performed even if performance has become more onerous, whether because the cost of performance has increased or because the value of what is to be received in return has diminished.

(2) If, however, performance of a contractual obligation or of an obligation arising from a unilateral juridical act becomes so onerous because of an exceptional change of circumstances that it would be manifestly unjust to hold the debtor to the obligation a court may:

   (a) vary the obligation in order to make it reasonable and equitable in the new circumstances; or

   (b) terminate the obligation at a date and on terms to be determined by the court.

(3) Paragraph (2) applies only if:

   (a) the change of circumstances occurred after the time when the obligation was incurred,

   (b) the debtor did not at that time take into account, and could not reasonably be expected to have taken into account, the possibility or scale of that change of circumstances;

   (c) the debtor did not assume, and cannot reasonably be regarded as having assumed, the risk of that change of circumstances; and

   (d) the debtor has attempted, reasonably and in good faith, to achieve by negotiation a reasonable and equitable adjustment of the terms regulating the obligation.

Chapter 2:
Performance

III. – 2:101: Place of performance

(1) If the place of performance of an obligation cannot be otherwise determined from the terms regulating the obligation it is:
- (a) in the case of a monetary obligation, the creditor's place of business;
- (b) in the case of any other obligation, the debtor's place of business.

(2) For the purposes of the preceding paragraph:
- (a) if a party has more than one place of business, the place of business is that which has the closest relationship to the obligation; and
- (b) if a party does not have a place of business, or the obligation does not relate to a business matter, the habitual residence is substituted.

(3) If, in a case to which paragraph (1) applies, a party causes any increase in the expenses incidental to performance by a change in place of business or habitual residence subsequent to the time when the obligation was incurred, that party must bear the increase.

III. – 2:102: Time of performance

(1) If the time at which, or a period of time within which, an obligation is to be performed cannot otherwise be determined from the terms regulating the obligation it must be performed within a reasonable time after it arises.

(2) If a period of time within which the obligation is to be performed can be determined from the terms regulating the obligation, the obligation may be performed at any time within that period chosen by the debtor unless the circumstances of the case indicate that the creditor is to choose the time.

III. – 2:103: Early performance

(1) A creditor may reject an offer to perform before performance is due unless the early performance would not cause the creditor unreasonable prejudice.

(2) A creditor's acceptance of early performance does not affect the time fixed for the performance by the creditor of any reciprocal obligation.

III. – 2:104: Order of performance

If the order of performance of reciprocal obligations cannot be otherwise determined from the terms regulating the obligations then, to the extent that the obligations can be performed simultaneously, the parties are bound to perform simultaneously unless the circumstances indicate otherwise.

III. – 2:105: Alternative obligations or methods of performance

(1) Where a debtor is bound to perform one of two or more obligations, or to perform an obligation in one of two or more ways, the choice belongs to the debtor, unless the terms regulating the obligations or obligation provide otherwise.

(2) If the party who is to make the choice fails to choose by the time when performance is due, then:

    (a) if the delay amounts to a fundamental non-performance, the right to choose passes to the other party;

    (b) if the delay does not amount to a fundamental non-performance, the other party may give a notice fixing an additional period of reasonable length in which the party to choose must do so. If the latter still fails to do so, the right to choose passes to the other party.

III. – 2:106: Performance entrusted to another

A debtor who entrusts performance of an obligation to another person remains responsible for performance.

III. – 2:107: Performance by a third person

(1) Where personal performance by the debtor is not required by the terms regulating the obligation, the creditor cannot refuse performance by a third person if:

    (a) the third person acts with the assent of the debtor; or

    (b) the third person has a legitimate interest in performing and the debtor has failed to perform or it is clear that the debtor will not perform at the time performance is due.

(2) Performance by a third person in accordance with paragraph (1) discharges the debtor except to the extent that the third person takes over the creditor's right by assignment or subrogation.

(3) Where personal performance by the debtor is not required and the creditor accepts performance of the debtor's obligation by a third party in circumstances not covered by paragraph (1) the debtor is discharged but the creditor is liable to the debtor for any loss caused by that acceptance.

III. – 2:108: Method of payment

(1) Payment of money due may be made by any method used in the ordinary course of business.

(2) A creditor who accepts a cheque or other order to pay or a promise to pay is presumed to do so only on condition that it will be honoured. The creditor may not enforce the original obligation to pay unless the order or promise is not honoured.

III. – 2:109: Currency of payment

(1) The debtor and the creditor may agree that payment is to be made only in a specified currency.

(2) In the absence of such agreement, a sum of money expressed in a currency other than that of the place where payment is due may be paid in the currency of that place according to the rate of exchange prevailing there at the time when payment is due.

(3) If, in a case falling within the preceding paragraph, the debtor has not paid at the time when payment is due, the creditor may require payment in the currency of the place where payment is due according to the rate of exchange prevailing there either at the time when payment is due or at the time of actual payment.

(4) Where a monetary obligation is not expressed in a particular currency, payment must be made in the currency of the place where payment is to be made.

III. – 2:110: Imputation of performance

(1) Where a debtor has to perform several obligations of the same nature and makes a performance which does not suffice to extinguish all of the obligations, then subject to paragraph (5), the debtor may at the time of performance notify the creditor of the obligation to which the performance is to be imputed.

(2) If the debtor does not make such a notification the creditor may, within a reasonable time and by notifying the debtor, impute the performance to one of the obligations.

(3) An imputation under paragraph (2) is not effective if it is to an obligation which is not yet due, or is illegal, or is disputed.

(4) In the absence of an effective imputation by either party, and subject to the following paragraph, the performance is imputed to that obligation which satisfies one of the following criteria in the sequence indicated:
  (a) the obligation which is due or is the first to fall due;
  (b) the obligation for which the creditor has the least security;
  (c) the obligation which is the most burdensome for the debtor;
  (d) the obligation which has arisen first.
  If none of the preceding criteria applies, the performance is imputed proportionately to all the obligations.

(5) In the case of a monetary obligation, a payment by the debtor is to be imputed, first, to expenses, secondly, to interest, and thirdly, to principal, unless the creditor makes a different imputation.

III. – 2:111: Property not accepted

(1) A person who has an obligation to deliver or return corporeal property other than money and who is left in possession of the property because of the creditor's failure to accept or retake the property, must take reasonable steps to protect and preserve it.

(2) The debtor may obtain discharge from the obligation to deliver or return:
  (a) by depositing the property on reasonable terms with a third person to be held to the order of the creditor, and notifying the creditor of this; or
  (b) by selling the property on reasonable terms after notice to the creditor, and paying the net proceeds to the creditor.

(3) Where, however, the property is liable to rapid deterioration or its preservation is unreasonably expensive, the debtor must take reasonable steps to dispose of it. The debtor may obtain discharge from the obligation to deliver or return by paying the net proceeds to the creditor.

(4) The debtor left in possession is entitled to be reimbursed or to retain out of the proceeds of sale any costs reasonably incurred.

III. – 2:112: Money not accepted

(1) Where a creditor fails to accept money properly tendered by the debtor, the debtor may after notice to the creditor obtain discharge from the obligation to pay by depositing the money to the order of the creditor in accordance with the law of the place where payment is due.

(2) Paragraph (1) applies, with appropriate adaptations, to money properly tendered by a third party in circumstances where the creditor is not entitled to refuse such performance.

III. – 2:113: Costs and formalities of performance

(1) The costs of performing an obligation are borne by the debtor.

(2) In the case of a monetary obligation the debtor's obligation to pay includes taking such steps and complying with such formalities as may be necessary to enable payment to be made.

III. – 2:114: Extinctive effect of performance

Full performance extinguishes the obligation if it is:

(a) in accordance with the terms regulating the obligation; or

(b) of such a type as by law to afford the debtor a good discharge.

Chapter 3:
Remedies for non-performance
Section 1:
General

III. – 3:101: Remedies available

(1) If an obligation is not performed by the debtor and the non-performance is not excused, the creditor may resort to any of the remedies set out in this Chapter.

(2) If the debtor's non-performance is excused, the creditor may resort to any of those remedies except enforcing specific performance and damages.

(3) The creditor may not resort to any of those remedies to the extent that the creditor caused the debtor's non-performance.

III. – 3:102: Cumulation of remedies

Remedies which are not incompatible may be cumulated. In particular, a creditor is not deprived of the right to damages by resorting to any other remedy.

III. – 3:103: Notice fixing additional period for performance

(1) In any case of non-performance of an obligation the creditor may by notice to the debtor allow an additional period of time for performance.

(2) During the additional period the creditor may withhold performance of the creditor's reciprocal obligations and may claim damages, but may not resort to any other remedy.

(3) If the creditor receives notice from the debtor that the debtor will not perform within that period, or if upon expiry of that period due performance has not been made, the creditor may resort to any available remedy.

III. – 3:104: Excuse due to an impediment

(1) A debtor's non-performance of an obligation is excused if it is due to an impediment beyond the debtor's control and if the debtor could not reasonably be expected to have avoided or overcome the impediment or its consequences.

(2) Where the obligation arose out of a contract or other juridical act, non-performance is not excused if the debtor could reasonably be expected to have taken the impediment into account at the time when the obligation was incurred.

(3) Where the excusing impediment is only temporary the excuse has effect for the period during which the impediment exists. However, if the delay amounts to a fundamental non-performance, the creditor may treat it as such.

(4) Where the excusing impediment is permanent the obligation is extinguished. Any reciprocal obligation is also extinguished. In the case of contractual obligations any restitutionary effects of extinction are regulated by the rules in Chapter 3, Section 5, Sub-section 4 (Restitution) with appropriate adaptations.

(5) The debtor must ensure that notice of the impediment and of its effect on the ability to perform reaches the creditor within a reasonable time after the debtor knew or could reasonably be expected to have known

of these circumstances. The creditor is entitled to damages for any loss resulting from the non-receipt of such notice.

III. – 3:105: Term excluding or restricting remedies

(1) A term of a contract or other juridical act which purports to exclude or restrict liability to pay damages for personal injury (including fatal injury) caused intentionally or by gross negligence is void.
(2) A term excluding or restricting a remedy for non-performance of an obligation, even if valid and otherwise effective, having regard in particular to the rules on unfair contract terms in Book II, Chapter 9, Section 4, may nevertheless not be invoked if it would be contrary to good faith and fair dealing to do so.

III. – 3:106: Notices relating to non-performance

(1) If the creditor gives notice to the debtor because of the debtor's non-performance of an obligation or because such non-performance is anticipated, and the notice is properly dispatched or given, a delay or inaccuracy in the transmission of the notice or its failure to arrive does not prevent it from having effect.
(2) The notice has effect from the time at which it would have arrived in normal circumstances.

III. – 3:107: Failure to notify non-conformity

(1) If, in the case of an obligation to supply goods or services, the debtor supplies goods or services which are not in conformity with the terms regulating the obligation, the creditor may not rely on the lack of conformity unless the creditor gives notice to the debtor within a reasonable time specifying the nature of the lack of conformity.
(2) The reasonable time runs from the time when the goods are supplied or the service is completed or from the time, if it is later, when the creditor discovered or could reasonably be expected to have discovered the non-conformity.
(3) The debtor is not entitled to rely on paragraph (1) if the failure relates to facts which the debtor knew or could reasonably be expected to have known and which the debtor did not disclose to the creditor.
(4) This Article does not apply where the creditor is a consumer.

Section 2:
Cure by debtor of non-conforming performance

III. – 3:201: Scope
This Section applies where a debtor's performance does not conform to the terms regulating the obligation.

III. – 3:202: Cure by debtor: general rules
(1) The debtor may make a new and conforming tender if that can be done within the time allowed for performance.
(2) If the debtor cannot make a new and conforming tender within the time allowed for performance but, promptly after being notified of the lack of conformity, offers to cure it within a reasonable time and at the debtor's own expense, the creditor may not pursue any remedy for non-performance, other than withholding performance, before allowing the debtor a reasonable period in which to attempt to cure the non-conformity.
(3) Paragraph (2) is subject to the provisions of the following Article.

III. – 3:203: When creditor need not allow debtor an opportunity to cure
The creditor need not, under paragraph (2) of the preceding Article, allow the debtor a period in which to attempt cure if:
(a) failure to perform a contractual obligation within the time allowed for performance amounts to a fundamental non-performance as defined in III. – 3:502 (2);
(b) the creditor has reason to believe that the debtor's performance was made with knowledge of the non-conformity and was not in accordance with good faith and fair dealing;
(c) the creditor has reason to believe that the debtor will be unable to effect the cure within a reasonable time and without significant inconvenience to the creditor or other prejudice to the creditor's legitimate interests; or
(d) cure would be inappropriate in the circumstances.

III. – 3:204: Consequences of allowing debtor opportunity to cure

(1) During the period allowed for cure the creditor may withhold performance of the creditor's reciprocal obligations, but may not resort to any other remedy.

(2) If the debtor fails to effect cure within the time allowed, the creditor may resort to any available remedy.

(3) Notwithstanding cure, the creditor retains the right to damages for any loss caused by the debtor's initial or subsequent non-performance or by the process of effecting cure.

Section 3:
Right to enforce performance

III. – 3:301: Monetary obligations

(1) The creditor is entitled to recover money payment of which is due.

(2) Where the creditor has not yet performed the reciprocal obligation for which payment will be due and it is clear that the debtor in the monetary obligation will be unwilling to receive performance, the creditor may nonetheless proceed with performance and may recover payment unless:

    (a) the creditor could have made a reasonable substitute transaction without significant effort or expense; or

    (b) performance would be unreasonable in the circumstances.

III. – 3:302: Non-monetary obligations

(1) The creditor is entitled to enforce specific performance of an obligation other than one to pay money.

(2) Specific performance includes the remedying free of charge of a performance which is not in conformity with the terms regulating the obligation.

(3) Specific performance cannot, however, be enforced where:

    (a) performance would be unlawful or impossible;

    (b) performance would be unreasonably burdensome or expensive; or

    (c) performance would be of such a personal character that it would be unreasonable to enforce it.

(4) The creditor loses the right to enforce specific performance if performance is not requested within a reasonable time after the creditor has become, or could reasonably be expected to have become, aware of the non-performance.

(5) The creditor cannot recover damages for loss or a stipulated payment for non-performance to the extent that the creditor has increased the loss or the amount of the payment by insisting unreasonably on specific performance in circumstances where the creditor could have made a reasonable substitute transaction without significant effort or expense.

III. – 3:303: Damages not precluded

The fact that a right to enforce specific performance is excluded under the preceding Article does not preclude a claim for damages.

Section 4:
Withholding performance

III. – 3:401: Right to withhold performance of reciprocal obligation

(1) A creditor who is to perform a reciprocal obligation at the same time as, or after, the debtor performs has a right to withhold performance of the reciprocal obligation until the debtor has tendered performance or has performed.

(2) A creditor who is to perform a reciprocal obligation before the debtor performs and who reasonably believes that there will be non-performance by the debtor when the debtor's performance becomes due may withhold performance of the reciprocal obligation for as long as the reasonable belief continues. However, the right to withhold performance is lost if the debtor gives an adequate assurance of due performance.

(3) A creditor who withholds performance in the situation mentioned in paragraph (2) has a duty to give notice of that fact to the debtor as soon as is reasonably practicable and is liable for any loss caused to the debtor by a breach of that duty.

(4) The performance which may be withheld under this Article is the whole or part of the performance as may be reasonable in the circumstances.

Section 5:
Termination

III. – 3:501: Scope and definition

(1) This Section applies only to contractual obligations and contractual relationships.
(2) In this Section "termination" means the termination of the contractual relationship in whole or in part and "terminate" has a corresponding meaning.

Sub-section 1:
Grounds for termination

III. – 3:502: Termination for fundamental non-performance

(1) A creditor may terminate if the debtor's non-performance of a contractual obligation is fundamental.
(2) A non-performance of a contractual obligation is fundamental if:
   (a) it substantially deprives the creditor of what the creditor was entitled to expect under the contract, as applied to the whole or relevant part of the performance, unless at the time of conclusion of the contract the debtor did not foresee and could not reasonably be expected to have foreseen that result; or
   (b) it is intentional or reckless and gives the creditor reason to believe that the debtor's future performance cannot be relied on.

III. – 3:503: Termination after notice fixing additional time for performance

(1) A creditor may terminate in a case of delay in performance of a contractual obligation which is not in itself fundamental if the creditor gives a notice fixing an additional period of time of reasonable length for performance and the debtor does not perform within that period.
(2) If the period fixed is unreasonably short, the creditor may terminate only after a reasonable period from the time of the notice.

III. – 3:504: Termination for anticipated non-performance

A creditor may terminate before performance of a contractual obligation is due if the debtor has declared that there will be a non-performance of the obligation, or it is otherwise clear that there will be such a non-performance, and if the non-performance would have been fundamental.

III. – 3:505: Termination for inadequate assurance of performance

A creditor who reasonably believes that there will be a fundamental non-performance of a contractual obligation by the debtor may terminate if the creditor demands an adequate assurance of due performance and no such assurance is provided within a reasonable time.

Sub-section 2:
Scope, exercise and loss of right to terminate

III. – 3:506: Scope of right when obligations divisible

(1) This Article applies where the debtor's obligations under the contract are to be performed in separate parts or are otherwise divisible.

(2) Where there is a ground for termination under this Section of a part to which a counter-performance can be apportioned, the creditor may terminate the contractual relationship so far as it relates to that part.

(3) The creditor may terminate the contractual relationship as a whole only if the creditor cannot reasonably be expected to accept performance of the other parts or there is a ground for termination in relation to the contractual relationship as a whole.

III. – 3:507: Notice of termination

(1) A right to terminate under this Section is exercised by notice to the debtor.

(2) Where a notice under III. – 3:503 (Termination after notice fixing additional time for performance) provides for automatic termination if the debtor does not perform within the period fixed by the notice, termination takes effect after that period or a reasonable length of time from the giving of notice (whichever is longer) without further notice.

III. – 3:508: Loss of right to terminate

(1) If performance has been tendered late or a tendered performance otherwise does not conform to the contract the creditor loses the right to terminate under this Section unless notice of termination is given within a reasonable time.

(2) Where the creditor has given the debtor a period of time to cure the non-performance under III. – 3:202 (Cure by debtor: general rules) the time mentioned in paragraph (1) begins to run from the expiry of that period. In other cases that time begins to run from the time when the creditor has become, or could reasonably be expected to have become, aware of the tender or the non-conformity.

(3) A creditor loses a right to terminate by notice under III. – 3:503 (Termination after notice fixing additional time for performance), III. – 3:504 (Termination for anticipated non-performance) or III. – 3:505 (Termination for inadequate assurance of performance) unless the creditor gives notice of termination within a reasonable time after the right has arisen.

Sub-section 3:
Effects of termination

III. – 3:509: Effect on obligations under the contract

(1) On termination under this Section, the outstanding obligations or relevant part of the outstanding obligations of the parties under the contract come to an end.

(2) Termination does not, however, affect any provision of the contract for the settlement of disputes or other provision which is to operate even after termination.

(3) A creditor who terminates under this Section retains existing rights to damages or a stipulated sum for non-performance and in addition has the same right to damages or a stipulated payment for non-performance as the creditor would have had if there had been non-performance of the now extinguished obligations of the debtor. In relation to such extinguished obligations the creditor is not regarded as having caused or contributed to the loss merely by exercising the right to terminate.

III. – 3:510: Property reduced in value

A party who terminates under this Section may reject property previously received from the other party if its value to the first party has been eliminated or fundamentally reduced as a result of the other party's non-performance. On such rejection any obligation to pay for the property is extinguished.

Sub-section 4:
Restitution

III. – 3:511: Restitution of benefits received by performance

(1) On termination under this Section a party (the recipient) who has received any benefit by the other's performance of obligations under the contract is obliged to return it. Where both parties have obligations to return, the obligations are reciprocal.

(2) If the performance was a payment of money, the amount received is to be repaid.

(3) To the extent that the benefit (not being money) is transferable, it is to be returned by transferring it. However, if a transfer would cause unreasonable effort or expense, the benefit may be returned by paying its value.

(4) To the extent that the benefit is not transferable it is to be returned by paying its value in accordance with III. – 3:513(Payment of value of benefit).

(5) The obligation to return a benefit extends to any natural or legal fruits received from the benefit.

III. – 3:512: When restitution not required

(1) Restitution is not required where the performance was due in separate parts or was otherwise divisible and what was received by each party resulted from due performance of a part for which counter-performance was duly made.

(2) Paragraph (1) does not, however, apply if what was received by the terminating party was properly rejected under III. – 3:510 (Property reduced in value) or if the value of a non-transferable benefit received by the terminating party has been eliminated or fundamentally reduced as a result of the other party's non-performance.

III. – 3:513: Payment of value of benefit

(1) The recipient is obliged to:
   - (a) pay the value (at the time of performance) of a benefit which is not transferable or which ceases to be transferable before the time when it is to be returned; and
   - (b) pay recompense for any reduction in the value of a returnable benefit as a result of a change in the condition of the benefit between the time of receipt and the time when it is to be returned.

(2) Where there was an agreed price the value of the benefit is that proportion of the price which the value of the actual performance bears to the value of the promised performance. Where no price was agreed the value of the benefit is the sum of money which a willing and capable provider and a willing and capable recipient, knowing of any non-conformity, would lawfully have agreed.

(3) The recipient's liability to pay the value of a benefit is reduced to the extent that as a result of a non-performance of an obligation owed by the other party to the recipient:
   - (a) the benefit cannot be returned in essentially the same condition as when it was received; or
   - (b) the recipient is compelled without compensation either to dispose of it or to sustain a disadvantage in order to preserve it.

(4) The recipient's liability to pay the value of a benefit is likewise reduced to the extent that it cannot be returned in the same condition as when it was received as a result of conduct of the recipient in the reasonable, but mistaken, belief that there was no non-conformity.

III. – 3:514: Use and improvements

(1) The recipient is obliged to pay a reasonable amount for any use which the recipient makes of the benefit except in so far as the recipient is liable under III. – 3:513 (Payment of value of benefit) paragraph (1) in respect of that use.

(2) A recipient who has improved a benefit which the recipient is obliged under this Section to return has a right to payment of the value of improvements if the other party can readily obtain that value by dealing with the benefit unless:
   - (a) the improvement was a non-performance of an obligation owed by the recipient to the other party; or

(b) the recipient made the improvement when the recipient knew or could reasonably be expected to know that the benefit would have to be returned.

III. – 3:515: Liabilities arising after time when return due

(1) The recipient is obliged to:
- (a) pay the value (at the time of performance) of a benefit which ceases to be transferable after the time when its return was due; and
- (b) pay recompense for any reduction in the value of a returnable benefit as a result of a change in the condition of the benefit after the time when its return was due.

(2) If the benefit is disposed of after the time when return was due, the value to be paid is the value of any proceeds, if this is greater.

(3) Other liabilities arising from non-performance of an obligation to return a benefit are unaffected.

Section 6:
Price reduction

III. – 3:601: Right to reduce price

(1) A creditor who accepts a performance not conforming to the terms regulating the obligation may reduce the price. The reduction is to be proportionate to the decrease in the value of what was received by virtue of the performance at the time it was made compared to the value of what would have been received by virtue of a conforming performance.

(2) A creditor who is entitled to reduce the price under the preceding paragraph and who has already paid a sum exceeding the reduced price may recover the excess from the debtor.

(3) A creditor who reduces the price cannot also recover damages for the loss thereby compensated but remains entitled to damages for any further loss suffered.

(4) This Article applies with appropriate adaptations to a reciprocal obligation of the creditor other than an obligation to pay a price.

Section 7:
Damages and interest

III. – 3:701: Right to damages
(1) The creditor is entitled to damages for loss caused by the debtor's non-performance of an obligation, unless the non-performance is excused.
(2) The loss for which damages are recoverable includes future loss which is reasonably likely to occur.
(3) "Loss" includes economic and non-economic loss. "Economic loss" includes loss of income or profit, burdens incurred and a reduction in the value of property. "Non-economic loss" includes pain and suffering and impairment of the quality of life.

III. – 3:702: General measure of damages
The general measure of damages for loss caused by non-performance of an obligation is such sum as will put the creditor as nearly as possible into the position in which the creditor would have been if the obligation had been duly performed. Such damages cover loss which the creditor has suffered and gain of which the creditor has been deprived.

III. – 3:703: Foreseeability
The debtor in an obligation which arises from a contract or other juridical act is liable only for loss which the debtor foresaw or could reasonably be expected to have foreseen at the time when the obligation was incurred as a likely result of the non-performance, unless the non-performance was intentional, reckless or grossly negligent.

III. – 3:704: Loss attributable to creditor
The debtor is not liable for loss suffered by the creditor to the extent that the creditor contributed to the non-performance or its effects.

III. – 3:705: Reduction of loss
(1) The debtor is not liable for loss suffered by the creditor to the extent that the creditor could have reduced the loss by taking reasonable steps.
(2) The creditor is entitled to recover any expenses reasonably incurred in attempting to reduce the loss.

III. – 3:706: Substitute transaction

A creditor who has terminated a contractual relationship in whole or in part under Section 5 and has made a substitute transaction within a reasonable time and in a reasonable manner may, in so far as entitled to damages, recover the difference between the price and the substitute transaction price as well as damages for any further loss.

III. – 3:707: Current price

Where the creditor has terminated a contractual relationship in whole or in part under Section 5 and has not made a substitute transaction but there is a current price for the performance, the creditor may, in so far as entitled to damages, recover the difference between the contract price and the price current at the time of termination as well as damages for any further loss.

III. – 3:708: Delay in payment of money

(1) If payment of a sum of money is delayed, whether or not the non-performance is excused, the creditor is entitled to interest on that sum from the time when payment is due to the time of payment at the average commercial bank short-term lending rate to prime borrowers prevailing for the contractual currency of payment at the place where payment is due.

(2) The creditor may in addition recover damages for any further loss.

III. – 3:709: When interest to be added to capital

(1) Interest payable according to the preceding Article is added to the outstanding capital every 12 months.

(2) Paragraph (1) of this Article does not apply if the parties have provided for interest upon delay in payment.

III. – 3:710: Stipulated payment for non-performance

(1) Where the terms regulating an obligation provide that a debtor who fails to perform the obligation is to pay a specified sum to the creditor for such non-performance, the creditor is entitled to that sum irrespective of the actual loss.

(2) However, despite any provision to the contrary, the sum so specified in a contract or other juridical act may be reduced to a reasonable amount where it is grossly excessive in relation to the loss resulting from the non-performance and the other circumstances.

III. – 3:711: Currency by which damages to be measured
Damages are to be measured by the currency which most appropriately reflects the creditor's loss.

Chapter 4:
Plurality of debtors and creditors
Section 1:
Plurality of debtors

III. – 4:101: Scope of Section
This Section applies where two or more debtors are bound to perform one obligation.

III. – 4:102: Solidary, divided and joint obligations
(1) An obligation is solidary when each debtor is bound to perform the obligation in full and the creditor may require performance from any of them until full performance has been received.
(2) An obligation is divided when each debtor is bound to perform only part of the obligation and the creditor may claim from each debtor only performance of that debtor's part.
(3) An obligation is joint when the debtors are bound to perform the obligation together and the creditor may require performance only from all of them together.

III. – 4:103: When different types of obligation arise
(1) Whether an obligation is solidary, divided or joint depends on the terms regulating the obligation.
(2) The default rule is that the liability of two or more debtors to perform the same obligation is solidary. This applies in particular where two or more persons are liable for the same damage.
(3) Incidental differences in the debtors' liabilities do not prevent solidarity.

III. – 4:104: Liability under divided obligations
Debtors bound by a divided obligation are liable in equal shares.

III. – 4:105: Joint obligations: special rule when money claimed for non-performance

Notwithstanding III. – 4:102 (Solidary, divided and joint obligations) paragraph (3), when money is claimed for non-performance of a joint obligation, the debtors have solidary liability for payment to the creditor.

III. – 4:106: Apportionment between solidary debtors

(1) As between themselves, solidary debtors are liable in equal shares.

(2) If two or more debtors have solidary liability for the same damage, their share of liability as between themselves is equal unless different shares of liability are more appropriate having regard to all the circumstances of the case and in particular to fault or to the extent to which a source of danger for which one of them was responsible contributed to the occurrence or extent of the damage.

III. – 4:107: Recourse between solidary debtors

(1) A solidary debtor who has performed more than that debtor's share may claim the excess from any of the other debtors to the extent of each debtor's unperformed share, together with a share of any costs reasonably incurred.

(2) A solidary debtor to whom paragraph (1) applies may also, subject to any prior right and interest of the creditor, exercise the rights and actions of the creditor, including any supporting security rights, to recover the excess from any of the other debtors to the extent of each debtor's unperformed share.

(3) If a solidary debtor who has performed more than that debtor's share is unable, despite all reasonable efforts, to recover contribution from another solidary debtor, the share of the others, including the one who has performed, is increased proportionally.

III. – 4:108: Performance, set-off and merger in solidary obligations

(1) Performance or set-off by a solidary debtor or set-off by the creditor against one solidary debtor discharges the other debtors in relation to the creditor to the extent of the performance or set-off.

(2) Merger of debts between a solidary debtor and the creditor discharges the other debtors only for the share of the debtor concerned.

III. – 4:109: Release or settlement in solidary obligations
(1) When the creditor releases, or reaches a settlement with, one solidary debtor, the other debtors are discharged of liability for the share of that debtor.
(2) As between solidary debtors, the debtor who is discharged from that debtor's share is discharged only to the extent of the share at the time of the discharge and not from any supplementary share for which that debtor may subsequently become liable under III. – 4:107 (Recourse between solidary debtors) paragraph (3).
(3) When the debtors have solidary liability for the same damage the discharge under paragraph (1) extends only so far as is necessary to prevent the creditor from recovering more than full reparation and the other debtors retain their rights of recourse against the released or settling debtor to the extent of that debtor's unperformed share.

III. – 4:110: Effect of judgment in solidary obligations
A decision by a court as to the liability to the creditor of one solidary debtor does not affect:
(a) the liability to the creditor of the other solidary debtors; or
(b) the rights of recourse between the solidary debtors under III. – 4:107 (Recourse between solidary debtors).

III. – 4:111: Prescription in solidary obligations
Prescription of the creditor's right to performance against one solidary debtor does not affect:
(a) the liability to the creditor of the other solidary debtors; or
(b) the rights of recourse between the solidary debtors under III. – 4:107 (Recourse between solidary debtors).

III. – 4:112: Opposability of other defences in solidary obligations
(1) A solidary debtor may invoke against the creditor any defence which another solidary debtor can invoke, other than a defence personal to that other debtor. Invoking the defence has no effect with regard to the other solidary debtors.
(2) A debtor from whom contribution is claimed may invoke against the claimant any personal defence that that debtor could have invoked against the creditor.

Section 2:
Plurality of creditors

III. – 4:201: Scope of Section
This Section applies where two or more creditors have a right to performance under one obligation.

III. – 4:202: Solidary, divided and joint rights
(1) A right to performance is solidary when any of the creditors may require full performance from the debtor and the debtor may perform to any of the creditors.
(2) A right to performance is divided when each creditor may require performance only of that creditor's share and the debtor owes each creditor only that creditor's share.
(3) A right to performance is joint when any creditor may require performance only for the benefit of all the creditors and the debtor must perform to all the creditors.

III. – 4:203: When different types of right arise
(1) Whether a right to performance is solidary, divided or communal depends on the terms regulating right.
(2) The default rule is that the right of co-creditors is divided.

III. – 4:204: Apportionment in cases of divided rights
Creditors whose rights are divided are entitled to equal shares.

III. – 4:205: Difficulties of performing in cases of joint rights
If one of the creditors who have joint rights to performance refuses to accept, or is unable to receive, the performance, the debtor may obtain discharge from the obligation by depositing the property or money with a third party according to III. – 2:111 (Property not accepted) or III. – 2:112 (Money not accepted).

III. – 4:206: Apportionment in cases of solidary rights
(I) Solidary creditors are entitled to equal shares.
(2) A creditor who has received more than that creditor's share must transfer the excess to the other creditors to the extent of their respective shares.

III. – 4:207: Regime of solidary rights
(I) A release granted to the debtor by one of the solidary creditors has no effect on the other solidary creditors.
(2) The rules of III. – 4:108 (Performance, set-off and merger in solidary obligations), III. – 4:110 (Effect of judgment in solidary obligations), III. – 4:111 (Prescription in solidary obligations) and III. – 4:112 (Opposability of other defences in solidary obligations) paragraph (I) apply, with appropriate adaptations, to solidary rights to performance.

Chapter 5:
Transfer of rights and obligations
Section I:
Assignment of rights
Sub-section I:
General

III. – 5:101: Scope of Section
(I) This Section applies to the assignment, by a contract or other juridical act, of a right to performance of an obligation.
(2) It does not apply to the transfer of a financial instrument or investment security where such transfer must be by entry in a register maintained by or for the issuer or where there are other requirements for transfer or restrictions on transfer.

III. – 5:102: Definitions
(I) An "assignment" of a right is the transfer of the right from one person (the "assignor") to another person (the "assignee").
(2) An "act of assignment" is a contract or other juridical act which is intended to effect a transfer of the right.
(3) Where part of a right is assigned, any reference in this Section to a right includes a reference to the assigned part of the right.

III. – 5:103: Priority of provisions on proprietary securities and trusts

(1) In relation to assignments for purposes of security, the provisions of Book IX apply and have priority over the provisions in this Chapter.

(2) In relation to assignments for purposes of a trust, or to or from a trust, the provisions of Book X apply and have priority over the provisions in this Chapter.

Sub-section 2:
Requirements for assignment

III. – 5:104: Basic requirements

(1) The requirements for an assignment of a right to performance are that:
    (a) the right exists;
    (b) the right is assignable;
    (c) there is a valid act of assignment of the right; and
    (d) the person purporting to assign the right is entitled to transfer it.

(2) Neither notice to the debtor nor the consent of the debtor to the assignment is required.

III. – 5:105: Assignability: general rule

(1) All rights to performance are assignable except where otherwise provided by law.

(2) A right to performance which is by law accessory to another right is not assignable separately from that right.

III. – 5:106: Future and unspecified rights

(1) A future right to performance may be the subject of an act of assignment but the transfer of the right depends on its coming into existence and being identifiable as the right to which the act of assignment relates.

(2) A number of rights to performance may be assigned without individual specification if, at the time when the assignment is to take place in relation to them, they are identifiable as rights to which the act of assignment relates.

III. – 5:107: Assignability in part

(1) A right to performance of a monetary obligation may be assigned in part.

(2) A right to performance of a non-monetary obligation may be assigned in part only if:
   (a) the debtor consents to the assignment; or
   (b) the right is divisible and the assignment does not render the obligation significantly more burdensome.

(3) Where a right is assigned in part the assignor is liable to the debtor for any increased costs which the debtor thereby incurs.

III. – 5:108: Assignability: effect of contractual prohibition

(1) A contractual prohibition of, or restriction on, the assignment of a right does not affect the assignability of the right.

(2) However, where a right is assigned in breach of such a prohibition or restriction:
   (a) the debtor may perform in favour of the assignor and is discharged by so doing; and
   (b) the debtor retains all rights of set-off against the assignor as if the right had not been assigned.

(3) Where the debtor is discharged under paragraph (2) by performing in favour of the assignor, the assignee's claim against the assignor for the proceeds has priority over the right of a competing claimant so long as the proceeds are held by the assignor and are reasonably identifiable from the other assets of the assignor.

(4) Paragraph (2) does not apply if:
   (a) the debtor has consented to the assignment; or
   (b) the debtor has caused the assignee to believe on reasonable grounds that there was no such prohibition or restriction.

[(5) If the assigned right is a right to payment for the provision of goods or services paragraph (2)(a) does not apply but, without prejudice to III. – 5:116 (Effect on defences and rights of set-off), the debtor can invoke against the assignee all rights of set-off retained against the assignor by virtue of paragraph (2)(b)]

(6) The fact that a right is assignable notwithstanding a contractual prohibition or restriction does not affect the assignor's liability to the debtor for any breach of the prohibition or restriction.

III. – 5:109: Assignability: rights personal to the creditor

(1) A right is not assignable if it is a right to a performance which the debtor, by reason of the nature of the performance or the relationship between the debtor and the creditor, could not reasonably be required to render to anyone except that creditor.

(2) Paragraph (1) does not apply if the debtor has consented to the assignment.

III. – 5:110: Act of assignment: formation and validity

(1) Subject to paragraphs (2) and (3), the rules of Book II on the formation and validity of contracts and other juridical acts apply to acts of assignment.

(2) The rules of Book IV.I on the formation and validity of contracts of donation apply to gratuitous acts of assignment.

(3) The rules of Book IX on the formation and validity of security agreements apply to acts of assignment for purposes of security.

III. – 5:111: Entitlement to assign

(1) Only the creditor (whether acting directly or through a representative) or a person authorised by law to transfer the right is entitled to assign a right.

(2) The requirement of entitlement in III. – 5:104 (Basic requirements) paragraph (1)(d) need not be satisfied at the time of the act of assignment but must be satisfied at the time the assignment is to take place.

III. – 5:112: Undertakings by assignor

(1) The undertakings in paragraphs (2) to (6) are included in the act of assignment unless the act of assignment or the circumstances indicate otherwise.

(2) The assignor undertakes that:
    (a) the assigned right exists or will exist at the time when the assignment is to take effect;
    (b) the assignor is entitled to assign the right or will be so entitled at the time when the assignment is to take effect.
    (c) the debtor has no defences against an assertion of the right;
    (d) the right will not be affected by any right of set-off available as between the assignor and the debtor; and

(e) the right has not been the subject of a prior assignment to another assignee and is not subject to any right in security in favour of any other person or to any other incumbrance.

(3) The assignor undertakes that any terms of a contract or other juridical act which have been disclosed to the assignee as terms regulating the right have not been modified and are not affected by any undisclosed agreement as to their meaning or effect which would be prejudicial to the assignee.

(4) The assignor undertakes that the terms of any contract or other juridical act from which the right arises will not be modified without the consent of the assignee unless the modification is provided for in the act of assignment or is one which is made in good faith and is of a nature to which the assignee could not reasonably object.

(5) The assignor undertakes not to conclude or grant any subsequent act of assignment of the same right which could lead to another person obtaining priority over the assignee.

(6) The assignor undertakes to transfer to the assignee, or to take such steps as are necessary to complete the transfer of, all transferable rights intended to secure the performance which are not already transferred by the assignment, and to transfer the proceeds of any non-transferable rights intended to secure the performance.

(7) The assignor does not represent that the debtor has, or will have, the ability to pay.

Sub-section 4:
Effects of assignment

III. – 5:113: New creditor
As soon as the assignment takes place the assignor ceases to be the creditor and the assignee becomes the creditor in relation to the right assigned.

III. – 5:114: When assignment takes place
(1) An assignment takes place when the requirements of III. – 5:104 (Basic requirements) are satisfied, or at such later time as the act of assignment may provide.

(2) However, an assignment of a right which was a future right at the time of the act of assignment is regarded as having taken place when all

requirements other than those dependent on the existence of the right were satisfied.

(3) Where the requirements of III. – 5:104 (Basic requirements) are satisfied in relation to successive acts of assignment at the same time, the earliest act of assignment takes effect unless it provides otherwise.

III. – 5:115: Rights transferred to assignee

(1) The assignment of a right to performance transfers to the assignee not only the primary right but also all accessory rights and transferable supporting security rights.

(2) Where the assignment of a right to performance of a contractual obligation is associated with the substitution of the assignee as debtor in respect of any obligation owed by the assignor under the same contract, this Article takes effect subject to III. – 5:301 (Transfer of contractual position).

III. – 5:116: Effect on defences and rights of set-off

(1) The debtor may invoke against the assignee all substantive and procedural defences to a claim based on the assigned right which the debtor could have invoked against the assignor.

(2) The debtor may not, however, invoke a defence against the assignee:
  (a) if the debtor has caused the assignee to believe that there was no such defence; or
  (b) if the defence is based on breach by the assignor of a prohibition or restriction on assignment.

(3) The debtor may invoke against the assignee all rights of set-off which would have been available against the assignor in respect of rights against the assignor:
  (a) existing at the time when the debtor could no longer obtain a discharge by performing to the assignor; or
  (b) closely connected with the assigned right.

III. – 5:117: Effect on place of performance

(1) Where the assigned right relates to an obligation to pay money at a particular place, the assignee may require payment at any place within the same country or, if that country is a Member State of the European Union, at any place within the European Union, but the assignor is

liable to the debtor for any increased costs which the debtor incurs by reason of any change in the place of performance.

(2) Where the assigned right relates to a non-monetary obligation to be performed at a particular place, the assignee may not require performance at any other place.

Sub-section 5:
Protection of debtor

III. – 5:118: Performance to person who is not the creditor

(1) The debtor is discharged by performing to the assignor so long as the debtor has not received a notice of assignment from either the assignor or the assignee and does not know that the assignor is no longer entitled to receive performance.

(2) Notwithstanding that the person identified as the assignee in a notice of assignment is not the creditor, the debtor is discharged by performing in good faith to that person.

III. – 5:119: Adequate proof of assignment

(1) A debtor who believes on reasonable grounds that the right has been assigned but who has not received a notice of assignment, may request the person who is believed to have assigned the right to provide a notice of assignment or a confirmation that the right has not been assigned or that the assignor is still entitled to receive payment.

(2) A debtor who has received a notice of assignment which is not in textual form on a durable medium or which does not give adequate information about the assigned right or the name and address of the assignee may request the person giving the notice to provide a new notice which satisfies these requirements.

(3) A debtor who has received a notice of assignment from the assignee but not from the assignor may request the assignee to provide reliable evidence of the assignment. Reliable evidence includes, but is not limited to, any statement in textual form on a durable medium emanating from the assignor indicating that the right has been assigned.

(4) A debtor who has made a request under this Article may withhold performance until the request is met.

Sub-section 6:
Priority

III. – 5:120: Competition between successive assignees

(1) Where there are successive purported assignments by the same person of the same right to performance the purported assignee whose assignment is first notified to the debtor has priority over any earlier assignee if at the time of the later assignment the assignee under that assignment neither knew nor could reasonably be expected to have known of the earlier assignment.

(2) The debtor is discharged by paying the first to notify even if aware of competing demands.

Section 2:
Substitution of new debtor

III. – 5:201: Substitution: general rules

(1) A third person may undertake with the agreement of the debtor and the creditor to be substituted as debtor, with the effect that the original debtor is discharged.

(2) A creditor may agree in advance to a future substitution. In such a case the substitution takes effect only when the creditor is given notice by the new debtor of the agreement between the new and the original debtor.

III. – 5:202: Effects of substitution on defences and securities

(1) The new debtor cannot invoke against the creditor any rights or defences arising from the relationship between the new debtor and the original debtor.

(2) The discharge of the original debtor also extends to any security of the original debtor given to the creditor for the performance of the obligation, unless the security is over an asset which is transferred to the new debtor as part of a transaction between the original and the new debtor.

(3) Upon discharge of the original debtor, a security granted by any person other than the new debtor for the performance of the obligation is

released, unless that other person agrees that it should continue to be available to the creditor.

(4) The new debtor may invoke against the creditor all defences which the original debtor could have invoked against the creditor.

Section 3:
Transfer of contractual position

III. – 5:301: Transfer of contractual position

(1) A party to a contractual relationship may agree with a third person that that person is to be substituted as a party to the relationship. In such a case the substitution takes effect only where, as a result of the other party's assent, the first party is discharged.

(2) To the extent that the substitution of the third person involves a transfer of rights, the provisions of Section 1 of this Chapter apply; to the extent that obligations are transferred, the provisions of Section 2 of this Chapter apply.

Chapter 6:
Set-off and merger
Section 1:
Set-off

III. – 6:101: Definitions

(1) "Set-off" is the process by which a debtor may reduce the amount owed to the creditor by an amount owed to the debtor by the creditor.

(2) In this Chapter, "right" means a right to performance of an obligation, unless the context otherwise requires.

III. – 6:102: Requirements for set-off

If two parties owe each other obligations of the same kind, either party may set off that party's right against the other party's right, if and to the extent that, at the time of set-off, the first party:

(a) is entitled to effect performance; and

(b) may demand the other party's performance.

III. – 6:103: Unascertained rights

(1) A debtor may not set off a right which is unascertained as to its existence or value unless the set-off will not prejudice the interests of the creditor.

(2) Where the rights of both parties arise from the same legal relationship it is presumed that the creditor's interests will not be prejudiced.

III. – 6:104: Foreign currency set-off

Where parties owe each other money in different currencies, each party may set off that party's right against the other party's right, unless the parties have agreed that the party declaring set-off is to pay exclusively in a specified currency.

III. – 6:105: Set-off by notice

The right of set-off is exercised by notice to the other party.

III. – 6:106: Two or more rights and obligations

(1) Where the party giving notice of set-off has two or more rights against the other party, the notice is effective only if it identifies the right to which it relates.

(2) Where the party giving notice of set-off has to perform two or more obligations towards the other party, the rules on imputation of performance apply with appropriate adaptations.

III. – 6:107: Effect of set-off

Set-off extinguishes the obligations, as far as they are coextensive, as from the time of notice.

III. – 6:108: Exclusion of right of set-off

Set-off cannot be effected:

(a) where it is excluded by agreement;

(b) against a right to the extent that that right is not capable of attachment; and

(c) against a right arising from an intentional wrongful act.

Section 2:
Merger of debts

III. – 6:201: Extinction of obligations by merger
(1) An obligation is extinguished if the same person becomes debtor and creditor in the same capacity.
(2) Paragraph (1) does not, however, apply if the effect would be to deprive a third person of a right.

Chapter 7:
Prescription
Section 1:
General provision

III. – 7:101: Rights subject to prescription
A right to performance of an obligation is subject to prescription by the expiry of a period of time in accordance with the rules in this Chapter.

Section 2:
Periods of prescription and their commencement

III. – 7:201: General period
The general period of prescription is three years.

III. – 7:202: Period for a right established by legal proceedings
(1) The period of prescription for a right established by judgment is ten years.
(2) The same applies to a right established by an arbitral award or other instrument which is enforceable as if it were a judgment.

III. – 7:203: Commencement
(1) The general period of prescription begins to run from the time when the debtor has to effect performance or, in the case of a right to damages, from the time of the act which gives rise to the right.

(2) Where the debtor is under a continuing obligation to do or refrain from doing something, the general period of prescription begins to run with each breach of the obligation.

(3) The period of prescription set out in III. – 7:202 (Period for a right established by legal proceedings) begins to run from the time when the judgment or arbitral award obtains the effect of res judicata, or the other instrument becomes enforceable, though not before the debtor has to effect performance.

Section 3:
Extension of period

III. – 7:301: Suspension in case of ignorance

The running of the period of prescription is suspended as long as the creditor does not know of, and could not reasonably be expected to know of:

(a) the identity of the debtor; or

(b) the facts giving rise to the right including, in the case of a right to damages, the type of damage.

III. – 7:302: Suspension in case of judicial and other proceedings

(1) The running of the period of prescription is suspended from the time when judicial proceedings to assert the right are begun.

(2) Suspension lasts until a decision has been made which has the effect of res judicata, or until the case has been otherwise disposed of. Where the proceedings end within the last six months of the prescription period without a decision on the merits, the period of prescription does not expire before six months have passed after the time when the proceedings ended.

(3) These provisions apply, with appropriate adaptations, to arbitration proceedings and to all other proceedings initiated with the aim of obtaining an instrument which is enforceable as if it were a judgment.

III. – 7:303: Suspension in case of impediment beyond creditor's control

(1) The running of the period of prescription is suspended as long as the creditor is prevented from pursuing proceedings to assert the right by an impediment which is beyond the creditor's control and which the creditor could not reasonably have been expected to avoid or overcome.

(2) Paragraph (1) applies only if the impediment arises, or subsists, within the last six months of the prescription period.

III. – 7:304: Postponement of expiry in case of negotiations

If the parties negotiate about the right, or about circumstances from which a claim relating to the right might arise, the period of prescription does not expire before one year has passed since the last communication made in the negotiations.

III. – 7:305: Postponement of expiry in case of incapacity

(1) If a person subject to an incapacity is without a representative, the period of prescription of a right held by or against that person does not expire before one year has passed after either the incapacity has ended or a representative has been appointed.

(2) The period of prescription of rights between a person subject to an incapacity and that person's representative does not expire before one year has passed after either the incapacity has ended or a new representative has been appointed.

III. – 7:306: Postponement of expiry: deceased's estate

Where the creditor or debtor has died, the period of prescription of a right held by or against the deceased's estate does not expire before one year has passed after the right can be enforced by or against an heir, or by or against a representative of the estate.

III. – 7:307: Maximum length of period

The period of prescription cannot be extended, by suspension of its running or postponement of its expiry under this Chapter, to more than ten years or, in case of rights to damages for personal injuries, to more than thirty years. This does not apply to suspension under III. – 7:302 (Suspension in case of judicial and other proceedings).

Section 4:
Renewal of period

III. – 7:401: Renewal by acknowledgement
(1) If the debtor acknowledges the right, vis-à-vis the creditor, by part payment, payment of interest, giving of security, or in any other manner, a new period of prescription begins to run.
(2) The new period is the general period of prescription, regardless of whether the right was originally subject to the general period of prescription or the ten year period under III. – 7:202 (Period for a right established by legal proceedings). In the latter case, however, this Article does not operate so as to shorten the ten year period.

III. – 7:402: Renewal by attempted execution
The ten year period of prescription laid down in III. – 7:202 (Period for a right established by legal proceedings) begins to run again with each reasonable attempt at execution undertaken by the creditor.

Section 5:
Effects of prescription

III. – 7:501: General effect
(1) After expiry of the period of prescription the debtor is entitled to refuse performance.
(2) Whatever has been paid or transferred by the debtor in performance of the obligation may not be reclaimed merely because the period of prescription had expired.

III. – 7:502: Effect on ancillary rights
The period of prescription for a right to payment of interest, and other rights of an ancillary nature, expires not later than the period for the principal right.

III. – 7:503: Effect on set-off

A right in relation to which the period of prescription has expired may nonetheless be set off, unless the debtor has invoked prescription previously or does so within two months of notification of set-off.

Section 6:
Modification by agreement

III. – 7:601: Agreements concerning prescription

(1) The requirements for prescription may be modified by agreement between the parties, in particular by either shortening or lengthening the periods of prescription.

(2) The period of prescription may not, however, be reduced to less than one year or extended to more than thirty years after the time of commencement set out in III. – 7:203 (Commencement).

Book IV
Specific contracts and the rights and obligations arising from them

Part A.
Sales

Chapter 1:
Scope of application and general provisions
Section 1:
Scope of application

IV. A. – 1:101: Contracts covered
(1) This Part of Book IV applies to contracts for the sale of goods.
(2) It applies with appropriate adaptations to:
    (a) contracts for the sale of electricity;
    (b) contracts for the sale of stocks, shares, investment securities and negotiable instruments;
    (c) contracts for the sale of other forms of incorporeal property, including rights to the performance of obligations, industrial and intellectual property rights and other transferable rights;
    (d) contracts conferring, in exchange for a price, rights in information or data, including software and databases;
    (e) contracts for the barter of goods or any of the other assets mentioned above.
(3) It does not apply to contracts for the sale or barter of immovable property or rights in immovable property.

IV. A. – 1:102: Goods to be manufactured or produced
A contract under which one party undertakes, for a price, to manufacture or produce goods for the other party and to transfer their ownership to the other party is to be considered as primarily a contract for the sale of the goods.

IV. A. – 1:103: Consumer goods guarantees
Chapter 6 applies to consumer goods guarantees associated with contracts for the sale of goods.

Section 2:
General provisions

IV. A. – 1:201: Goods
In this Part of Book IV:
(a) the word "goods" includes goods which at the time of the conclusion of the contract do not yet exist; and
(b) references to goods, other than in IV. A. – 1:101 (Contracts covered) itself, are to be taken as referring also to the other assets mentioned in paragraph (2) of that Article.

IV. A. – 1:202: Contract for sale
A contract for the "sale" of goods is a contract under which one party, the seller, undertakes to another party, the buyer, to transfer the ownership of the goods to the buyer, or to a third person, either immediately on conclusion of the contract or at some future time, and the buyer undertakes to pay the price.

IV. A. – 1:203: Contract for barter
(1) A contract for the "barter" of goods is a contract under which each party undertakes to transfer the ownership of goods, either immediately on conclusion of the contract or at some future time, in return for the transfer of ownership of other goods.
(2) Each party is considered to be the buyer with respect to the goods to be received and the seller with respect to the goods or assets to be transferred.

IV. A. – 1:204: Consumer contract for sale
For the purpose of this Part of Book IV, a consumer contract for sale is a contract for sale in which the seller is a business and the buyer is a consumer.

Section 3:
Derogation

IV. A. – 1:301: Rules not mandatory unless otherwise stated

The parties may exclude the application of any of the rules in this Part of
Book IV or derogate from or vary their effects, except as otherwise provided
in this Part.

Chapter 2:
Obligations of the seller
Section 1:
Overview

IV. A. – 2:101: Overview of obligations of the seller

The seller must:
(a) transfer the ownership of the goods;
(b) deliver the goods;
(c) transfer such documents representing or relating to the goods as may
    be required by the contract; and
(d) ensure that the goods conform to the contract.

Section 2:
Delivery of the goods

IV. A. – 2:201: Delivery

(1) The seller fulfils the obligation to deliver by making the goods, or
    where it is agreed that the seller need only deliver documents repre-
    senting the goods, the documents, available to the buyer.
(2) If the contract involves carriage of the goods by a carrier or series of
    carriers, the seller fulfils the obligation to deliver by handing over the
    goods to the first carrier for transmission to the buyer and by transfer-
    ring to the buyer any document necessary to enable the buyer to take
    over the goods from the carrier holding the goods.
(3) In this Article, any reference to the buyer includes a third person to
    whom delivery is to be made in accordance with the contract.

IV. A. – 2:202: Place and time for delivery

(1) The place and time for delivery are determined by III. – 2:101 (Place of performance) and III. – 2:102 (Time of performance) as modified by this Article.

(2) If the performance of the obligation to deliver requires the transfer of documents representing the goods, the seller must transfer them at such a time and place and in such a form as is required by the contract.

(3) If in a consumer contract for sale the contract involves carriage of goods by a carrier or a series of carriers and the consumer is given a time for delivery, the goods must be received from the last carrier or made available for collection from that carrier by that time.

IV. A. – 2:203: Cure in case of early delivery

(1) If the seller has delivered goods before the time for delivery, the seller may, up to that time, deliver any missing part or make up any deficiency in the quantity of the goods delivered, or deliver goods in replacement of any non-conforming goods delivered or otherwise remedy any lack of conformity in the goods delivered, provided that the exercise of this right does not cause the buyer unreasonable inconvenience or unreasonable expense.

(2) If the seller has transferred documents before the time required by the contract, the seller may, up to that time, cure any lack of conformity in the documents, provided that the exercise of this right does not cause the buyer unreasonable inconvenience or unreasonable expense.

(3) This Article does not preclude the buyer from claiming damages, in accordance with Book III, Chapter 3, Section 7 (Damages and interest), for any loss not remedied by the seller's cure.

IV. A. – 2:204: Carriage of the goods

(1) If the contract requires the seller to arrange for carriage of the goods, the seller must make such contracts as are necessary for carriage to the place fixed by means of transportation appropriate in the circumstances and according to the usual terms for such transportation.

(2) If the seller, in accordance with the contract, hands over the goods to a carrier and if the goods are not clearly identified to the contract by markings on the goods, by shipping documents or otherwise, the seller must give the buyer notice of the consignment specifying the goods.

(3) If the contract does not require the seller to effect insurance in respect of the carriage of the goods, the seller must, at the buyer's request, provide the buyer with all available information necessary to enable the buyer to effect such insurance.

Section 3:
Conformity of the goods

IV. A. – 2:301: Conformity with the contract

The goods do not conform with the contract unless they:

(a) are of the quantity, quality and description required by the contract;

(b) are contained or packaged in the manner required by the contract;

(c) are supplied along with any accessories, installation instructions or other instructions required by the contract; and

(d) comply with the remaining Articles of this Section.

IV. A. – 2:302: Fitness for purpose, qualities, packaging

The goods must:

(a) be fit for any particular purpose made known to the seller at the time of the conclusion of the contract, except where the circumstances show that the buyer did not rely, or that it was unreasonable for the buyer to rely, on the seller's skill and judgement;

(b) be fit for the purposes for which goods of the same description would ordinarily be used;

(c) possess the qualities of goods which the seller held out to the buyer as a sample or model;

(d) be contained or packaged in the manner usual for such goods or, where there is no such manner, in a manner adequate to preserve and protect the goods;

(e) be supplied along with such accessories, installation instructions or other instructions as the buyer may reasonably expect to receive; and

(f) possess such qualities and performance capabilities as the buyer may reasonably expect.

IV. A. – 2:303: Statements by third persons

The goods must possess the qualities and performance capabilities held out in any statement on the specific characteristics of the goods made about them by a person in earlier links of the business chain, the producer or the producer's representative which forms part of the terms of the contract by virtue of II. – 9:102 (Certain pre-contractual statements regarded as contract terms).

IV. A. – 2:304: Incorrect installation under a consumer contract for sale

Where goods supplied under a consumer contract for sale are incorrectly installed, any lack of conformity resulting from the incorrect installation is deemed to be a lack of conformity of the goods if:

(a) the goods were installed by the seller or under the seller's responsibility; or

(b) the goods were intended to be installed by the consumer and the incorrect installation was due to a shortcoming in the installation instructions.

IV. A. – 2:305: Third party rights or claims in general

The goods must be free from any right or claim of a third party. However, if such right or claim is based on industrial property or other intellectual property, the seller's obligation is governed by the following Article.

IV. A. – 2:306: Third party rights or claims based on industrial property or other intellectual property

(1) The goods must be free from any right or claim of a third party which is based on industrial property or other intellectual property and of which at the time of the conclusion of the contract the seller knew or could reasonably be expected to have known.

(2) However, paragraph (1) does not apply where the right or claim results from the seller's compliance with technical drawings, designs, formulae or other such specifications furnished by the buyer.

IV. A. – 2:307: Buyer's knowledge of lack of conformity

(1) The seller is not liable under IV. A. – 2:302 (Fitness for purpose, qualities, packaging), IV. A. – 2:305 (Third party rights or claims in general) or IV. A. – 2:306 (Third party rights or claims based on industrial property or other intellectual property) if, at the time of the conclusion of the contract, the buyer knew or could reasonably be assumed to have known of the lack of conformity.

(2) The seller is not liable under IV. A. – 2:304 (Incorrect installation in a consumer contract for sale) sub-paragraph (b) if, at the time of the conclusion of the contract, the buyer knew or could reasonably be assumed to have known of the shortcoming in the installation instructions.

IV. A. – 2:308: Relevant time for establishing conformity

(1) The seller is liable for any lack of conformity which exists at the time when the risk passes to the buyer, even if the lack of conformity becomes apparent only after that time.

(2) In a consumer contract for sale, any lack of conformity which becomes apparent within six months of the time when risk passes to the buyer is presumed to have existed at that time unless this is incompatible with the nature of the goods or the nature of the lack of conformity.

(3) In a case governed by IV.A – 2:304 (Incorrect installation in a consumer contract for sale) any reference in paragraphs (1) or (2) to the time when risk passes to the buyer is to be read as a reference to the time when the installation is complete.

IV. A. – 2:309: Limits on derogation from conformity rights in a consumer contract for sale

In a consumer contract for sale, any contractual term or agreement concluded with the seller before a lack of conformity is brought to the seller's attention which directly or indirectly waives or restricts the rights resulting from the seller's obligation to ensure that the goods conform to the contract is not binding on the consumer.

Chapter 3:
Obligations of the buyer
Section 1:
Overview

IV. A. – 3:101: Overview of obligations of the buyer

The buyer must:

(a) pay the price;

(b) take delivery of the goods; and

(c) take over documents representing or relating to the goods as may be required by the contract.

IV. A. – 3:102: Determination of form, measurement or other features

(1) If under the contract the buyer is to specify the form, measurement or other features of the goods, or the time or manner of their delivery, and fails to make such specification either within the time agreed upon or within a reasonable time after receipt of a request from the seller, the seller may, without prejudice to any other rights, make the specification in accordance with any requirements of the buyer that may be known to the seller.

(2) A seller who makes such a specification must inform the buyer of the details of the specification and must fix a reasonable time within which the buyer may make a different specification. If, after receipt of such a communication, the buyer fails to do so within the time so fixed, the specification made by the seller is binding.

Section 2:
Payment of the price

IV. A. – 3:201: Place and time for payment

The place and time for payment are determined by III. – 2:101 (Place of performance) and III. – 2:102 (Time of performance).

IV. A. – 3:202: Formalities of payment

The buyer's obligation to pay the price includes taking such steps and complying with such formalities as may be necessary to enable payment to be made.

IV. A. – 3:203: Price fixed by weight

If the price is fixed according to the weight of the goods, in case of doubt it is to be determined by the net weight.

Section 3:
Taking delivery of the goods

IV. A. – 3:301: Taking delivery
The buyer fulfils the obligation to take delivery by:
(a) doing all the acts which could reasonably be expected in order to enable the seller to perform the obligation to deliver; and
(b) taking over the goods, or the documents representing the goods, as required by the contract.

IV. A. – 3:302: Early delivery and delivery of excess quantity
(1) If the seller delivers all or part of the goods before the time fixed, the buyer may take delivery or, except where acceptance of the tender would not unreasonably prejudice the buyer's interests, refuse to take delivery.
(2) If the seller delivers a quantity of goods greater than that provided for by the contract, the buyer may retain or refuse the excess quantity.
(3) If the buyer retains the excess quantity it is deemed to have been supplied under the contract and must be paid for at the contractual rate.
(4) In a consumer contract for sale paragraph (3) does not apply if the buyer believes on reasonable grounds that the seller has delivered the excess quantity intentionally and without error, knowing that it had not been ordered. In such a case the rules on unsolicited goods apply.

Chapter 4:
Remedies
Section 1:
Remedies of the parties in general

IV. A. – 4:101: Application of Book III
If a party fails to perform an obligation under the contract, the other party may exercise the remedies provided in Book III, Chapter 3, except as otherwise provided in this Chapter.

IV. A. – 4:102: Limits on derogation from remedies for non-conformity in a consumer contract for sale

In a consumer contract for sale, any contractual term or agreement concluded with the seller before a lack of conformity is brought to the seller's attention which directly or indirectly waives or restricts the remedies of the buyer provided in Book III, Chapter 3 (Remedies for Non-performance), as modified in this Chapter, in respect of the lack of conformity is not binding on the consumer.

Section 2:
Remedies of the buyer for lack of conformity

IV. A. – 4:201: Overview of remedies

When the goods do not conform to the contract the buyer is entitled, subject to the provisions of Book III and of this Chapter:

(a) to have the lack of conformity remedied by repair or replacement in accordance with III. – 3:302 (Non-monetary obligations);

(b) to withhold performance under III. – 3:401 (Right to withhold performance of reciprocal obligation);

(c) to terminate the contractual relationship under Book III, Chapter 3, Section 5 (Termination);

(d) to reduce the price under Book III, Chapter 3, Section 6 (Price reduction); or

(e) to damages under Book III, Chapter 3, Section 7 (Damages and interest).

IV. A. – 4:202: Termination by consumer for lack of conformity

In a consumer contract for sale, the buyer may terminate the contractual relationship for non-performance under Book III, Chapter 3, Section 5 (Termination) in the case of any lack of conformity, unless the lack of conformity is minor.

IV. A. – 4:203: Limitation of liability for damages of non-business sellers

(1) If the seller is a natural person acting for purposes not related to that person's trade, business or profession, the buyer is not entitled to claim damages for lack of conformity exceeding the contract price.

(2) The seller is not entitled to rely on paragraph (1) if the lack of conformity relates to facts of which the seller, at the time when the risk passed to the buyer, knew or could reasonably be expected to have known and which the seller did not disclose to the buyer before that time.

Section 3:
Requirements of examination and notification

IV. A. – 4:301: Examination of the goods

(1) The buyer should examine the goods, or cause them to be examined, within as short a period as is reasonable in the circumstances. Failure to do so may result in the buyer losing, under III. – 3:107 (Failure to notify non-conformity) as supplemented by IV. A. – 4:302 (Notification of lack of conformity), the right to rely on the lack of conformity.

(2) If the contract involves carriage of the goods, examination may be deferred until after the goods have arrived at their destination.

(3) If the goods are redirected in transit, or redispatched by the buyer before the buyer has had a reasonable opportunity to examine them, and at the time of the conclusion of the contract the seller knew or could reasonably be expected to have known of the possibility of such redirection or redispatch, examination may be deferred until after the goods have arrived at the new destination.

(4) This Article does not apply to a consumer contract for sale.

IV. A. – 4:302: Notification of lack of conformity

(1) In a contract between two businesses the rule in III. – 3:107 (Failure to notify non-conformity) requiring notification of a lack of conformity within a reasonable time is supplemented by the following rules.

(2) The buyer in any event loses the right to rely on a lack of conformity if the buyer does not give the seller notice of the lack of conformity at the latest within two years from the time at which the goods were actually handed over to the buyer in accordance with the contract.

(3) If the parties have agreed that the goods must remain fit for a particular purpose or for their ordinary purpose during a fixed period of time, the period for giving notice under paragraph (2) does not expire before the end of the agreed period.

(4) Paragraph (2) does not apply in respect of third party claims or rights pursuant to IV. A. – 2:305 (Third party rights or claims in general) and IV. A. – 2:306 (Third party rights or claims based on industrial property or other intellectual property) .

IV. A. – 4:303: Notification of partial delivery

The buyer does not have to notify the seller that not all the goods have been delivered, if the buyer has reason to believe that the remaining goods will be delivered.

IV. A. – 4:304: Seller's knowledge of lack of conformity

The seller is not entitled to rely on the provisions of IV. A. – 4:301 (Examination of the goods) or IV. A. – 4:302 (Notification of lack of conformity) if the lack of conformity relates to facts of which the seller knew or could reasonably be expected to have known and which the seller did not disclose to the buyer.

Chapter 5:
Passing of risk
Section 1:
General provisions

IV. A. – 5:101: Effect of passing of risk

Loss of, or damage to, the goods after the risk has passed to the buyer does not discharge the buyer from the obligation to pay the price, unless the loss or damage is due to an act or omission of the seller.

IV. A. – 5:102: Time when risk passes

(1) The risk passes when the buyer takes over the goods or the documents representing them.
(2) However, if the contract relates to goods not then identified, the risk does not pass to the buyer until the goods are clearly identified to the contract, whether by markings on the goods, by shipping documents, by notice given to the buyer or otherwise.
(3) The rule in paragraph (1) is subject to the Articles in Section 2 of this Chapter.

IV. A. – 5:103: Passing of risk in a consumer contract for sale

(1) In a consumer contract for sale, the risk does not pass until the buyer takes over the goods.

(2) Paragraph (1) does not apply if the buyer has failed to perform the obligation to take over the goods and the non-performance is not excused under III. – 3:104 (Excuse due to an impediment) in which case IV. A. – 5:201 (Goods placed at buyer's disposal) applies.

(3) Except in so far as provided in the preceding paragraph, Section 2 of this Chapter does not apply to a consumer contract for sale.

(4) The parties may not, to the detriment of the consumer, exclude the application of this Article or derogate from or vary its effects.

Section 2:
Special rules

IV. A. – 5:201: Goods placed at buyer's disposal

(1) If the goods are placed at the buyer's disposal and the buyer is aware of this, the risk passes to the buyer from the time when the goods should have been taken over, unless the buyer was entitled to withhold taking of delivery under III. – 3:401 (Right to withhold performance of reciprocal obligation).

(2) If the goods are placed at the buyer's disposal at a place other than a place of business of the seller, the risk passes when delivery is due and the buyer is aware of the fact that the goods are placed at the buyer's disposal at that place.

IV. A. – 5:202: Carriage of the goods

(1) This Article applies to any contract of sale which involves carriage of goods.

(2) If the seller is not bound to hand over the goods at a particular place, the risk passes to the buyer when the goods are handed over to the first carrier for transmission to the buyer in accordance with the contract.

(3) If the seller is bound to hand over the goods to a carrier at a particular place, the risk does not pass to the buyer until the goods are handed over to the carrier at that place.

(4) The fact that the seller is authorised to retain documents controlling the disposition of the goods does not affect the passing of the risk.

IV. A. – 5:203: Goods sold in transit

(1) This Article applies to any contract of sale which involves goods sold in transit.

(2) The risk passes to the buyer at the time the goods are handed over to the first carrier. However, if the circumstances so indicate, the risk passes to the buyer as from the time of the conclusion of the contract.

(3) If at the time of the conclusion of the contract the seller knew or could reasonably be expected to have known that the goods had been lost or damaged and did not disclose this to the buyer, the loss or damage is at the risk of the seller.

Chapter 6:
Consumer goods guarantees

IV. A. – 6:101: Definition of a consumer goods guarantee

(1) A consumer goods guarantee means any undertaking of a type mentioned in the following paragraph given to a consumer in connection with a consumer contract for the sale of goods:

    (a) by a producer or a person in later links of the business chain; or

    (b) by the seller in addition to the seller's obligations as seller of the goods.

(2) The undertaking may be that:

    (a) apart from misuse, mistreatment or accident the goods will remain fit for their ordinary purpose for a specified period of time, or otherwise;

    (b) the goods will meet the specifications set out in the guarantee document or in associated advertising; or

    (c) subject to any conditions stated in the guarantee,

        (i) the goods will be repaired or replaced;

        (ii) the price paid for the goods will be reimbursed in whole or in part; or

        (iii) some other remedy will be provided.

IV. A. – 6:102: Binding nature of the guarantee

(1) A consumer goods guarantee, whether contractual or in the form of a unilateral undertaking, is binding in favour of the first buyer, and in the case of a unilateral undertaking is so binding without acceptance not-

withstanding any provision to the contrary in the guarantee document or the associated advertising.

(2) If not otherwise provided in the guarantee document, the guarantee is also binding without acceptance in favour of every owner of the goods within the duration of the guarantee.

(3) Any requirement in the guarantee whereby it is conditional on the fulfilment by the guarantee holder of any formal requirement, such as registration or notification of purchase, is not binding on the consumer.

IV. A. – 6:103: Guarantee document

(1) A person who gives a consumer goods guarantee must (unless such a document has already been provided to the buyer) provide the buyer with a guarantee document which:

   (a) states that the buyer has legal rights which are not affected by the guarantee;

   (b) points out the advantages of the guarantee for the buyer in comparison with the conformity rules;

   (c) lists all the essential particulars necessary for making claims under the guarantee, notably:

      – the name and address of the guarantor;

      – the name and address of the person to whom any notification is to be made and the procedure by which the notification is to be made;

      – any territorial limitations to the guarantee;

   (d) is drafted in plain, intelligible language; and

   (e) is drafted in the same language as that in which the goods were offered.

(2) The guarantee document must be in textual form on a durable medium and be available and accessible to the buyer.

(3) The validity of the guarantee is not affected by any failure to comply with paragraphs (1) and (2), and accordingly the guarantee holder can still rely on the guarantee and require it to be honoured.

(4) If the obligations under paragraphs (1) and (2) are not observed the guarantee holder may, without prejudice to any right to damages which may be available, require the guarantor to provide a guarantee document which conforms to those requirements.

(5) The parties may not, to the detriment of the consumer, exclude the application of this Article or derogate from or vary its effects.

IV. A. – 6:104: Coverage of the guarantee

If the guarantee document does not specify otherwise:

(a) the period of the guarantee is 5 years or the estimated life-span of the goods, whichever is shorter;

(b) the guarantor's obligations become effective if, for a reason other than misuse, mistreatment or accident, the goods at any time during the period of the guarantee become unfit for their ordinary purpose or cease to possess such qualities and performance capabilities as the guarantee holder may reasonably expect;

(c) the guarantor is obliged, if the conditions of the guarantee are satisfied, to repair or replace the goods; and

(d) all costs involved in invoking and performing the guarantee are to be borne by the guarantor.

IV. A. – 6:105: Guarantee limited to specific parts

A consumer goods guarantee relating only to a specific part or specific parts of the goods must clearly indicate this limitation in the guarantee document; otherwise the limitation is not binding on the consumer.

IV. A. – 6:106: Exclusion or limitation of the guarantor's liability

The guarantee may exclude or limit the guarantor's liability under the guarantee for any failure of or damage to the goods caused by failure to maintain the goods in accordance with instructions, provided that the exclusion or limitation is clearly set out in the guarantee document.

IV. A. – 6:107: Burden of proof

(1) Where the guarantee holder invokes a consumer goods guarantee within the period covered by the guarantee the burden of proof is on the guarantor that:

(a) the goods met the specifications set out in the guarantee document or in associated advertisements; and

(b) any failure of or damage to the goods is due to misuse, mistreatment, accident, failure to maintain, or other cause for which the guarantor is not responsible.

(2) The parties may not, to the detriment of the consumer, exclude the application of this Article or derogate from or vary its effects.

IV. A. – 6:108: Prolongation of the guarantee period

(1) If any defect or failure in the goods is remedied under the guarantee then the guarantee is prolonged for a period equal to the period during which the guarantee holder could not use the goods due to the defect or failure.

(2) The parties may not, to the detriment of the consumer, exclude the application of this Article or derogate from or vary its effects.

Part B.
Lease of goods

Chapter 1:
Scope of application and general provisions

IV. B. – 1:101: Lease of goods

(1) This Part of Book IV applies to contracts for the lease of goods.

(2) A contract for the lease of goods is a contract under which one party, the lessor, undertakes to provide the other party, the lessee, with a temporary right of use of goods in exchange for rent. The rent may be in the form of money or other value.

(3) This Part of Book IV does not apply to contracts where the parties have agreed that ownership will be transferred after a period with right of use even if the parties have described the contract as a lease.

(4) The application of this Part of Book IV is not excluded by the fact that the contract has a financing purpose, the lessor has the role as a financing party, or the lessee has an option to become owner of the goods.

(5) This Part of Book IV regulates only the contractual relationship arising from a contract for lease.

IV. B. – 1:102: Consumer contract for the lease of goods

For the purpose of this Part of Book IV, a consumer contract for the lease of goods is a contract for the lease of goods in which the lessor is a business and the lessee is a consumer.

Chapter 2:
Lease period

IV. B. – 2:101: Start of lease period
(1) The lease period starts:
  (a) at the time determinable from the terms agreed by the parties;
  (b) if a time frame within which the lease period is to start can be determined, at any time chosen by the lessor within that time frame unless the circumstances of the case indicate that the lessee is to choose the time;
  (c) in any other case, a reasonable time after the conclusion of the contract, at the request of either party.
(2) The lease period starts at the time when the lessee takes control of the goods if this is earlier than the starting time under paragraph (1).

IV. B. – 2:102: End of lease period
(1) A definite lease period ends at the time determinable from the terms agreed by the parties. A definite lease period cannot be terminated unilaterally beforehand by giving notice.
(2) An indefinite lease period ends at the time specified in a notice of termination given by either party.
(3) A notice under paragraph (2) is effective only if the time specified in the notice of termination is in compliance with the terms agreed by the parties or, if no period of notice can be determined from such terms, a reasonable time after the notice has reached the other party.

IV. B. – 2:103: Tacit prolongation
(1) A lease period is prolonged for an indefinite period if:
  (a) the lessee, with the lessor's knowledge, has continued to use the goods after the expiry of the lease period;
  (b) the use has continued for a period equal to that required for an effective notice of termination; and
  (c) the circumstances are not inconsistent with the tacit consent of both parties to such prolongation.
(2) Either party can prevent tacit prolongation by giving notice to the other before tacit prolongation takes effect. The notice need only indicate

that the party regards the lease period as having expired on the expiry date.

(3) Where the lease period is prolonged under this Article, the period during which the contract of lease has effect is also prolonged accordingly. The other terms of the contract are not changed by the prolongation.

(4) Notwithstanding the second sentence of paragraph (3), where the rent prior to prolongation was calculated so as to take into account amortisation of the cost of the goods by the lessee, the rent payable following prolongation is limited to what is reasonable having regard to the amount already paid.

(5) In the case of a consumer contract for the lease of goods the parties may not, to the detriment of the consumer, exclude the application of paragraph (4) or derogate from or vary its effects.

(6) Prolongation under this Article does not increase or extend security rights provided by third parties.

Chapter 3:
Obligations of the lessor

IV. B. – 3:101: Availability of the goods

(1) The lessor must make the goods available for the lessee's use at the start of the lease period and at the place determined by III. – 2:101 (Place of performance).

(2) Notwithstanding the rule in the previous paragraph, the lessor must make the goods available for the lessee's use at the lessee's place of business or, as the case may be, at the lessee's habitual residence if the lessor, on the specifications of the lessee, acquires the goods from a supplier selected by the lessee.

(3) The seller must ensure that the goods remain available for the lessee's use throughout the lease period, free from any right or claim of a third party which prevents or is otherwise likely to interfere with the lessee's use of the goods in accordance with the contract.

(4) The lessor's obligations when the goods are lost or damaged during the lease period are regulated by IV. B. – 3:104 (Conformity of the goods during the lease period).

IV. B. – 3:102: Conformity with the contract at the start of the lease period

(1) The lessor must ensure that the goods conform with the contract at the start of the lease period.

(2) The goods do not conform with the contract unless they:

(a) are of the quantity, quality and description required by the terms agreed by the parties;

(b) are contained or packaged in the manner required by the terms agreed by the parties;

(c) are supplied along with any accessories, installation instructions or other instructions required by the terms agreed by the parties; and

(d) comply with the following Article.

IV. B. – 3:103: Fitness for purpose, qualities, packaging etc.

The goods do not conform with the contract unless they:

(a) are fit for any particular purpose made known to the lessor at the time of the conclusion of the contract, except where the circumstances show that the lessee did not rely, or that it was unreasonable for the lessee to rely, on the lessor's skill and judgement;

(b) are fit for the purposes for which goods of the same description would ordinarily be used;

(c) possess the qualities of goods which the lessor held out to the lessee as a sample or model;

(d) are contained or packaged in the manner usual for such goods or, where there is no such manner, in a manner adequate to preserve and protect the goods;

(e) are supplied along with such accessories, installation instructions or other instructions as the lessee could reasonably expect to receive; and

(f) possess such qualities and performance capabilities as the lessee may reasonably expect.

IV. B. – 3:104: Conformity of the goods during the lease period

(1) The lessor must ensure that throughout the lease period, and subject to normal wear and tear, the goods:

(a) remain of the quantity, quality and description required by the contract; and

(b) remain fit for the purposes of the lease, even where this requires modifications to the goods.

(2) Paragraph (1) does not apply where the rent is calculated so as to take into account the amortisation of the cost of the goods by the lessee.

(3) Nothing in paragraph (1) affects the lessee's obligations under IV. B. – 5:104 (Handling the goods in accordance with the contract) paragraph (1)(c).

IV. B. – 3:105: Incorrect installation under a consumer contract for the lease of goods

Where, under a consumer contract for the lease of goods, the goods are incorrectly installed, any lack of conformity resulting from the incorrect installation is deemed to be a lack of conformity of the goods if:

(a) the goods were installed by the lessor or under the lessor's responsibility; or

(b) the goods were intended to be installed by the consumer and the incorrect installation was due to shortcomings in the installation instructions.

IV. B. – 3:106: Limits on derogation from conformity rights in a consumer contract for lease

In the case of a consumer contract for the lease of goods, any contractual term or agreement concluded with the lessor before a lack of conformity is brought to the lessor's attention which directly or indirectly waives or restricts the rights resulting from the lessor's obligation to ensure that the goods conform to the contract is not binding on the consumer.

IV. B. – 3:107: Obligations on return of the goods

The lessor must:

(a) take all the steps which may reasonably be expected in order to enable the lessee to perform the obligation to return the goods; and

(b) accept return of the goods as required by the contract.

Chapter 4:
Remedies of the lessee

IV. B. – 4:101: Overview of remedies of lessee

If the lessor fails to perform an obligation under the contract, the lessee may be entitled, according to Book III, Chapter 3 and the rules of this Chapter:

(a) to enforce specific performance of the obligation;
(b) to withhold performance of the reciprocal obligation;
(c) to terminate the lease;
(d) to reduce the rent;
(e) to damages and interest.

IV. B. – 4:102: Rules on remedies mandatory in consumer contract

(1) In the case of a consumer contract for the lease of goods the parties may not, to the detriment of the consumer, exclude the application of the rules of this Chapter or derogate from or vary their effects.

(2) Notwithstanding paragraph (1), the parties may agree on a limitation of the lessor's liability for loss related to the lessee's trade, business or profession. Such a term may not, however, be invoked if it would be contrary to good faith and fair dealing to do so.

IV. B. – 4:103: Lessee's right to have lack of conformity remedied

(1) The lessee may have any lack of conformity of the goods remedied, and recover any expenses reasonably incurred, to the extent that the lessee is entitled to enforce specific performance according to III. – 3:302 (Non-monetary obligations).

(2) Nothing in the preceding paragraph affects the lessor's right to cure the lack of conformity according to Book III, Chapter 3, Section 2.

IV. B. – 4:104: Rent reduction

(1) The lessee may reduce the rent for a period in which the value of the lessor's performance is decreased due to delay or lack of conformity, to the extent that the reduction in value is not caused by the lessee.

(2) The rent may be reduced even for periods in which the lessor retains the right to perform or cure according to III. – 3:103 (Notice fixing additional time for performance), III. – 3:202 (Cure by debtor: general

rules) paragraph (2) and III. – 3:204 (Consequences of allowing debtor opportunity to cure)).

(3) Notwithstanding the rule in paragraph (1), the lessee may lose the right to reduce the rent for a period according to IV. B. – 4:106 (Notification of lack of conformity).

IV. B. – 4:105: Substitute transaction by lessee

Where the lessee has terminated the lease under Book III, Chapter 3, Section 5 (Termination) and has made a substitute transaction within a reasonable time and in a reasonable manner, the lessee may, where entitled to damages, recover the difference between the value of the terminated lease and the value of the substitute transaction, as well as any further loss.

IV. B. – 4:106: Notification of lack of conformity

(1) The lessee cannot resort to remedies for lack of conformity unless notification is given to the lessor. Where notification is not timely, the lack of conformity is disregarded for a period corresponding to the unreasonable delay. Notification is always considered timely where it is given within a reasonable time after the lessee has become, or could reasonably be expected to have become, aware of the lack of conformity.

(2) When the lease period has ended the rules in III. – 3:107 (Failure to notify non-conformity) apply.

(3) The lessor is not entitled to rely on the provisions of paragraphs (1) and (2) if the lack of conformity relates to facts of which the lessor knew or could reasonably be expected to have known and which the lessor did not disclose to the lessee.

IV. B. – 4:107: Remedies channelled towards supplier of the goods

(1) This Article applies where:
   (a) the lessor, on the specifications of the lessee, acquires the goods from a supplier selected by the lessee;
   (b) the lessee, in providing the specifications for the goods and selecting the supplier, does not rely primarily on the skill and judgement of the lessor;
   (c) the lessee approves the terms of the supply contract;
   (d) the supplier's obligations under the supply contract are owed, by law or by contract, to the lessee as a party to the supply contract or as if the lessee were a party to that contract; and

(e) the supplier's obligations owed to the lessee cannot be varied without the consent of the lessee.

(2) The lessee cannot claim performance from the lessor, reduce the rent or claim damages or interest from the lessor, for late delivery or for lack of conformity, unless non-performance results from an act or omission of the lessor.

(3) The provision in paragraph (2) does not preclude:

(a) any right of the lessee to reject the goods, to terminate the lease under Book III, Chapter 3, Section 5 (Termination) or, prior to acceptance of the goods, to withhold rent to the extent that the lessee could have resorted to these remedies as a party to the supply contract; or

(b) any remedy of the lessee where a third party right or claim prevents, or is otherwise likely to interfere with, the lessee's continuous use of the goods in accordance with the contract.

(4) The lessee cannot terminate the lessee's contractual relationship with the supplier under the supply contract without the consent of the lessor.

Chapter 5:
Obligations of the lessee

IV. B. – 5:101: Obligation to pay rent

(1) The lessee must pay the rent.

(2) Where the rent cannot be determined from the terms agreed by the parties, from any other applicable rule of law or from usages or practices, it is a monetary sum determined in accordance with II. – 9:104 (Determination of price).

(3) The rent accrues from the start of the lease period.

IV. B. – 5:102: Time for payment

Rent is payable:

(a) at the end of each period for which the rent is agreed;

(b) if the rent is not agreed for certain periods, at the expiry of a definite lease period; or

(c) if no definite lease period is agreed and the rent is not agreed for certain periods, at the end of reasonable intervals.

IV. B. – 5:103: Acceptance of goods
The lessee must:
(a) take all steps reasonably to be expected in order to enable the lessor to perform the obligation to make the goods available at the start of the lease period; and
(b) take control of the goods as required by the contract.

IV. B. – 5:104: Handling the goods in accordance with the contract
(1) The lessee must:
  (a) observe the requirements and restrictions which follow from the terms agreed by the parties;
  (b) handle the goods with the care which can reasonably be expected in the circumstances, taking into account the duration of the lease period, the purpose of the lease and the character of the goods; and
  (c) take all measures which could ordinarily be expected to become necessary in order to preserve the normal standard and functioning of the goods, in so far as is reasonable, taking into account the duration of the lease period, the purpose of the lease and the character of the goods.
(2) Where the rent is calculated so as to take into account the amortisation of the cost of the goods by the lessee, the lessee must, during the lease period, keep the goods in the condition they were in at the start of the lease period, subject to any wear and tear which is normal for that kind of goods.

IV. B. – 5:105: Intervention to avoid danger or damage to the goods
(1) The lessee must take such measures for the maintenance and repair of the goods as would ordinarily be carried out by the lessor, if the measures are necessary to avoid danger or damage to the goods, and it is impossible or impracticable for the lessor, but not for the lessee, to ensure these measures are taken.
(2) The lessee has a right against the lessor to indemnification or, as the case may be, reimbursement in respect of an obligation or expenditure (whether of money or other assets) in so far as reasonably incurred for the purposes of the measures.

IV. B. – 5:106: Compensation for maintenance and improvements

(1) The lessee cannot claim compensation for maintenance of or improvements to the goods.

(2) Paragraph (1) does not exclude or restrict any claim the lessee may have for damages or any right or claim the lessee may have under IV. B. – 4:103 (Lessee's right to have lack of conformity remedied), IV. B. – 5:105 (Intervention to avoid danger or damage to the goods) or Book VIII (Acquisition and loss of ownership in movables).

IV. B. – 5:107: Obligation to inform

(1) The lessee must inform the lessor of any damage or danger to the goods, and of any right or claim of a third party, if these circumstances would normally give rise to a need for action on the part of the lessor.

(2) The lessee must inform the lessor under paragraph (1) within a reasonable time after the lessee first becomes aware of the circumstances and their character.

(3) The lessee is presumed to be aware of the circumstances and their character if the lessee could reasonably be expected to be so aware.

IV. B. – 5:108: Repairs and inspections by the lessor

(1) The lessee, if given reasonable notice where possible, must tolerate the carrying out by the lessor of repair work and other work on the goods which is necessary in order to preserve the goods, remove defects and prevent danger. This obligation does not preclude the lessee from reducing the rent in accordance with IV. B. – 4:104 (Rent reduction).

(2) The lessee must tolerate the carrying out of work on the goods which does not fall under paragraph (1), unless there is good reason to object.

(3) The lessee must tolerate inspection of the goods for the purposes indicated in paragraph (1). The lessee must also accept inspection of the goods by a prospective lessee during a reasonable period prior to expiry of the lease.

IV. B. – 5:109: Obligation to return the goods

At the end of the lease period the lessee must return the goods to the place where they were made available for the lessee.

Chapter 6:
Remedies of the lessor

IV. B. – 6:101: Overview of remedies of lessor
If the lessee fails to perform an obligation under the contract, the lessor may be entitled, according to Book III, Chapter 3 (Remedies for non-performance) and the provisions of this Chapter:

(a) to enforce performance of the obligation;
(b) to withhold performance of the reciprocal obligation;
(c) to terminate the lease;
(d) to damages and interest.

IV. B. – 6:102: Consumer contract for the lease of goods
In the case of a consumer contract for the lease of goods the parties may not, to the detriment of the consumer, exclude the application of the rules of this Chapter or derogate from or vary their effects.

IV. B. – 6:103: Right to enforce performance of monetary obligations
(1) The lessor is entitled to recover payment of rent and other sums due.
(2) Where the lessor has not yet made the goods available to the lessee and it is clear that the lessee will be unwilling to take control of the goods, the lessor may nonetheless proceed with performance and may recover payment unless:
    (a) the lessor could have made a reasonable substitute transaction without significant effort or expense; or
    (b) performance would be unreasonable in the circumstances.
(3) Where the lessee has taken control of the goods, the lessor may recover payment of any sums due under the contract. This includes future rent, unless the lessee wishes to return the goods and it would be reasonable for the lessor to accept their return.

IV. B. – 6:104: Substitute transaction by lessor
Where the lessor has terminated the lease under Book III, Chapter 3, Section 5 (Termination) and has made a substitute transaction within a reasonable time and in a reasonable manner, the lessor may, where entitled to damages, recover the difference between the value of the terminated lease and the value of the substitute transaction, as well as any further loss.

IV. B. – 6:105: Reduction of liability in consumer contract for the lease of goods

(1) In the case of a consumer contract for the lease of goods, the lessor's claim for damages may be reduced to the extent that the loss is mitigated by insurance covering the goods, or to the extent that loss would have been mitigated by insurance, in circumstances where it is reasonable to expect the lessor to take out such insurance.

(2) The rule in paragraph (1) applies in addition to the rules in Book III, Chapter 3, Section 7.

Chapter 7:
New parties and sublease

IV. B. – 7:101: Change in ownership and substitution of lessor

(1) Where ownership passes from the lessor to a new owner, the new owner of the goods is substituted as a party to the lease if the lessee has possession of the goods at the time ownership passes. The former owner remains subsidiarily liable for the non-performance of the obligations under the contract for lease as a personal security provider.

(2) A reversal of the passing of ownership puts the parties back in their original positions except as regards performance already rendered at the time of reversal.

(3) The rules in the preceding paragraphs apply accordingly where the lessor has acted as holder of a right other than ownership.

IV. B. – 7:102: Assignment of lessee's rights to performance

The lessee's rights to performance of the lessor's obligations under the contract for lease cannot be assigned without the lessor's consent.

IV. B. – 7:103: Sublease

(1) The lessee may not sublease the goods without the lessor's consent.

(2) If consent to a sublease is withheld without good reason, the lessee may terminate the lease by giving a reasonable period of notice.

(3) In the case of a sublease, the lessee remains liable for the performance of the lessee's obligations under the contract for lease.

Part C.
Services

Chapter 1:
General provisions
Section 1:
Scope

IV. C. – 1:101: Supply of a service
(1) This Part of Book IV applies:
   (a) to contracts under which one party, the service provider, under-
       takes to supply a service to the other party, the client, in exchange
       for a price; and
   (b) with appropriate adaptations, to contracts under which the service
       provider undertakes to supply a service to the client otherwise than
       in exchange for a price.
(2) It applies in particular to contracts for construction, processing, stor-
    age, design, information or advice, and treatment.

IV. C. – 1:102: Exclusions
This Part does not apply to contracts in so far as they are for transport,
insurance, the provision of a security or the supply of a financial product or
a financial service.

Section 2:
Other general provisions

IV. C. – 1:201: Structure
(1) Chapter 2 of this Part applies in relation to all service contracts within
    the scope of this Part, including contracts for construction, processing,
    storage, design, information or advice, and treatment.
(2) Chapters 3 to 8 contain more specific rules in relation to contracts for
    construction, processing, storage, design, information or advice, and
    treatment.
(3) In the case of any conflict the rules in Chapters 3 to 8 prevail over the
    rules in Chapter 2.

IV. C. – 1:202: Derogation

The parties may exclude the application of any of the rules in this Part of Book IV or derogate from or vary their effects, except as otherwise provided in this Part.

Chapter 2:
Rules applying to service contracts in general

IV. C. – 2:101: Price

Where the service provider is a business, a price is payable unless the circumstances indicate otherwise.

IV. C. – 2:102: Pre-contractual duties to warn

(1) The service provider is under a pre-contractual duty to warn the client if the service provider becomes aware of a risk that the service requested:
- (a) may not achieve the result stated or envisaged by the client,
- (b) may damage other interests of the client, or
- (c) may become more expensive or take more time than reasonably expected by the client.

(2) The duty to warn in paragraph (1) does not apply if the client:
- (a) already knows of the risks referred to in paragraph (1); or
- (b) could reasonably be expected to know of them.

(3) If a risk referred to in paragraph (1) materialises and the service provider was in breach of the duty to warn of it, a subsequent change of the service by the service provider under IV. C. – 2:109 (Unilateral variation of the service contract) which is based on the materialisation of the risk is of no effect unless the service provider proves that the client, if duly warned, would have entered into a contract anyway. This is without prejudice to any other remedies, including remedies for mistake, which the client may have.

(4) The client is under a pre-contractual duty to warn the service provider if the client becomes aware of unusual facts which are likely to cause the service to become more expensive or time-consuming than expected by the service provider or to cause any danger to the service provider or others when performing the service.

(5) If the facts referred to under paragraph (4) occur and the service provider was not duly warned, the service provider is entitled to:
  (a) damages for the loss the service provider sustained as a consequence of the failure to warn; and
  (b) an adjustment of the time allowed for performance of the service.
(6) For the purpose of paragraph (1), the service provider is presumed to be aware of the risks mentioned if they should be obvious from all the facts and circumstances known to the service provider, considering the information which the service provider must collect about the result stated or envisaged by the client and the circumstances in which the service is to be carried out.
(7) For the purpose of paragraph (2)(b) the client cannot reasonably be expected to know of a risk merely because the client was competent, or was advised by others who were competent, in the relevant field, unless such other person acted as the agent of the client, in which case II. – 1:105 (Imputed knowledge etc.) applies.
(8) For the purpose of paragraph (4), the client is presumed to be aware of the facts mentioned if they should be obvious from all the facts and circumstances known to the client without investigation.

IV. C. – 2:103: Obligation to co-operate

(1) The obligation of co-operation requires in particular:
  (a) the client to answer reasonable requests by the service provider for information in so far as this may reasonably be considered necessary to enable the service provider to perform the obligations under the contract;
  (b) the client to give directions regarding the performance of the service in so far as this may reasonably be considered necessary to enable the service provider to perform the obligations under the contract;
  (c) the client, in so far as the client is to obtain permits or licences, to obtain these at such time as may reasonably be considered necessary to enable the service provider to perform the obligations under the contract;
  (d) the service provider to give the client a reasonable opportunity to determine whether the service provider is performing the obligations under the contract; and

(e) the parties to co-ordinate their respective efforts in so far as this may reasonably be considered necessary to perform their respective obligations under the contract.

(2) If the client fails to perform the obligations under paragraph (1)(a) or (b), the service provider may either withhold performance or base performance on the expectations, preferences and priorities the client could reasonably be expected to have, given the information and directions which have been gathered, provided that the client is warned in accordance with IV. C. – 2:108 (Contractual obligation of the service provider to warn).

(3) If the client fails to perform the obligations under paragraph (1) causing the service to become more expensive or to take more time than agreed on in the contract, the service provider is entitled to:
(a) damages for the loss the service provider sustained as a consequence of the non-performance; and
(b) an adjustment of the time allowed for supplying the service.

IV. C. – 2:104: Subcontractors, tools and materials

(1) The service provider may subcontract the performance of the service in whole or in part without the client's consent, unless personal performance is required by the contract.

(2) Any subcontractor so engaged by the service provider must be of adequate competence.

(3) The service provider must ensure that any tools and materials used for the performance of the service are in conformity with the contract and the applicable statutory rules, and fit to achieve the particular purpose for which they are to be used.

(4) In so far as subcontractors are nominated by the client or tools and materials are provided by the client, the responsibility of the service provider is governed by IV. C. – 2:107 (Directions of the client) and IV. C. – 2:108 (Contractual obligation of the service provider to warn).

IV. C. – 2:105: Obligation of skill and care

(1) The service provider must perform the service:
(a) with the care and skill which a reasonable service provider would exercise under the circumstances; and
(b) in conformity with any statutory or other binding legal rules which are applicable to the service.

(2) If the service provider professes a higher standard of care and skill the provider must exercise that care and skill.

(3) If the service provider is, or purports to be, a member of a group of professional service providers for which standards have been set by a relevant authority or by that group itself, the service provider must exercise the care and skill expressed in those standards.

(4) In determining the care and skill the client is entitled to expect, regard is to be had, among other things, to:

    (a) the nature, the magnitude, the frequency and the foreseeability of the risks involved in the performance of the service for the client;

    (b) if damage has occurred, the costs of any precautions which would have prevented that damage or similar damage from occurring;

    (c) whether the service provider is a business;

    (d) whether a price is payable and, if one is payable, its amount; and

    (e) the time reasonably available for the performance of the service.

(5) The obligations under this Article require in particular the service provider to take reasonable precautions in order to prevent the occurrence of damage as a consequence of the performance of the service.

IV. C. – 2:106: Obligation to achieve result

(1) The supplier of a service must achieve the specific result stated or envisaged by the client at the time of the conclusion of the contract, provided that in the case of a result envisaged but not stated:

    (a) the result envisaged was one which the client could reasonably be expected to have envisaged; and

    (b) the client had no reason to believe that there was a substantial risk that the result

would not be achieved by the service.

(2) In so far as ownership of anything is transferred to the client under the service contract, it must be transferred free from any right or claim of a third party. Articles IV. A. – 2:305 (Third party rights or claims in general) and IV. A. – 2:306 (Third party rights or claims based on industrial property or other intellectual property) apply with any appropriate adaptations.

IV. C. – 2:107: Directions of the client

(1) The service provider must follow all timely directions of the client regarding the performance of the service, provided that the directions:

(a) are part of the contract itself or are specified in any document to which the contract refers; or

(b) result from the realisation of choices left to the client by the contract; or

(c) result from the realisation of choices initially left open by the parties.

(2) If non-performance of one or more of the obligations of the service provider under IV. C. – 2:105 (Obligation of skill and care) or IV.C – 2:106 (Obligation to achieve result) is the consequence of following a direction which the service provider is obliged to follow under paragraph (1), the service provider is not liable under those Articles, provided that the client was duly warned under IV. C. – 2:108 (Contractual obligation of the service provider to warn).

(3) If the service provider perceives a direction falling under paragraph (1) to be a variation of the contract under IV. C. – 2:109 (Unilateral variation of the service contract) the service provider must warn the client accordingly. Unless the client then revokes the direction without undue delay, the service provider must follow the direction and the direction is deemed to be a variation of the contract.

IV. C. – 2:108: Contractual obligation of the service provider to warn

(1) The service provider must warn the client if the service provider becomes aware of a risk that the service requested:

(a) may not achieve the result stated or envisaged by the client at the time of conclusion of the contract;

(b) may damage other interests of the client; or

(c) may become more expensive or take more time than agreed on in the contract

either as a result of following information or directions given by the client or collected in preparation for performance, or as a result of the occurrence of any other risk.

(2) The service provider must take reasonable measures to ensure that the client understands the content of the warning.

(3) The obligation to warn in paragraph (1) does not apply if the client:

(a) already knows of the risks referred to in paragraph (1); or

(b) could reasonably be expected to know of them.

(4) If a risk referred to in paragraph (1) materialises and the service provider did not perform the obligation to warn the client of it, a notice of variation by the service provider under IV. C. – 2:109 (Unilateral variation of the service contract) based on the materialisation of that risk is without effect.

(5) For the purpose of paragraph (1), the service provider is presumed to be aware of the risks mentioned if they should be obvious from all the facts and circumstances known to the service provider without investigation.

(6) For the purpose of paragraph (3)(b), the client cannot reasonably be expected to know of a risk merely because the client was competent, or was advised by others who were competent, in the relevant field, unless such other person acted as the agent of the client, in which case II. – 1:105 (Imputed knowledge etc.) applies.

IV. C. – 2:109: Unilateral variation of the service contract

(1) Without prejudice to the client's right to terminate under IV. C. – 2:111 (Client's right to terminate), either party may, by notice to the other party, change the service to be provided, if such a change is reasonable taking into account:
   (a) the result to be achieved;
   (b) the interests of the client;
   (c) the interests of the service provider; and
   (d) the circumstances at the time of the change.

(2) A change is regarded as reasonable only if it is:
   (a) necessary in order to enable the service provider to act in accordance with IV. C. – 2:105 (Obligation of skill and care) or, as the case may be, IV. C. – 2:106 (Obligation to achieve result);
   (b) the consequence of a direction given in accordance with paragraph (1) of IV. C. – 2:107 (Directions of the client) and not revoked without undue delay after receipt of a warning in accordance with paragraph (3) of that Article;
   (c) a reasonable response to a warning from the service provider under IV. C. – 2:108 (Contractual obligation of the service provider to warn); or
   (d) required by a change of circumstances which would justify a variation of the service provider's obligations under III. – 1:110 (Variation or termination by court on a change of circumstances).

(3) Any additional price due as a result of the change has to be reasonable and is to be determined using the same methods of calculation as were used to establish the original price for the service.

(4) In so far as the service is reduced, the loss of profit, the expenses saved and any possibility that the service provider may be able to use the released capacity for other purposes are to be taken into account in the calculation of the price due as a result of the change.

(5) A change of the service may lead to an adjustment of the time of performance proportionate to the extra work required in relation to the work originally required for the performance of the service and the time span determined for performance of the service.

IV. C. – 2:110: Client's obligation to notify anticipated non-conformity

(1) The client must notify the service provider if the client becomes aware during the period for performance of the service that the service provider will fail to perform the obligation under IV. C. – 2:106 (Obligation to achieve result).

(2) The client is presumed to be so aware if from all the facts and circumstances known to the client without investigation the client has reason to be so aware.

(3) If a non-performance of the obligation under paragraph (1) causes the service to become more expensive or to take more time than agreed on in the contract, the service provider is entitled to:

(a) damages for the loss the service provider sustains as a consequence of that failure; and

(b) an adjustment of the time allowed for performance of the service.

IV. C. – 2:111: Client's right to terminate

(1) The client may terminate the contractual relationship at any time by giving notice to the service provider.

(2) The effects of termination are governed by III. – 1:109 (Variation or termination by notice) paragraph (3).

(3) When the client was justified in terminating the relationship no damages are payable for so doing.

(4) When the client was not justified in terminating the relationship, the termination is nevertheless effective but the service provider may claim damages in accordance with the rules in Book III.

(5) For the purposes of this Article, the client is justified in terminating the relationship if the client:
  (a) was entitled to terminate the relationship under the express terms of the contract and observed any requirements laid down in the contract for doing so;
  (b) was entitled to terminate the relationship under Book III, Chapter 3, Section 5 (Termination); or
  (c) was entitled to terminate the relationship under III. – 1:109 (Variation or termination by notice) paragraph (2) and gave a reasonable period of notice as required by that provision.

Chapter 3:
Construction

IV. C. – 3:101: Scope
(1) This Chapter applies to contracts under which one party, the constructor, undertakes to construct a building or other immovable structure, or to materially alter an existing building or other immovable structure, following a design provided by the client.
(2) It applies with appropriate adaptations to contracts under which the constructor undertakes:
  (a) to construct a movable or incorporeal thing, following a design provided by the client; or
  (b) to construct a building or other immovable structure, to materially alter an existing building or other immovable structure, or to construct a movable or incorporeal thing, following a design provided by the constructor.

IV. C. – 3:102: Obligation of client to co-operate
The obligation of co-operation requires in particular the client to:
(a) provide access to the site where the construction has to take place in so far as this may reasonably be considered necessary to enable the constructor to perform the obligations under the contract; and
(b) provide the components, materials and tools, in so far as they must be provided by the client, at such time as may reasonably be considered necessary to enable the constructor to perform the obligations under the contract.

IV. C. – 3:103: Obligation to prevent damage to structure

The constructor must take reasonable precautions in order to prevent any damage to the structure.

IV. C. – 3:104: Conformity

(1) The constructor must ensure that the structure is of the quality and description required by the contract. Where more than one structure is to be made, the quantity also must be in conformity with the contract.

(2) The structure does not conform to the contract unless it is:

    (a) fit for any particular purpose expressly or impliedly made known to the constructor at the time of the conclusion of the contract or at the time of any variation in accordance with IV. C. – 2:109 (Unilateral variation of the service contract) pertaining to the issue in question; and

    (b) fit for the particular purpose or purposes for which a structure of the same description would ordinarily be used.

(3) The client is not entitled to invoke a remedy for non-conformity if a direction provided by the client under IV. C. – 2:107 (Directions of the client) is the cause of the non-conformity and the constructor performed the obligation to warn pursuant to IV. C. – 2:108 (Contractual obligation of the service provider to warn).

IV. C. – 3:105: Inspection, supervision and acceptance

(1) The client may inspect or supervise the tools and materials used in the construction process, the process of construction and the resulting structure in a reasonable manner and at any reasonable time, but is not bound to do so.

(2) If the parties agree that the constructor has to present certain elements of the tools and materials used, the process or the resulting structure to the client for acceptance, the constructor may not proceed with the construction before having been allowed by the client to do so.

(3) Absence of, or inadequate, inspection, supervision or acceptance does not relieve the constructor wholly or partially from liability. This rule also applies when the client is under a contractual obligation to inspect, supervise or accept the structure or the construction of it.

IV. C. – 3:106: Handing-over of the structure

(1) If the constructor regards the structure, or any part of it which is fit for independent use, as sufficiently completed and wishes to transfer control over it to the client, the client must accept such control within a reasonable time after being notified. The client may refuse to accept the control when the structure, or the relevant part of it, does not conform to the contract and such non-conformity makes it unfit for use.

(2) Acceptance by the client of the control over the structure does not relieve the constructor wholly or partially from liability. This rule also applies when the client is under a contractual obligation to inspect, supervise or accept the structure or the construction of it.

(3) This Article does not apply if, under the contract, control is not to be transferred to the client.

IV. C. – 3:107: Payment of the price

(1) The price or a proportionate part of it is payable when the constructor transfers the control of the structure or a part of it to the client in accordance with the preceding Article.

(2) However, where work remains to be done under the contract on the structure or relevant part of it after such transfer the client may withhold such part of the price as is reasonable until the work is completed.

(3) If, under the contract, control is not to be transferred to the client, the price is payable when the work has been completed, the constructor has so informed the client and the client has had a chance to inspect the structure.

IV. C. – 3:108: Risks

(1) This Article applies if the structure is destroyed or damaged due to an event which the constructor could not have avoided or overcome and the constructor cannot be held accountable for the destruction or damage.

(2) In this Article the "relevant time" is:
   (a) where the control of the structure is to be transferred to the client, the time when such control has been, or should have been, transferred in accordance with IV. C. – 3:106 (Handing over of the structure);
   (b) in other cases, the time when the work has been completed and the constructor has so informed the client.

(3) When the situation mentioned in paragraph (1) has been caused by an event occurring before the relevant time and it is still possible to perform:

(a) the constructor still has to perform or, as the case may be, perform again;

(b) the client is only obliged to pay for the constructor's performance under (a);

(c) the time for performance is extended in accordance with paragraph (6) of IV. C. – 2:109 (Unilateral variation of the service contract);

(d) the rules of III. – 3:104 (Excuse due to an impediment) may apply to the constructor's original performance; and

(e) the constructor is not obliged to compensate the client for losses to materials provided by the client.

(4) When the situation mentioned in paragraph (1) has been caused by an event occurring before the relevant time, and it is no longer possible to perform:

(a) the client does not have to pay for the service rendered;

(b) the rules of III. – 3:104 (Excuse due to an impediment) may apply to the constructor's performance; and

(c) the constructor is not obliged to compensate the client for losses to materials provided by the client, but is obliged to return the structure or what remains of it to the client.

(5) When the situation mentioned in paragraph (1) has been caused by an event occurring after the relevant time:

(a) the constructor does not have to perform again; and

(b) the client remains obliged to pay the price.

Chapter 4:
Processing

IV. C. – 4:101: Scope

(1) This Chapter applies to contracts under which one party, the processor, undertakes to perform a service on an existing movable or incorporeal thing or to an immovable structure for another party, the client. It does not, however, apply to construction work on an existing building or other immovable structure.

(2) This Chapter applies in particular to contracts under which the processor undertakes to repair, maintain or clean an existing movable or incorporeal thing or immovable structure.

IV. C. – 4:102: Obligation of client to co-operate
The obligation to co-operate requires in particular the client to:
(a) hand over the thing or to give the control of it to the processor, or to give access to the site where the service is to be performed in so far as may reasonably be considered necessary to enable the processor to perform the obligations under the contract; and
(b) in so far as they must be provided by the client, provide the components, materials and tools in time to enable the processor to perform the obligations under the contract.

IV. C. – 4:103: Obligation to prevent damage to thing being processed
The processor must take reasonable precautions in order to prevent any damage to the thing being processed.

IV. C. – 4:104: Inspection and supervision
(1) If the service is to be performed at a site provided by the client, the client may inspect or supervise the tools and material used, the performance of the service and the thing on which the service is performed in a reasonable manner and at any reasonable time, but is not bound to do so.
(2) Absence of, or inadequate inspection or supervision does not relieve the processor wholly or partially from liability. This rule also applies when the client is under a contractual obligation to accept, inspect or supervise the processing of the thing.

IV. C. – 4:105: Return of the thing processed
(1) If the processor regards the service as sufficiently completed and wishes to return the thing or the control of it to the client, the client must accept such return or control within a reasonable time after being notified. The client may refuse to accept the return or control when the thing is not fit for use in accordance with the particular purpose for which the client had the service performed, provided that such purpose

was made known to the processor or that the processor otherwise has reason to know of it.

(2) The processor must return the thing or the control of it within a reasonable time after being so requested by the client.

(3) Acceptance by the client of the return of the thing or the control of it does not relieve the processor wholly or partially from liability for non-performance.

(4) If, by virtue of the rules on the acquisition of property, the processor has become the owner of the thing, or a share in it, as a consequence of the performance of the obligations under the contract, the processor must transfer ownership of the thing or share when the thing is returned.

IV. C. – 4:106: Payment of the price

(1) The price is payable when the processor transfers the thing or the control of it to the client in accordance with IV. C. – 4:105 (Return of the thing processed) or the client, without being entitled to do so, refuses to accept the return of the thing.

(2) However, where work remains to be done under the contract on the thing after such transfer or refusal the client may withhold such part of the price as is reasonable until the work is completed.

(3) If, under the contract, the thing or the control of it is not to be transferred to the client, the price is payable when the work has been completed and the processor has so informed the client.

IV. C. – 4:107: Risks

(1) This Article applies if the thing is destroyed or damaged due to an event which the processor could not have avoided or overcome and the processor cannot be held accountable for the destruction or damage.

(2) If, prior to the event mentioned in paragraph (1), the processor had indicated that the processor regarded the service as sufficiently completed and that the processor wished to return the thing or the control of it to the client:

(a) the processor is not required to perform again; and

(b) the client must pay the price.

The price is due when the processor returns the remains of the thing, if any, or the client indicates that the client does not want the remains. In the latter case, the processor may dispose of the remains at the client's expense. This provision does not apply if the client was entitled to refuse the return of the thing under paragraph (1) of IV. C. – 4:105 (Return of the thing processed).

(3) If the parties had agreed that the processor would be paid for each period which has elapsed, the client is obliged to pay the price for each period which has elapsed before the event mentioned in paragraph (1) occurred.

(4) If, after the event mentioned in paragraph (1), performance of the obligations under the contract is still possible for the processor:

(a) the processor still has to perform or, as the case may be, perform again;

(b) the client is only obliged to pay for the processor's performance under (a); the processor's entitlement to a price under paragraph (3) is not affected by this provision;

(c) the client is obliged to compensate the processor for the costs the processor has to incur in order to acquire materials replacing the materials supplied by the client, unless the client on being so requested by the processor supplies these materials; and

(d) if need be, the time for performance is extended in accordance with paragraph (6) of IV. C. – 2:109 (Unilateral variation of the service contract).

This paragraph is without prejudice to the client's right to terminate the contractual relationship under IV. C. – 2:111 (Client's right to terminate).

(5) If, in the situation mentioned in paragraph (1), performance of the obligations under the contract is no longer possible for the processor:

(a) the client does not have to pay for the service rendered; the processor's entitlement to a price under paragraph (3) is not affected by this provision; and

(b) the processor is obliged to return to the client the thing and the materials supplied by the client or what remains of them, unless the client indicates that the client does not want the remains. In the latter case, the processor may dispose of the remains at the client's expense.

IV. C. – 4:108: Limitation of liability

In a contract between two businesses, a term restricting the processor's liability for non-performance to the value of the thing, had the service been performed correctly, is presumed to be fair for the purposes of II. – 9:406 (Meaning of "unfair" in contracts between businesses) except to the extent that it restricts liability for damage caused intentionally or by way of grossly negligent behaviour on the part of the processor or any person for whose actions the processor is responsible.

Chapter 5:
Storage

IV. C. – 5:101: Scope

(1) This Chapter applies to contracts under which one party, the storer, undertakes to store a movable or incorporeal thing for another party, the client.

(2) This Chapter does not apply to the storage of:
  (a) immovable structures;
  (b) movable or incorporeal things during transportation; and
  (c) money or securities (except in the circumstances mentioned in paragraph (7) of IV. C. – 5:110 (Liability of the hotel-keeper)) or rights.

IV. C. – 5:102: Storage place and subcontractors

(1) The storer, in so far as the storer provides the storage place, must provide a place fit for storing the thing in such a manner that the thing can be returned in the condition the client may expect.

(2) The storer may not subcontract the performance of the service without the client's consent.

IV. C. – 5:103: Protection and use of the thing stored

(1) The storer must take reasonable precautions in order to prevent unnecessary deterioration, decay or depreciation of the thing stored.

(2) The storer may use the thing handed over for storage only if the client has agreed to such use.

IV. C. – 5:104: Return of the thing stored

(1) Without prejudice to any other obligation to return the thing, the storer must return the thing at the agreed time or, where the contractual relationship is terminated before the agreed time, within a reasonable time after being so requested by the client.

(2) The client must accept the return of the thing when the storage obligation comes to an end and when acceptance of return is properly requested by the storer.

(3) Acceptance by the client of the return of the thing does not relieve the storer wholly or partially from liability for non-performance.

(4) If the client fails to accept the return of the thing at the time provided under paragraph (2), the storer has the right to sell the thing in accordance with III. – 2:111 (Property not accepted), provided that the storer has given the client reasonable warning of the storer's intention to do so.

(5) If, during storage, the thing bears fruit, the storer must hand this fruit over when the thing is returned to the client.

(6) If, by virtue of the rules on the acquisition of ownership, the storer has become the owner of the thing, the storer must return a thing of the same kind and the same quality and quantity and transfer ownership of that thing. This Article applies with appropriate adaptations to the substituted thing.

(7) This Article applies with appropriate adaptations if a third party who holds sufficient title to receive the thing requests its return.

IV. C. – 5:105: Conformity

(1) The storage of the thing does not conform with the contract unless the thing is returned in the same condition as it was in when handed over to the storer.

(2) If, given the nature of the thing or the contract, it cannot reasonably be expected that the thing is returned in the same condition, the storage of the thing does not conform with the contract if the thing is not returned in such condition as the client could reasonably expect.

(3) If, given the nature of the thing or the contract, it cannot reasonably be expected that the same thing is returned, the storage of the thing does not conform with the contract if the thing which is returned is not in the same condition as the thing which was handed over for storage, or if it is not of the same kind, quality and quantity, or if ownership of the thing is not transferred in accordance with paragraph (6) of IV. C. – 5:104 (Return of the thing stored).

IV. C. – 5:106: Payment of the price

(1) The price is payable at the time when the thing is returned to the client in accordance with IV. C. – 5:104 (Return of the thing stored) or the client, without being entitled to do so, refuses to accept the return of the thing.

(2) The storer may withhold the thing until the client pays the price. III. – 3:401 (Right to withhold performance of reciprocal obligation) applies accordingly.

IV. C. – 5:107: Post-storage obligation to inform

After the ending of the storage, the storer must inform the client of:

(a) any damage which has occurred to the thing during storage; and

(b) the necessary precautions which the client must take before using or transporting the thing, unless the client could reasonably be expected to be aware of the need for such precautions.

IV. C. – 5:108: Risks

(1) This Article applies if the thing is destroyed or damaged due to an event which the storer could not have avoided or overcome and if the storer cannot be held accountable for the destruction or damage.

(2) If, prior to the event, the storer had notified the client that the client was required to accept the return of the thing, the client must pay the price. The price is due when the storer returns the remains of the thing, if any, or the client indicates to the storer that the client does not want those remains.

(3) If, prior to the event, the storer had not notified the client that the client was required to accept the return of the thing:

    (a) if the parties had agreed that the storer would be paid for each period of time which has elapsed, the client must pay the price for each period which has elapsed before the event occurred;

    (b) if further performance of the obligations under the contract is still possible for the storer, the storer is required to continue performance, without prejudice to the client's right to terminate the contractual relationship under IV. C. – 2:111 (Client's right to terminate);

    (c) if performance of the obligations under the contract is no longer possible for the storer the client does not have to pay for the service rendered except to the extent that the storer is entitled to a price under subparagraph (a); and the storer must return to the client the remains of the thing unless the client indicates that the client does not want those remains.

(4) If the client indicates to the storer that the client does not want the remains of the thing, the storer may dispose of the remains at the client's expense.

IV. C. – 5:109: Limitation of liability

In a contract between two businesses, a term restricting the storer's liability for non-performance to the value of the thing is presumed to be fair for the purposes of II. – 9:406 (Meaning of unfair in contracts between businesses), except to the extent that it restricts liability for damage caused intentionally or by way of grossly negligent conduct on the part of the storer or any person for whose actions the storer is responsible.

IV. C. – 5:110: Liability of the hotel-keeper

(1) A hotel-keeper is liable as a storer for any damage to, or destruction or loss of, a thing brought to the hotel by any guest who stays at the hotel and has sleeping accommodation there.

(2) For the purposes of paragraph (1) a thing is regarded as brought to the hotel:
  (a) if it is at the hotel during the time when the guest has the use of sleeping accommodation there;
  (b) if the hotel-keeper or a person for whose actions the hotel-keeper is responsible takes charge of it outside the hotel during the period for which the guest has the use of the sleeping accommodation at the hotel; or
  (c) if the hotel-keeper or a person for whose actions the hotel-keeper is responsible takes charge of it whether at the hotel or outside it during a reasonable period preceding or following the time when the guest has the use of sleeping accommodation at the hotel.

(3) The hotel-keeper is not liable in so far as the damage, destruction or loss is caused by:
  (a) a guest or any person accompanying, employed by or visiting the guest;
  (b) an impediment beyond the hotel-keeper's control; or
  (c) the nature of the thing.

(4) A term excluding or limiting the liability of the hotel-keeper is unfair for the purposes of Book II, Chapter 9, Section 4 if it excludes or limits liability in a case where the hotel-keeper, or a person for whose actions the hotel-keeper is responsible, causes the damage, destruction or loss intentionally or by way of grossly negligent conduct.

(5) Except where the damage, destruction or loss is caused intentionally or by way of grossly negligent conduct of the hotel-keeper or a person for whose actions the hotel-keeper is responsible, the guest is required to inform the hotel-keeper of the damage, destruction or loss without undue delay. If the guest fails to inform the hotel-keeper without undue delay, the hotel-keeper is not liable.

(6) The hotel-keeper has the right to withhold any thing referred to in paragraph (1) until the guest has met any claim the hotel-keeper has against the guest with respect to accommodation, food, drink and so-licited services performed for the guest in the hotel-keeper's profession-al capacity.

(7) This Article does not apply if and to the extent that a separate storage contract is concluded between the hotel-keeper and any guest for any thing brought to the hotel. A separate storage contract is deemed to have been concluded if a thing is handed over for storage to the hotel-keeper.

Chapter 6:
Design

IV. C. – 6:101: Scope

(1) This Chapter applies to contracts under which one party, the designer, undertakes to design for another party, the client:

    (a) an immovable structure which is to be constructed by or on behalf of the client; or

    (b) a movable or incorporeal thing or service which is to be construct-ed or performed by or on behalf of the client.

(2) A contract under which one party undertakes to design and to supply a service which consists of carrying out the design is to be considered as primarily a contract for the supply of the subsequent service.

IV. C. – 6:102: Pre-contractual duty to warn

The designer's pre-contractual duty to warn requires in particular the designer to warn the client in so far as the designer lacks special expertise in specific problems which require the involvement of specialists.

IV. C. – 6:103: Obligation of skill and care

The designer's obligation of skill and care requires in particular the designer to:

(a) attune the design work to the work of other designers who contracted with the client, to enable there to be an efficient performance of all services involved;

(b) integrate the work of other designers which is necessary to ensure that the design will conform to the contract;

(c) include any information for the interpretation of the design which is necessary for a user of the design of average competence (or a specific user made known to the designer at the conclusion of the contract) to give effect to the design;

(d) enable the user of the design to give effect to the design without violation of public law rules or interference based on justified third-party rights of which the designer knows or could reasonably be expected to know; and

(e) provide a design which allows economic and technically efficient realisation.

IV. C. – 6:104: Conformity

(1) The design does not conform to the contract unless it enables the user of the design to achieve a specific result by carrying out the design with the skill and care which could reasonably be expected.

(2) The client is not entitled to invoke a remedy for non-conformity if a direction provided by the client under IV. C. – 2:107 (Directions of the client) is the cause of the non-conformity and the designer performed the obligation to warn under IV. C. – 2:108 (Contractual obligation of the service provider to warn).

IV. C. – 6:105: Handing over of the design

(1) In so far as the designer regards the design, or a part of it which is fit for carrying out independently from the completion of the rest of the design, as sufficiently completed and wishes to transfer the design to the

client, the client must accept it within a reasonable time after being notified.

(2) The client may refuse to accept the design when it, or the relevant part of it, does not conform to the contract and such non-conformity amounts to a fundamental non-performance.

IV. C. – 6:106: Records

(1) After performance of both parties' other contractual obligations, the designer must, on request by the client, hand over all relevant documents or copies of them.

(2) The designer must store, for a reasonable time, relevant documents which are not handed over. Before destroying the documents, the designer must offer them again to the client.

IV. C. – 6:107: Limitation of liability

In contracts between two businesses, a term restricting the designer's liability for non-performance to the value of the structure, thing or service which is to be constructed or performed by or on behalf of the client following the design, is presumed to be fair for the purposes of II. – 9:406 (Meaning of "unfair" in contracts between businesses) except to the extent that it restricts liability for damage caused intentionally or by grossly negligent conduct on the part of the designer or any person for whose actions the designer is responsible.

Chapter 7:
Information and advice

IV. C. – 7:101: Scope

(1) This Chapter applies to contracts under which one party, the provider, undertakes to provide information or advice to another party, the client.

(2) This Chapter does not apply in relation to treatment in so far as Chapter 8 (Treatment) contains more specific rules on the obligation to inform.

(3) In the remainder of this Chapter any reference to information includes a reference to advice.

IV. C. – 7:102: Obligation to collect preliminary data

(1) The provider must, in so far as this may reasonably be considered necessary for the performance of the service, collect data about:

    (a) the particular purpose for which the client requires the information;

    (b) the client's preferences and priorities in relation to the information;

    (c) the decision the client can be expected to make on the basis of the information; and

    (d) the personal situation of the client.

(2) In case the information is intended to be passed on to a group of persons, the data to be collected must relate to the purposes, preferences, priorities and personal situations that can reasonably be expected from individuals within such a group.

(3) In so far as the provider must obtain data from the client, the provider must explain what the client is required to supply.

IV. C. – 7:103: Obligation to acquire and use expert knowledge

The provider must acquire and use the expert knowledge to which the provider has or should have access as a professional information provider or adviser, in so far as this may reasonably be considered necessary for the performance of the service.

IV. C. – 7:104: Obligation of skill and care

(1) The provider's obligation of skill and care requires in particular the provider to:

    (a) take reasonable measures to ensure that the client understands the content of the information;

    (b) act with the care and skill that a reasonable information provider would demonstrate under the circumstances when providing evaluative information; and

    (c) in any case where the client is expected to make a decision on the basis of the information, inform the client of the risks involved, in so far as such risks could reasonably be expected to influence the client's decision.

(2) When the provider expressly or impliedly undertakes to provide the client with a recommendation to enable the client to make a subsequent decision, the provider must:

(a) base the recommendation on a skilful analysis of the expert knowledge to be collected in relation to the purposes, priorities, preferences and personal situation of the client;

(b) inform the client of alternatives the provider can personally provide relating to the subsequent decision and of their advantages and risks, as compared with those of the recommended decision; and

(c) inform the client of other alternatives the provider cannot personally provide, unless the provider expressly informs the client that only a limited range of alternatives is offered or this is apparent from the situation.

IV. C. – 7:105: Conformity

(1) The provider must provide information which is of the quantity, quality and description required by the contract.

(2) The factual information provided by the information provider to the client must be a correct description of the actual situation described.

IV. C. – 7:106: Records

In so far as this may reasonably be considered necessary, having regard to the interest of the client, the provider must keep records regarding the information provided in accordance with this Chapter and make such records or excerpts from them available to the client on reasonable request.

IV. C. – 7:107: Conflict of interest

(1) When the provider expressly or impliedly undertakes to provide the client with a recommendation to enable the client to make a subsequent decision, the provider must disclose any possible conflict of interest which might influence the performance of the provider's obligations.

(2) So long as the contractual obligations have not been completely performed, the provider may not enter into a relationship with another party which may give rise to a possible conflict with the interests of the client, without full disclosure to the client and the client's explicit or implicit agreement.

IV. C. – 7:108: Influence of ability of the client

(1) The involvement in the supply of the service of other persons on the client's behalf or the mere competence of the client does not relieve the provider of any obligation under this Chapter.

(2) The provider is relieved of those obligations if the client already has knowledge of the information or if the client has reason to know of the information.

(3) For the purpose of paragraph (2), the client has reason to know if the information should be obvious to the client without investigation.

IV. C. – 7:109: Causation

If the provider knows or could reasonably be expected to know that a subsequent decision will be based on the information to be provided, and if the client makes such a decision and suffers loss as a result, any non-performance of an obligation under the contract by the provider is presumed to have caused the loss if the client proves that, if the provider had provided all information required, it would have been reasonable for the client to have seriously considered making an alternative decision.

Chapter 8:
Treatment

IV. C. – 8:101: Scope

(1) This Chapter applies to contracts under which one party, the treatment provider, undertakes to provide medical treatment for another party, the patient.

(2) It applies with appropriate adaptations to contracts under which the treatment provider undertakes to provide any other service in order to change the physical or mental condition of a person.

(3) Where the patient is not the contracting party, the patient is regarded as a third party on whom the contract confers rights corresponding to the obligations of the treatment provider imposed by this Chapter.

IV. C. – 8:102: Preliminary assessment

The treatment provider must, in so far as this may reasonably be considered necessary for the performance of the service:

(a) interview the patient about the patient's health condition, symptoms, previous illnesses, allergies, previous or other current treatment and the patient's preferences and priorities in relation to the treatment;

(b) carry out the examinations necessary to diagnose the health condition of the patient; and

(c) consult with any other treatment providers involved in the treatment of the patient.

IV. C. – 8:103: Obligations regarding instruments, medicines, materials, installations and premises

(1) The treatment provider must use instruments, medicines, materials, installations and premises which are of at least the quality demanded by accepted and sound professional practice, which conform to applicable statutory rules, and which are fit to achieve the particular purpose for which they are to be used.

(2) The parties may not, to the detriment of the patient, exclude the application of this Article or derogate from or vary its effects.

IV. C. – 8:104: Obligation of skill and care

(1) The treatment provider's obligation of skill and care requires in particular the treatment provider to provide the patient with the care and skill which a reasonable treatment provider exercising and professing care and skill would demonstrate under the given circumstances.

(2) If the treatment provider lacks the experience or skill to treat the patient with the required degree of skill and care, the treatment provider must refer the patient to a treatment provider who can.

(3) The parties may not, to the detriment of the patient, exclude the application of this Article or derogate from or vary its effects.

IV. C. – 8:105: Obligation to inform

(1) The treatment provider must, in order to give the patient a free choice regarding treatment, inform the patient about, in particular:

(a) the patient's existing state of health;

(b) the nature of the proposed treatment;

(c) the advantages of the proposed treatment;

(d) the risks of the proposed treatment;

(e) the alternatives to the proposed treatment, and their advantages and risks as compared to those of the proposed treatment; and

(f) the consequences of not having treatment.

(2) The treatment provider must, in any case, inform the patient about any risk or alternative which might reasonably influence the patient's de-

cision on whether to give consent to the proposed treatment or not. It is presumed that a risk might reasonably influence that decision if its materialisation would lead to serious detriment to the patient. Unless otherwise provided, the obligation to inform is subject to the provisions of Chapter 7 (Information and Advice).

(3) The information must be provided in a way understandable to the patient.

IV. C. – 8:106: Obligation to inform in case of unnecessary or experimental treatment

(1) If the treatment is not necessary for the preservation or improvement of the patient's health, the treatment provider must disclose all known risks.

(2) If the treatment is experimental, the treatment provider must disclose all information regarding the objectives of the experiment, the nature of the treatment, its advantages and risks and the alternatives, even if only potential.

(3) The parties may not, to the detriment of the patient, exclude the application of this Article or derogate from or vary its effects.

IV. C. – 8:107: Exceptions to the obligation to inform

(1) Information which would normally have to be provided by virtue of the obligation to inform may be withheld from the patient:
   (a) if there are objective reasons to believe that it would seriously and negatively influence the patient's health or life; or
   (b) if the patient expressly states a wish not to be informed, provided that the non-disclosure of the information does not endanger the health or safety of third parties.

(2) The obligation to inform need not be performed where treatment must be provided in an emergency. In such a case the treatment provider must, so far as possible, provide the information later.

IV. C. – 8:108: Obligation not to treat without consent

(1) The treatment provider must not carry out treatment unless the patient has given prior informed consent to it.

(2) The patient may revoke consent at any time.

(3) In so far as the patient is incapable of giving consent, the treatment provider must not carry out treatment unless:

    (a) informed consent has been obtained from a person or institution legally entitled to take decisions regarding the treatment on behalf of the patient; or

    (b) any rules or procedures enabling treatment to be lawfully given without such consent have been complied with; or

    (c) the treatment must be provided in an emergency.

(4) In the situation described in paragraph (3), the treatment provider must not carry out treatment without considering, so far as possible, the opinion of the incapable patient with regard to the treatment and any such opinion expressed by the patient before becoming incapable.

(5) In the situation described in paragraph (3), the treatment provider may carry out only such treatment as is intended to improve the health condition of the patient.

(6) In the situation described in paragraph (2) of IV. C. – 8:106 (Obligation to inform in case of unnecessary or experimental treatment), consent must be given in an express and specific way.

(7) The parties may not, to the detriment of the patient, exclude the application of this Article or derogate from or vary its effects.

IV. C. – 8:109: Records

(1) The treatment provider must create adequate records of the treatment. Such records must include, in particular, information collected in any preliminary interviews, examinations or consultations, information regarding the consent of the patient and information regarding the treatment performed.

(2) The treatment provider must, on reasonable request:

    (a) give the patient, or if the patient is incapable of giving consent, the person or institution legally entitled to take decisions on behalf of the patient, access to the records; and

    (b) answer, in so far as reasonable, questions regarding the interpretation of the records.

(3) If the patient has suffered injury and claims that it is a result of non-performance by the treatment provider of the obligation of skill and care and the treatment provider fails to comply with paragraph (2), non-performance of the obligation of skill and care and a causal link between such non-performance and the injury are presumed.

(4) The treatment provider must keep the records, and give information about their interpretation, during a reasonable time of at least 10 years after the treatment has ended, depending on the usefulness of these records for the patient or the patient's heirs or representatives and for future treatments. Records which can reasonably be expected to be important after the reasonable time must be kept by the treatment provider after that time. If for any reason the treatment provider ceases activity, the records must be deposited or delivered to the patient for future consultation.

(5) The parties may not, to the detriment of the patient, exclude the application of paragraphs (1) to (4) or derogate from or vary their effects.

(6) The treatment provider may not disclose information about the patient or other persons involved in the patient's treatment to third parties unless disclosure is necessary in order to protect third parties or the public interest. The treatment provider may use the records in an anonymous way for statistical, educational or scientific purposes.

IV. C. – 8:110: Remedies for non-performance

With regard to any non-performance of an obligation under a contract for treatment, Book III, Chapter 3 (Remedies for Non-performance) and IV. C. – 2:111 (Client's right to terminate) apply with the following adaptations:

(a) the treatment provider may not withhold performance or terminate the contractual relationship under that Chapter if this would seriously endanger the health of the patient; and

(b) in so far as the treatment provider has the right to withhold performance or to terminate the contractual relationship and is planning to exercise that right, the treatment provider must refer the patient to another treatment provider.

IV. C. – 8:111: Obligations of treatment-providing organisations

(1) If, in the process of performance of the obligations under the treatment contract, activities take place in a hospital or on the premises of another treatment-providing organisation, and the hospital or that other treatment-providing organisation is not a party to the treatment contract, it must make clear to the patient that it is not the contracting party.

(2) Where the treatment provider cannot be identified, the hospital or treatment-providing organisation in which the treatment took place is

treated as the treatment provider unless the hospital or treatment-providing organisation informs the patient, within a reasonable time, of the identity of the treatment provider.

(3) The parties may not, to the detriment of the patient, exclude the application of this Article or derogate from or vary its effects.

Part D.
Mandate

Chapter 1:
General provisions

IV. D. – 1:101: Scope

(1) This Part of Book IV applies to contracts (mandate contracts) under which:

    (a) a person, the representative, is authorised and instructed (mandated) by another person, the principal, to conclude a contract between the principal and a third party or otherwise affect the legal position of the principal in relation to a third party; and

    (b) the representative undertakes, in exchange for a price, to act on behalf of, and in accordance with the directions of, the principal.

(2) This Part applies only to the internal relationship between the principal and the representative (the mandate relationship). It does not apply to the relationship between the principal and the third party or the relationship between the representative and the third party.

(3) This Part applies with appropriate adaptations:

    (a) to contracts and unilateral juridical acts under which the representative is to represent the principal otherwise than in exchange for a price;

    (b) to contracts under which the representative is instructed to, and undertakes to, perform the obligations which are meant to lead to the conclusion of the prospective contract but in which the representative is not authorised from the start to actually conclude that prospective contract; and

(c) to contracts and unilateral juridical acts under which the representative is merely authorised but not instructed or obliged to act, but nevertheless does act.

(4) Contracts to which, in accordance with paragraph (3)(b), this Part applies and to which Part C (Services) of this Book applies, are to be regarded primarily as mandate contracts.

(5) This Part does not apply to mandate contracts pertaining to investment services and activities as defined by Directive 2004/30/EC, OJ L 145/1, as subsequently amended or replaced.

IV. D. – 1:102: Definitions

In this Part:

(a) the 'mandate' of the representative is the authorisation and instruction given by the principal as modified by any subsequent direction;

(b) the 'authority' of a representative is the power to affect the principal's legal position;

(c) the 'prospective contract' is the contract the representative is authorised and instructed to conclude on behalf of the principal and any reference to the prospective contract includes a reference to any other juridical act which the representative is authorised and instructed to do on behalf of the principal;

(d) a mandate for direct representation is a mandate under which the representative is to act in the name of the principal, or otherwise in such a way as to indicate an intention to affect the principal's legal position;

(e) a mandate for indirect representation is a mandate under which the representative is to act in the representative's own name or otherwise in such a way as not to indicate an intention to affect the principal's legal position;

(f) a 'direction' is a decision by the principal pertaining to the performance of the obligations under the mandate contract or to the contents of the prospective contract that is given at the time the mandate contract is concluded or, in accordance with the mandate, at a later moment;

(g) the 'third party' is the party with whom the prospective contract is concluded by the representative on behalf of the principal;

(h) the 'revocation' of the mandate of the representative is the decision of the principal to no longer authorise and instruct the representative to act on behalf of the principal.

IV. D. – 1:103: Duration

A mandate contract may be concluded:

(a) for an indefinite period of time;

(b) for a fixed period; or

(c) for a particular task.

IV. D. – 1:104: Revocation of the mandate

(1) Unless the following Article applies, the mandate of the representative can be revoked by the principal at any time by giving notice to the representative.

(2) The termination of the mandate relationship has the effect of a revocation of the mandate of the representative.

(3) The parties may not, to the detriment of the principal, exclude the application of this Article or derogate from or vary its effects, unless the requirements of the following Article are met.

IV. D. – 1:105: Irrevocable mandate

(1) In derogation of the preceding Article, the mandate of the representative cannot be revoked by the principal if the mandate is given:

    (a) in order to safeguard a legitimate interest of the representative other than the interest in the payment of the price; or

    (b) in the common interest of the parties to another legal relationship, whether or not these parties are all parties to the mandate contract, and the irrevocability of the mandate of the representative is meant to properly safeguard the interest of one or more of these parties.

(2) The mandate may nevertheless be revoked if:

    (a) the mandate is irrevocable under paragraph (1)(a) and:

        (i) the contractual relationship from which the legitimate interest of the representative originates is terminated for non-performance by the representative; or

        (ii) there is a fundamental non-performance by the representative of the obligations under the mandate contract; or

        (iii) there is an extraordinary and serious reason for the principal to terminate under IV. D. – 6:103 (Termination by principal for extraordinary and serious reason); or

    (b) the mandate is irrevocable under paragraph (1)(b) and:

        (i) the parties in whose interest the mandate is irrevocable have agreed to the revocation of the mandate;

    (ii) the relationship referred to in paragraph (1)(b) is terminated;

    (iii) the representative commits a fundamental non-performance of the obligations under the mandate contract, provided that the representative is replaced without undue delay by another representative in conformity with the terms regulating the legal relationship between the principal and the other party or parties; or

    (iv) there is an extraordinary and serious reason for the principal to terminate under IV. D. – 6:103 (Termination by principal for extraordinary and serious reason), provided that the representative is replaced without undue delay by another representative in conformity with the terms regulating the legal relationship between the principal and the other party or parties.

(3) Where the revocation of the mandate is not allowed under this Article, a notice of revocation is without effect.

(4) This Article does not apply if the mandate relationship is terminated under Chapter 7 of this Part.

Chapter 2:
Main obligations of the principal

IV. D. – 2:101: Obligation to co-operate

The obligation to co-operate under III. – 1:104 (Co-operation) requires the principal in particular to:

(a) answer requests by the representative for information in so far as such information is needed to allow the representative to perform the obligations under the mandate contract;

(b) give a direction regarding the performance of the obligations under the mandate contract in so far as this is required under the mandate contract or follows from a request for a direction under IV. D. – 4:102 (Request for direction).

IV. D. – 2:102: Price

(1) The principal must pay a price if the representative performs the obligations under the mandate contract in the course of a business, unless the principal expected and could reasonably have expected the representative to perform the obligations otherwise than in exchange for a price.

(2) The price is payable as of the moment the representative has affected the legal relations of the principal in accordance with the mandate contract and given account of that.

(3) If the parties had agreed on payment of a price for services rendered, the mandate relationship has terminated and the prospective contract has not been concluded, the price is payable as of the moment the representative has given account of the performance of the obligations under the mandate contract.

(4) When the principal has concluded the prospective contract directly or another person appointed by the principal has concluded the prospective contract on the principal's behalf, the representative is entitled to the price or a proportionate part thereof if the conclusion of the prospective contract can be attributed in full or in part to the representative's performance of the obligations under the mandate contract.

(5) When the prospective contract is concluded after the mandate relationship has terminated, the principal must pay the price if payment of a price based solely on the conclusion of the prospective contract was agreed and:
   (a) the conclusion of the prospective contract can be attributed mainly to the representative's performance of the obligations under the mandate contract; and
   (b) the prospective contract is concluded within a reasonable period after the mandate relationship has terminated.

IV. D. – 2:103: Expenses incurred by representative

(1) When the representative is entitled to a price, the price is presumed to include the reimbursement of the expenses the representative has incurred in the performance of the obligations under the mandate contract.

(2) When the representative is not entitled to a price or when the parties have agreed that the expenses will be paid separately, the principal must reimburse the representative for the expenses the representative has incurred in the performance of the obligations under the mandate contract, when and in so far as the representative acted reasonably when incurring the expenses.

(3) The representative is entitled to reimbursement of expenses under paragraph (2) as from the time when the expenses are incurred and the representative has given account of the expenses.

(4) If the mandate relationship has terminated and the prospective contract is not concluded, the representative is entitled to reimbursement of the expenses incurred in the performance of the obligations under the mandate contract. Paragraph (3) applies accordingly.

Chapter 3:
Performance by the representative
Section 1:
Main obligations of representative

IV. D. – 3:101: Obligation to act in accordance with mandate
Before and during the negotiations and in the conclusion of the prospective contract the representative must act in accordance with the mandate.

IV. D. – 3:102: Obligation to act in interests of principal
(1) The representative must act in accordance with the interests of the principal, in so far as these have been communicated to the representative or the representative could reasonably be expected to be aware of them.
(2) The representative must request information from the principal as to the principal's interests which the representative is not aware of when such information is needed to allow the proper performance of the obligations under the mandate contract.

IV. D. – 3:103: Obligation of skill and care
(1) The representative must perform the obligations under the mandate contract with the care and skill that the principal is entitled to expect under the circumstances.
(2) If the representative professes a higher standard of care and skill the representative must exercise that care and skill.
(3) If the representative is, or purports to be, a member of a group of professional representatives for which standards exist that have been set by a relevant authority or by that group itself, the representative must exercise the care and skill expressed in these standards.
(4) In determining the care and skill the principal is entitled to expect, regard is to be had, among other things, to:

(a) the nature, the magnitude, the frequency and the foreseeability of the risks involved in the performance of the obligations;

(b) whether the obligations are performed by a business;

(c) whether a price is payable and, if one is payable, its amount; and

(d) the time reasonably available for the performance of the obligations.

Section 2:
Consequences of acting beyond mandate

IV. D. – 3:201: Acting beyond mandate

(1) The representative may act in a way not covered by the mandate if:

(a) the representative has reasonable ground for so acting on behalf of the principal; and

(b) the representative does not have a reasonable opportunity to discover the principal's wishes in the particular circumstances; and

(c) the representative does not know and could not reasonably be expected to know that the act in the particular circumstances is against the principal's wishes.

(2) As between the representative and the principal an act within paragraph (1) is regarded as being covered by the mandate.

(3) In relation to third parties the consequences of an act within paragraph (1) are governed by Book III, Chapter 6 (Representation).

IV. D. – 3:202: Consequences of ratification

Where, in circumstances not covered by the preceding Article, the representative has acted beyond the mandate in concluding the prospective contract on behalf of the principal, ratification of that contract by the principal absolves the representative from liability to the principal, unless the principal without undue delay after ratification notifies the representative that the principal reserves remedies for the non-performance by the representative.

Section 3:
Conclusion of prospective contract by other person

IV. D. – 3:301: Exclusivity not presumed

The principal is free to conclude the prospective contract directly or to appoint another representative to conclude it.

IV. D. – 3:302: Subcontracting

(1) The representative may subcontract the performance of the obligations under the mandate contract in whole or in part without the principal's consent, unless personal performance is required by the contract.

(2) Any subcontractor so engaged by the representative must be of adequate competence.

(3) In accordance with III. – 2:106 (Performance entrusted to another) the representative remains responsible for performance.

Section 4:
Obligation to inform principal

IV. D. – 3:401: Information about progress of performance

During the performance of the obligations under the mandate contract the representative must in so far as is reasonable under the circumstances inform the principal of the existence of and the progress in the negotiations leading to the possible conclusion of the prospective contract.

IV. D. – 3:402: Giving account to principal

(1) The representative must without undue delay inform the principal of the conclusion of the prospective contract.

(2) The representative must give an account to the principal:
    (a) of the manner in which the obligations under the mandate contract have been performed; and
    (b) of money spent or received or expenses incurred by the representative in performing the obligations under the mandate contract.

(3) Paragraph (2) applies with appropriate adaptations if the mandate relationship is terminated in accordance with Chapters 6 and 7 and the prospective contract has not been concluded.

IV. D. – 3:403: Communication of identity of third party

(1) The representative must communicate the name and address of the third party to the principal on the principal's demand.

(2) Paragraph (1) does not apply in the case of a mandate for indirect representation.

Chapter 4:
Directions and changes
Section 1:
Directions

IV. D. – 4:101: Directions given by principal

(1) The principal is entitled to give directions to the representative.

(2) The representative must follow directions by the principal.

(3) The representative must warn the principal if a direction:
    (a) has the effect that the conclusion of the prospective contract would become significantly more expensive or take significantly more time than agreed upon in the mandate contract; or
    (b) is inconsistent with the purpose of the mandate contract or may otherwise be detrimental to the interests of the principal.

(4) Unless the principal revokes the direction without undue delay after having been so warned by the representative, the direction is to be regarded as a change of the mandate contract under IV. D. – 4:201 (Changes of the mandate contract).

IV. D. – 4:102: Request for a direction

(1) The representative must ask for a direction on obtaining information which requires the principal to make a decision pertaining to the performance of the obligations under the mandate contract or the content of the prospective contract.

(2) The representative must ask for a direction if the mandate contract does not determine whether the mandate is for direct representation or indirect representation.

IV. D. – 4:103: Consequences of failure to give a direction

(1) If the principal fails to give a direction when required to do so under the mandate contract or under paragraph (1) of the preceding Article, the

representative may, in so far as relevant, resort to any of the remedies
under Book III, Chapter 3 (Remedies for Non-Performance); or
  (a) base performance upon the expectations, preferences and priorities
      the principal may reasonably be expected to have, given the infor-
      mation and directions that have been gathered; and
  (b) claim a proportionate adjustment of the price and of the time al-
      lowed or required for the conclusion of the prospective contract.
(2) If the principal fails to give a direction under paragraph (2) of the pre-
    ceding Article, the representative may choose direct representation or
    indirect representation or may withhold performance under III. – 3:401
    (Right to withhold performance of reciprocal obligation).
(3) The adjusted price that is to be paid under paragraph (1)(b) must be
    reasonable and is to be determined using the same methods of calcu-
    lation as were used to establish the original price for the conclusion of
    the prospective contract.

IV. D. – 4:104: No time to ask or wait for direction
(1) If the representative is required to ask for a direction under IV. D. –
    4:102 (Request for a direction) but needs to act before being able to
    contact the principal and to ask for a direction, or needs to act before
    the direction is given, the representative may base performance upon
    the expectations, preferences and priorities the principal may reason-
    ably be expected to have, given the information and directions that
    have been gathered.
(2) In the situation referred to in paragraph (1), the representative may
    claim a proportionate adjustment of the price and of the time allowed
    or required for the conclusion of the prospective contract in so far as
    such an adjustment is reasonable given the circumstances of the case.

Section 2:
Changes of the mandate contract

IV. D. – 4:201: Changes of the mandate contract
(1) The mandate contract is changed if the principal:
  (a) significantly changes the mandate of the representative; or

    (b) does not revoke a direction without undue delay after having been warned in accordance with paragraph (3) of IV. D. – 4:101 (Directions given by principal).

(2) In the case of a change of the mandate contract under paragraph (1) the representative may claim:

    (a) a proportionate adjustment of the price and of the time allowed or required for the conclusion of the prospective contract; or

    (b) damages in accordance with III. – 3:702 (General measure of damages) to put the representative as nearly as possible into the position in which the representative would have been if the mandate contract had not been changed.

(3) In the case of a change of the mandate contract under paragraph (1) the representative may also terminate the mandate relationship by giving notice of termination for extraordinary and serious reason under IV. D. – 6:105 (Termination by representative for extraordinary and serious reason), unless the change is minor or it enlarges the possibilities for the representative to conclude the prospective contract.

(4) The adjusted price that is to be paid under paragraph (2)(a) must be reasonable and is to be determined using the same methods of calculation as were used to establish the original price for the conclusion of the prospective contract.

Chapter 5:
Conflict of interest

IV. D. – 5:101: Self-contracting

(1) The representative may not become the principal's counterparty to the prospective contract.

(2) The representative may nevertheless become the counterparty if:

    (a) this is agreed by the parties in the mandate contract;

    (b) the representative has disclosed an intention to become the counterparty and

        (i) the principal subsequently expresses consent; or

        (ii) the principal does not object to the representative becoming the counterparty after having been requested to indicate consent or a refusal of consent;

(c) the principal otherwise knew, or could reasonably be expected to have known, of the representative becoming the counterparty and the principal did not object within a reasonable time; or

(d) the content of the prospective contract is so precisely determined in the mandate contract that there is no risk that the interests of the principal may be disregarded.

(3) If the principal is a consumer, the representative may only become the counterparty if:

(a) the representative has disclosed that information and the principal has given express consent to the representative becoming the counterparty to the particular prospective contract; or

(b) the content of the prospective contract is so precisely determined in the mandate contract that there is no risk that the interests of the principal may be disregarded.

(4) The parties may not, to the detriment of the principal, exclude the application of paragraph (3) or derogate from or vary its effects.

(5) If the representative has become the counterparty, the representative is not entitled to a price for services rendered as a representative.

IV. D. – 5:102: Double mandate

(1) The representative may not act as the representative of both the principal and the principal's counterparty to the prospective contract.

(2) The representative may nevertheless act as the representative of both the principal and the counterparty if:

(a) this is agreed by the parties in the mandate contract;

(b) the representative has disclosed an intention to act as the representative of the counterparty and the principal

(i) subsequently expresses consent; or

(ii) does not object to the representative acting as the representative of the counterparty after having been requested to indicate consent or a refusal of consent;

(c) the principal otherwise knew, or could reasonably be expected to have known, of the representative acting as the representative of the counterparty and the principal did not object within a reasonable time; or

(d) the content of the prospective contract is so precisely determined in the mandate contract that there is no risk that the interests of the principal may be disregarded.

(3) If the principal is a consumer, the representative may only act as the representative of both the principal and of the counterparty if:

    (a) the representative has disclosed that information and the principal has given express consent to the representative acting also as the representative of the counterparty to the particular prospective contract; or

    (b) the content of the prospective contract is so precisely determined in the mandate contract that there is no risk that the interests of the principal may be disregarded.

(4) The parties may not, to the detriment of the principal, exclude the application of paragraph (3) or derogate from or vary its effects.

(5) If and in so far as the representative has acted in accordance with the previous paragraphs, the representative is entitled to the price.

Chapter 6:
Termination by notice other than for non-performance

IV. D. – 6:101: Termination by notice in general

(1) Either party may terminate the mandate relationship at any time by giving notice to the other.

(2) For the purposes of paragraph (1), a revocation of the mandate of the representative is treated as termination.

(3) Termination of the mandate relationship is not effective if the mandate of the representative is irrevocable under IV. D. – 1:105 (Irrevocable mandate).

(4) The effects of termination are governed by III. – 1:109 (Variation or termination by notice) paragraph (3).

(5) When the party giving the notice was justified in terminating the relationship no damages are payable for so doing.

(6) When the party giving the notice was not justified in terminating the relationship, the termination is nevertheless effective but the other party is entitled to damages in accordance with the rules in Book III.

(7) For the purposes of this Article the party giving the notice is justified in terminating the relationship if that party:

    (a) was entitled to terminate the relationship under the express terms of the contract and observed any requirements laid down in the contract for doing so;

(b) was entitled to terminate the relationship under Book III, Chapter 3, Section 5 (Termination); or

(c) was entitled to terminate the relationship under any other Article of the present Chapter and observed any requirements laid down in such Article for doing so.

IV. D. – 6:102: Termination by principal when relationship is to last for indefinite period or when mandate is for a particular task

(1) The principal may terminate the mandate relationship at any time by giving notice of reasonable length if the mandate contract has been concluded for an indefinite period or for a particular task.

(2) Paragraph (1) does not apply if the mandate is irrevocable.

(3) The parties may not, to the detriment of the principal, exclude the application of this Article or derogate from or vary its effects, unless the conditions set out under IV. D. – 1:105 (Irrevocable mandate) are met.

IV. D. – 6:103: Termination by principal for extraordinary and serious reason

(1) The principal may terminate the mandate relationship by giving notice for extraordinary and serious reason.

(2) No period of notice is required.

(3) For the purposes of this Article, the death or incapacity of the person who, at the time of conclusion of the mandate contract, the parties had intended to execute the representative's obligations under the mandate contract, constitutes an extraordinary and serious reason.

(4) This Article applies with appropriate adaptations if the successors of the principal terminate the mandate relationship in accordance with IV. D. – 7:103 (Death of the principal).

(5) The parties may not, to the detriment of the principal or the principal's successors, exclude the application of this Article or derogate from or vary its effects.

IV. D. – 6:104: Termination by representative when relationship is to last for indefinite period or when it is gratuitous

(1) The representative may terminate the mandate relationship at any time by giving notice of reasonable length if the mandate contract has been concluded for an indefinite period.

(2) The representative may terminate the mandate relationship by giving notice of reasonable length if the representative is to represent the principal otherwise than in exchange for a price.

(3) The parties may not, to the detriment of the representative, exclude the application of paragraph (1) of this Article or derogate from or vary its effects.

IV. D. – 6:105: Termination by representative for extraordinary and serious reason

(1) The representative may terminate the mandate relationship by giving notice for extraordinary and serious reason.

(2) No period of notice is required.

(3) For the purposes of this Article an extraordinary and serious reason includes:
  (a) a change of the mandate contract under IV. D. – 4:201 (Changes of the mandate contract);
  (b) the death or incapacity of the principal; and
  (c) the death or incapacity of the person who, at the time of conclusion of the mandate contract, the parties had intended to execute the representative's obligations under the mandate contract.

(4) The parties may not, to the detriment of the representative, exclude the application of this Article or derogate from or vary its effects.

Chapter 7:
Other provisions on termination

IV. D. – 7:101: Conclusion of the prospective contract

(1) If the mandate contract was concluded solely for the conclusion of a specific prospective contract the mandate relationship terminates when the representative has concluded the prospective contract and the representative has informed the principal of that in accordance with paragraph (1) of IV. D. – 3:402 (Giving account to principal).

(2) If the mandate contract was concluded solely for the conclusion of a specific prospective contract the mandate relationship terminates when the principal or another representative appointed by the principal has concluded the prospective contract. In such case, the conclusion

of the prospective contract is treated as a notice under IV. D. – 6:101 (Termination by notice in general).

IV. D. – 7:102: Expiry of fixed period
(1) If the mandate contract was concluded for a definite period the mandate relationship terminates when that period expires.
(2) If the parties continue performance of the obligations under the mandate contract after the definite period has expired, the parties are treated as having concluded a mandate contract for an indefinite period.
(3) If the mandate relationship has terminated under paragraph (1) the representative is entitled to reimbursement of the reasonable costs incurred.
(4) If payment of a price based on a particular rate was agreed, the representative is entitled to payment of the price on the basis of that rate.

IV. D. – 7:103: Death of the principal
(1) The death of the principal does not end the mandate relationship.
(2) Both the representative and the successors of the principal may terminate the mandate relationship by giving notice of termination for extraordinary and serious reason under IV. D. – 6:103 (Termination by principal for extraordinary and serious reason) or IV. D. – 6:105 (Termination by representative for extraordinary and serious reason).

IV. D. – 7:104: Death of the representative
(1) The death of the representative ends the mandate relationship.
(2) The expenses and any other payments due at the date of death remain payable.

Part E.
Commercial agency, franchise and distributorship

Chapter 1:
General provisions
Section 1:
Scope

IV. E. – 1:101: Contracts covered
(1) This Part of Book IV applies to contracts for the establishment and regulation of a commercial agency, franchise or distributorship and with appropriate adaptations to other contracts under which a party engaged in business independently is to use skills and efforts to bring another party's products on to the market.
(2) In this Part, "products" includes goods and services.

Section 2:
Other general provisions

IV. E. – 1:201: Priority rules
In the case of any conflict:
(a) the rules in this Part prevail over the rules in Part D (Mandate); and
(b) the rules in Chapters 3 to 5 of this Part prevail over the rules in Chapter 2 of this Part.

IV. E. – 1:202: Derogation
The parties may exclude the application of any of the rules in this Part or derogate from or vary their effects, except as otherwise provided in this Part.

Chapter 2:
Rules applying to all contracts within the scope of this part
Section 1:
Pre-contractual information duty

IV. E. – 2:101: Pre-contractual information duty
A party who is engaged in negotiations for a contract within the scope of this Part has a duty to provide the other party, a reasonable time before the contract is concluded and so far as required by good commercial practice, with such information as is sufficient to enable the other party to decide on a reasonably informed basis whether or not to enter into a contract of the type and on the terms under consideration.

Section 2:
Obligations of the parties

IV. E. – 2:201: Co-operation
The parties to a contract within the scope of this Part of Book IV must collaborate actively and loyally and co-ordinate their respective efforts in order to achieve the objectives of the contract.

IV. E. – 2:202: Information during the performance
During the period of the contractual relationship each party must provide the other in due time with all the information which the first party has and the second party needs in order to achieve the objectives of the contract.

IV. E. – 2:203: Confidentiality
(1) A party who receives confidential information from the other must keep such information confidential and must not disclose the information to third parties either during or after the period of the contractual relationship.
(2) A party who receives confidential information from the other must not use such information for purposes other than the objectives of the contract.

(3) Any information which a party already possessed or which has been disclosed to the general public, and any information which must necessarily be disclosed to customers as a result of the operation of the business, is not regarded as confidential information for this purpose.

Section 3:
Termination of contractual relationship

IV. E. – 2:301: Contract for a definite period
(1) A party is free not to renew a contract for a definite period. If a party has given notice in due time that it wishes to renew the contract, the contract will be renewed for an indefinite period unless the other party gives that party notice, not later than a reasonable time before the expiry of the contract period, that it is not to be renewed.
(2) Where the obligations under a contract for a definite period continue to be performed by both parties after the contract period has expired, the contract becomes a contract for an indefinite period.

IV. E. – 2:302: Contract for an indefinite period
(1) Either party to a contract for an indefinite period may terminate the contractual relationship by giving notice to the other.
(2) If the notice provides for termination after a period of reasonable length no damages are payable under IV. E. – 2:303 (Damages for termination with inadequate notice). If the notice provides for immediate termination or termination after a period which is not of reasonable length damages are payable under that Article.
(3) Whether a period of notice is of reasonable length depends, among other factors, on:
    (a) the time the contractual relationship has lasted;
    (b) reasonable investments made;
    (c) the time it will take to find a reasonable alternative; and
    (d) usages.
(4) A period of notice of one month for each year during which the contractual relationship has lasted, with a maximum of 36 months, is presumed to be reasonable.

(5) The period of notice for the principal, the franchisor or the supplier is to be no shorter than one month for the first year, two months for the second, three months for the third, four months for the fourth, five months for the fifth and six months for the sixth and subsequent years during which the contractual relationship has lasted. Parties may not exclude the application of this provision or derogate from or vary its effects.

(6) Agreements on longer periods than those laid down in paragraphs (4) and (5) are valid provided that the agreed period to be observed by the principal, franchisor or supplier is no shorter than that to be observed by the commercial agent, the franchisee or the distributor.

(7) In relation to contracts within the scope of this Part, the rules in this Article replace those in paragraph (2) of III. – 1:109 (Variation or termination by notice). Paragraph (3) of that Article governs the effects of termination.

IV. E. – 2:303: Damages for termination with inadequate notice

(1) Where a party terminates a contractual relationship under IV. E. – 2:302 (Contract for indefinite period) but does not give a reasonable period of notice the other party is entitled to damages.

(2) The general measure of damages is such sum as corresponds to the benefit which the other party would have obtained during the extra period for which the relationship would have lasted if a reasonable period of notice had been given.

(3) The yearly benefit is presumed to be equal to the average benefit which the aggrieved party has obtained from the contract during the previous 3 years or, if the contractual relationship has lasted for a shorter period, during that period.

(4) The general rules on damages for non-performance in Book III, Chapter 3, Section 7 apply with any appropriate adaptations.

IV. E. – 2:304: Termination for non-performance

(1) Any term of a contract within the scope of this Part whereby a party may terminate the contractual relationship for non-performance which is not fundamental is without effect.

(2) The parties may not exclude the application of this Article or derogate from or vary its effects.

IV. E. – 2:305: Indemnity for goodwill

(1) When the contractual relationship comes to an end for any reason (including termination by either party for fundamental non-performance), a party is entitled to an indemnity from the other party for goodwill if and to the extent that:

    (a) the first party has significantly increased the other party's volume of business and the other party continues to derive substantial benefits from that business; and

    (b) the payment of the indemnity is reasonable.

(2) The grant of an indemnity does not prevent a party from seeking damages under IV. E. – 2:303 (Damages for termination with inadequate notice).

IV. E. – 2:306: Stock, spare parts and materials

If the contract is avoided, or the contractual relationship terminated, by either party, the party whose products are being brought on to the market must repurchase the other party's remaining stock, spare parts and materials at a reasonable price, unless the other party can reasonably resell them.

Section 4:
Other general provisions

IV. E. – 2:401: Right of retention

In order to secure its rights to remuneration, compensation, damages and indemnity the party who is bringing the products on to the market has a right of retention over the movables of the other party which are in its possession as a result of the contract, until the other party has performed its obligations.

IV. E. – 2:402: Signed document available on request

(1) Each party is entitled to receive from the other, on request, a signed statement in textual form on a durable medium setting out the terms of the contract.

(2) The parties may not exclude the application of this Article or derogate from or vary its effects.

Chapter 3:
Commercial agency
Section 1:
General

IV. E. – 3:101: Scope

This Chapter applies to contracts under which one party, the commercial
agent, agrees to act on a continuing basis as a self-employed intermediary
to negotiate or to conclude contracts on behalf of another party, the principal, and the principal agrees to remunerate the agent for those activities.

Section 2:
Obligations of the commercial agent

IV. E. – 3:201: Negotiate and conclude contracts

The commercial agent must make reasonable efforts to negotiate contracts
on behalf of the principal and to conclude the contracts which the agent
was instructed to conclude.

IV. E. – 3:202: Instructions

The commercial agent must follow the principal's reasonable instructions,
provided they do not substantially affect the agent's independence.

IV. E. – 3:203: Information by agent during the performance

The obligation to inform requires the commercial agent in particular to
provide the principal with information concerning:
(a) contracts negotiated or concluded;
(b) market conditions;
(c) the solvency of and other characteristics relating to clients.

IV. E. – 3:204: Accounting

(1) The commercial agent must maintain proper accounts relating to the
    contracts negotiated or concluded on behalf of the principal.
(2) If the agent represents more than one principal, the agent must main-
    tain independent accounts for each principal.

(3) If the principal has important reasons to doubt that the agent maintains proper accounts, the agent must allow an independent accountant to have reasonable access to the agent's books upon the principal's request. The principal must pay for the services of the independent accountant.

Section 3:
Obligations of the principal

IV. E. – 3:301: Commission during the agency
(1) The commercial agent is entitled to commission on any contract concluded with a client during the period covered by the agency, if:
    (a) the contract has been concluded
        (i) as a result of the commercial agent's efforts;
        (ii) with a third party whom the commercial agent has previously acquired as a client for contracts of the same kind; or
        (iii) with a client belonging to a certain geographical area or group of clients with which the commercial agent was entrusted; and
    (b) either
        (i) the principal has or should have performed the principal's obligations under the contract; or
        (ii) the client has performed the client's obligations under the contract or justifiably withholds performance.
(2) The parties may not, to the detriment of the commercial agent, exclude the application of paragraph (1)(b)(ii) or derogate from or vary its effects.

IV. E. – 3:302: Commission after the agency has ended
(1) The commercial agent is entitled to commission on any contract concluded with a client after the agency has ended, if:
    (a) either
        (i) the contract with the client is mainly the result of the commercial agent's efforts during the period covered by the agency contract, and the contract with the client was concluded within a reasonable period after the agency ended; or
        (ii) the requirements of paragraph (1) of IV. E. – 3:301 (Commission during the agency) would have been satisfied except that

the contract with the client was not concluded during the period of the agency, and the client's offer reached the principal or the commercial agent before the agency ended; and

(b) either

(i) the principal has or should have performed the principal's obligations under the contract; or

(ii) the client has performed the client's obligations under the contract or justifiably withholds the client's performance.

(2) The parties may not, to the detriment of the commercial agent, exclude the application of paragraph (1)(b)(ii) or derogate from or vary its effects.

IV. E. – 3:303: Conflicting entitlements of successive agents

The commercial agent is not entitled to the commission referred to in IV. E. – 3:301 (Commission during the agency) if a previous commercial agent is entitled to that commission under IV.E – 3:302 (Commission after the agency has ended), unless it is reasonable that the commission is shared between the two commercial agents.

IV. E. – 3:304: When commission is to be paid

(1) The principal must pay the commercial agent's commission not later than the last day of the month following the quarter in which the agent became entitled to it.

(2) The parties may not, to the detriment of the commercial agent, exclude the application of this Article or derogate from or vary its effects.

IV. E. – 3:305: Entitlement to commission extinguished

(1) The commercial agent's entitlement to commission under IV. E. – 3:301 (Commission during the agency) and IV. E. – 3:302 (Commission after the agency has ended) can be extinguished only if and to the extent that it is established that the client's contractual obligations will not be performed for a reason for which the principal is not accountable.

(2) Upon the extinguishing of the commercial agent's entitlement to commission, the commercial agent must refund any commission already received.

(3) The parties may not, to the detriment of the commercial agent, exclude the application of paragraph (1) or derogate from or vary its effects.

IV. E. – 3:306: Remuneration

Any remuneration which wholly or partially depends upon the number or value of contracts is presumed to be commission within the meaning of this Chapter.

IV. E. – 3:307: Information by principal during the performance

The obligation to inform requires the principal in particular to provide the commercial agent with information concerning:

(a) characteristics of the goods or services; and

(b) prices and conditions of sale or purchase.

IV. E. – 3:308: Information on acceptance, rejection and non-performance

(1) The principal must inform the commercial agent, within a reasonable period, of:
(a) the principal's acceptance or rejection of a contract which the commercial agent has negotiated on the principal's behalf; and
(b) any non-performance of obligations under a contract which the commercial agent has negotiated or concluded on the principal's behalf.

(2) The parties may not, to the detriment of the commercial agent, exclude the application of this Article or derogate from or vary its effects.

IV. E. – 3:309: Warning of decreased volume of contracts

(1) The principal must warn the commercial agent within a reasonable time when the principal foresees that the volume of contracts that the principal will be able to conclude will be significantly lower than the commercial agent could reasonably have expected.

(2) For the purpose of paragraph (1) the principal is presumed to foresee what the principal could reasonably be expected to foresee.

(3) The parties may not, to the detriment of the commercial agent, exclude the application of this Article or derogate from or vary its effects.

IV. E. – 3:310: Information on commission

(1) The principal must supply the commercial agent in reasonable time with a statement of the commission to which the commercial agent is entitled. This statement must set out how the amount of the commission has been calculated.

(2) For the purpose of calculating commission, the principal must provide the commercial agent upon request with an extract from the principal's books.

(3) The parties may not, to the detriment of the commercial agent, exclude the application of this Article or derogate from or vary its effects.

IV. E. – 3:311: Accounting

(1) The principal must maintain proper accounts relating to the contracts negotiated or concluded by the commercial agent.

(2) If the principal has more than one commercial agent, the principal must maintain independent accounts for each commercial agent.

(3) The principal must allow an independent accountant to have reasonable access to the principal's books upon the commercial agent's request, if:

(a) the principal does not comply with the principal's obligations under paragraphs (1) or (2) of IV. E. – 3:310 (Information on commission); or

(b) the commercial agent has important reasons to doubt that the principal maintains proper accounts.

IV. E. – 3:312: Amount of indemnity

(1) The commercial agent is entitled to an indemnity for goodwill on the basis of IV. E. – 2:305 (Indemnity for goodwill) amounting to:

(a) the average commission on contracts with new clients and on the increased volume of business with existing clients calculated for the last 12 months, multiplied by:

(b) the number of years the principal is likely to continue to derive benefits from these contracts in the future.

(2) The resulting indemnity must be amended to take account of:

(a) the probable attrition of clients, based on the average rate of migration in the commercial agent's territory; and

(b) the discount required for early payment, based on average interest rates.

(3) In any case, the indemnity must not exceed one year's remuneration, calculated from the commercial agent's average annual remuneration over the preceding five years or, if the contractual relationship has been in existence for less than five years, from the average during the period in question.

(4) The parties may not, to the detriment of the commercial agent, exclude the application of this Article or derogate from or vary its effects.

IV. E. – 3:313: Del credere clause

(1) An agreement whereby the commercial agent guarantees that a client will pay the price of the products forming the subject-matter of the contract which the commercial agent has negotiated or concluded (del credere clause) is valid only if and to the extent that the agreement:
  (a) is in textual form on a durable medium;
  (b) covers particular contracts which were negotiated or concluded by the commercial agent or such contracts with particular clients who are specified in the agreement; and
  (c) is reasonable with regard to the interests of the parties.
(2) The commercial agent is entitled to be paid a commission of a reasonable amount on contracts to which the del credere guarantee applies (del credere commission).

Chapter 4:
Franchise
Section 1:
General

IV. E. – 4:101: Scope

This Chapter applies to contracts under which one party, the franchisor, grants the other party, the franchisee, in exchange for remuneration, the right to conduct a business (franchise business) within the franchisor's network for the purposes of supplying certain products on the franchisee's behalf and in the franchisee's name, and under which the franchisee has the right and the obligation to use the franchisor's tradename or trade mark or other intellectual property rights, know-how and business method.

IV. E. – 4:102: Pre-contractual information

(1) The duty under IV. E. – 2:101 (Pre-contractual information duty) requires the franchisor in particular to provide the franchisee with adequate and timely information concerning:
  (a) the franchisor's company and experience;
  (b) the relevant intellectual property rights;

    (c) the characteristics of the relevant know-how;

    (d) the commercial sector and the market conditions;

    (e) the particular franchise method and its operation;

    (f) the structure and extent of the franchise network;

    (g) the fees, royalties or any other periodical payments; and

    (h) the terms of the contract.

(2) Even if the franchisor's non-compliance with paragraph (1) does not give rise to a mistake for which the contract could be avoided under II. – 7:201 (Mistake), the franchisee may recover damages in accordance with paragraphs (2) and (3) of II. – 7:214 (Damages for loss), unless the franchisor had reason to believe that the information was adequate or had been given in reasonable time.

(3) The parties may not exclude the application of this Article or derogate from or vary its effects.

IV. E. – 4:103: Co-operation

The parties to a contract within the scope of this Chapter may not exclude the application of IV. E. – 2:201 (Co-operation) or derogate from or vary its effects.

Section 2:
Obligations of the franchisor

IV. E. – 4:201: Intellectual property rights

(1) The franchisor must grant the franchisee a right to use the intellectual property rights to the extent necessary to operate the franchise business.

(2) The franchisor must make reasonable efforts to ensure the undisturbed and continuous use of the intellectual property rights.

(3) The parties may not exclude the application of this Article or derogate from or vary its effects.

IV. E. – 4:202: Know-how

(1) Throughout the duration of the contractual relationship the franchisor must provide the franchisee with the know-how which is necessary to operate the franchise business.

(2) The parties may not exclude the application of this Article or derogate from or vary its effects.

IV. E. – 4:203: Assistance
(1) The franchisor must provide the franchisee with assistance in the form of training courses, guidance and advice, in so far as necessary for the operation of the franchise business, without additional charge for the franchisee.
(2) The franchisor must provide further assistance, in so far as reasonably requested by the franchisee, at a reasonable cost.

IV. E. – 4:204: Supply
(1) When the franchisee is obliged to obtain the products from the franchisor, or from a supplier designated by the franchisor, the franchisor must ensure that the products ordered by the franchisee are supplied within a reasonable time, in so far as practicable and provided that the order is reasonable.
(2) Paragraph (1) also applies to cases where the franchisee, although not legally obliged to obtain the products from the franchisor or from a supplier designated by the franchisor, is in fact required to do so.
(3) The parties may not exclude the application of this Article or derogate from or vary its effects.

IV. E. – 4:205: Information by franchisor during the performance
The obligation to inform requires the franchisor in particular to provide the franchisee with information concerning:
(a) market conditions;
(b) commercial results of the franchise network;
(c) characteristics of the products;
(d) prices and terms for the supply of products;
(e) any recommended prices and terms for the re-supply of products to customers;
(f) relevant communication between the franchisor and customers in the territory; and
(g) advertising campaigns.

IV. E. – 4:206: Warning of decreased supply capacity

(1) When the franchisee is obliged to obtain the products from the franchisor, or from a supplier designated by the franchisor, the franchisor must warn the franchisee within a reasonable time when the franchisor foresees that the franchisor's supply capacity or the supply capacity of the designated suppliers will be significantly less than the franchisee had reason to expect.

(2) For the purpose of paragraph (1) the franchisor is presumed to foresee what the franchisor could reasonably be expected to foresee.

(3) Paragraph (1) also applies to cases where the franchisee, although not legally obliged to obtain the products from the franchisor or from a supplier designated by the franchisor, is in fact required to do so.

(4) The parties may not, to the detriment of the franchisee, exclude the application of this Article or derogate from or vary its effects.

IV. E. – 4:207: Reputation of network and advertising

(1) The franchisor must make reasonable efforts to promote and maintain the reputation of the franchise network.

(2) In particular, the franchisor must design and co-ordinate the appropriate advertising campaigns aiming at the promotion of the franchise network.

(3) The activities of promotion and maintenance of the reputation of the franchise network are to be carried out without additional charge to the franchisee.

Section 3:
Obligations of the franchisee

IV. E. – 4:301: Fees, royalties and other periodical payments

(1) The franchisee must pay to the franchisor fees, royalties or other periodical payments agreed upon in the contract.

(2) If fees, royalties or any other periodical payments are to be determined unilaterally by the franchisor, II. – 9:105 (Unilateral determination by a party) applies.

IV. E. – 4:302: Information by franchisee during the performance

The obligation under IV. E. – 2:202 (Information during the performance) requires the franchisee in particular to provide the franchisor with information concerning:

(a) claims brought or threatened by third parties in relation to the franchisor's intellectual property rights; and

(b) infringements by third parties of the franchisor's intellectual property rights.

IV. E. – 4:303: Business method and instructions

(1) The franchisee must make reasonable efforts to operate the franchise business according to the business method of the franchisor.

(2) The franchisee must follow the franchisor's reasonable instructions in relation to the business method and the maintenance of the reputation of the network.

(3) The franchisee must take reasonable care not to harm the franchise network.

(4) The parties may not exclude the application of this Article or derogate from or vary its effects.

IV. E. – 4:304: Inspection

(1) The franchisee must grant the franchisor reasonable access to the franchisee's premises to enable the franchisor to check that the franchisee is complying with the franchisor's business method and instructions.

(2) The franchisee must grant the franchisor reasonable access to the accounting books of the franchisee.

Chapter 5:
Distributorship
Section 1:
General

IV. E. – 5:101: Scope and definitions

(1) This Chapter applies to contracts (distribution contracts) under which one party, the supplier, agrees to supply the other party, the distributor, with products on a continuing basis and the distributor agrees to pur-

chase them, or to take and pay for them, and to supply them to others in the distributor's name and on the distributor's behalf.

(2) An exclusive distribution contract is a distribution contract under which the supplier agrees to supply products to only one distributor within a certain territory or to a certain group of customers.

(3) A selective distribution contract is a distribution contract under which the supplier agrees to supply products, either directly or indirectly, only to distributors selected on the basis of specified criteria.

(4) An exclusive purchasing contract is a distribution contract under which the distributor agrees to purchase, or to take and pay for, products only from the supplier or from a party designated by the supplier.

Section 2:
Obligations of the supplier

IV. E. – 5:201: Obligation to supply
The supplier must supply the products ordered by the distributor in so far as it is practicable and provided that the order is reasonable.

IV. E. – 5:202: Information by supplier during the performance
The obligation under IV. E. – 2:202 (Information during the performance) requires the supplier to provide the distributor with information concerning:
(a) the characteristics of the products;
(b) the prices and terms for the supply of the products;
(c) any recommended prices and terms for the re-supply of the products to customers;
(d) any relevant communication between the supplier and customers; and
(e) any advertising campaigns relevant to the operation of the business.

IV. E. – 5:203: Warning by supplier of decreased supply capacity
(1) The supplier must warn the distributor within a reasonable time when the supplier foresees that the supplier's supply capacity will be significantly less than the distributor had reason to expect.
(2) For the purpose of paragraph (1) the supplier is presumed to foresee what the supplier could reasonably be expected to foresee.
(3) In exclusive purchasing contracts, the parties may not exclude the application of this Article or derogate from or vary its effects.

IV. E. – 5:204: Advertising materials

The supplier must provide the distributor at a reasonable price with all the advertising materials the supplier has which are needed for the proper distribution and promotion of the products.

IV. E. – 5:205: The reputation of the products

The supplier must make reasonable efforts not to damage the reputation of the products.

Section 3:
Obligations of the distributor

IV. E. – 5:301: Obligation to distribute

In exclusive distribution contracts and selective distribution contracts the distributor must, so far as practicable, make reasonable efforts to promote the products.

IV. E. – 5:302: Information by distributor during the performance

In exclusive distribution contracts and selective distribution contracts, the obligation under IV. E. – 2:202 (Information during the performance) requires the distributor to provide the supplier with information concerning:

(a) claims brought or threatened by third parties in relation to the supplier's intellectual property rights; and

(b) infringements by third parties of the supplier's intellectual property rights.

IV. E. – 5:303: Warning by distributor of decreased requirements

(1) In exclusive distribution contracts and selective distribution contracts, the distributor must warn the supplier within a reasonable time when the distributor foresees that the distributor's requirements will be significantly less than the supplier had reason to expect.

(2) For the purpose of paragraph (1) the distributor is presumed to foresee what the distributor could reasonably be expected to foresee.

IV. E. – 5:304: Instructions

In exclusive distribution contracts and selective distribution contracts, the distributor must follow reasonable instructions from the supplier which are designed to secure the proper distribution of the products or to maintain the reputation or the distinctiveness of the products.

IV. E. – 5:305: Inspection

In exclusive distribution contracts and selective distribution contracts, the distributor must provide the supplier with reasonable access to the distributor's premises to enable the supplier to check that the distributor is complying with the standards agreed upon in the contract and with reasonable instructions given.

IV. E. – 5:306: The reputation of the products

In exclusive distribution contracts and selective distribution contracts, the distributor must make reasonable efforts not to damage the reputation of the products.

Part F.
Loans
[In preparation]

Part G.
Personal security

Chapter 1:
Common rules

IV. G. – 1:101: Definitions

For the purposes of this Part:

(a) a "dependent personal security" is an obligation by a security provider which is assumed in favour of a creditor in order to secure a present or future obligation of the debtor owed to the creditor and performance of which is due only if, and to the extent that, performance of the latter obligation is due;

(b) an "independent personal security" is an obligation by a security provider which is assumed in favour of a creditor for the purposes of security and which is expressly or impliedly declared not to depend upon another person's obligation owed to the creditor;

(c) the "security provider" is the person who assumes the obligations towards the creditor for the purposes of security;

(d) the "debtor" is the person who owes the secured obligation, if any, to the creditor, and, in provisions relating to purported obligations, includes an apparent debtor;

(e) a "co-debtorship for security purposes" is an obligation owed by two or more debtors in which one of the debtors, the security provider, assumes the obligation primarily for purposes of security towards the creditor;

(f) a "global security" is a dependent personal security which is assumed in order to secure all the debtor's obligations towards the creditor or the debit balance of a current account or a security of a similar extent; and

(g) "proprietary security" covers security rights in all kinds of property, whether movable or immovable, tangible or intangible.

IV. G. – 1:102: Scope

(1) This Part applies to any type of voluntarily assumed personal security and, in particular, to:
   (a) dependent personal securities, including those assumed by binding comfort letters;
   (b) independent personal securities, including those assumed by stand-by letters of credit; and
   (c) co-debtorship for security purposes.

(2) This Part does not apply to insurance contracts. In the case of a guarantee insurance, this Part applies only if and in so far as the insurer has issued a document containing a personal security in favour of the creditor.

(3) This Part does not affect the rules on the aval and the security endorsement of negotiable instruments, but does apply to security for obligations resulting from such an aval or security endorsement.

IV. G. – 1:103: Freedom of contract

The parties may exclude the application of any of the rules in this Part or derogate from or vary their effects, except as otherwise provided in Chapter 4 of this Part.

IV. G. – 1:104: Creditor's acceptance

(1) If the parties intend to create the security by contract, the creditor is regarded as accepting an offer of security as soon as the offer reaches the creditor, unless the offer requires express acceptance, or the creditor without undue delay rejects it or reserves time for consideration.

(2) A personal security can also be assumed by a unilateral promise or undertaking intended to be legally binding without acceptance. The rules of this Part apply with any appropriate adaptations.

IV. G. – 1:105: Interpretation

Where there is doubt about the meaning of a term regulating a security, and this term is supplied by a security provider acting for remuneration, an interpretation of the term against the security provider is to be preferred.

IV. G. – 1:106: Co-debtorship for security purposes

A co-debtorship for security purposes is subject to the rules of Chapters 1 and 4 and, subsidiarily, to the rules in Book III, Chapter 4, Section 1 (Plurality of debtors).

IV. G. – 1:107: Several security providers: solidary liability towards creditor

(1) To the extent that several providers of personal security have secured the same obligation or the same part of an obligation or have assumed their undertakings for the same security purpose, each security provider assumes within the limits of that security provider's undertaking to the creditor solidary liability together with the other security providers. This rule also applies if these security providers in assuming their securities have acted independently.

(2) Paragraph (1) applies with appropriate adaptations if proprietary security has been provided by the debtor or a third person in addition to the personal security.

IV. G. – 1:108: Several security providers: internal recourse

(1) In the cases covered by the preceding Article recourse between several providers of personal security or between providers of personal security and of proprietary security is governed by III. – 4:107 (Recourse between solidary debtors), subject to the following paragraphs.

(2) Subject to paragraph (8), the proportionate share of each security provider for the purposes of that Article is determined according to the rules in paragraphs (3) to (7).

(3) Unless the security providers have otherwise agreed, as between themselves each security provider is liable in the same proportion that the maximum risk assumed by that security provider bore to the total of the maximum risks assumed by all the security providers. The relevant time is that of the creation of the last security.

(4) For personal security, the maximum risk is determined by the agreed maximum amount of the security. In the absence of an agreed maximum amount, the amount of the secured obligation or, if a current account has been secured, the credit limit is decisive. If the secured obligation is not limited, its final balance is decisive.

(5) For proprietary security, the maximum risk is determined by the agreed maximum amount of the security. In the absence of an agreed maximum amount, the value of the assets serving as security is decisive.

(6) If the maximum amount in the case of paragraph (4) first sentence or the maximum amount or the value, respectively, in the case of paragraph (5) is higher than the amount of the secured obligation at the time of creation of the last security, the latter determines the maximum risk.

(7) In the case of an unlimited personal security securing an unlimited credit the maximum risk of other limited personal or proprietary security rights which exceed the final balance of the secured credit is limited to the latter.

(8) The rules in paragraphs (3) to (7) do not apply to proprietary security provided by the debtor and to security providers who, at the time when the creditor was satisfied, were not liable towards the latter.

IV. G. – 1:109: Several security providers: recourse against debtor

(1) Any security provider who has satisfied a claim for recourse of another security provider is subrogated to this extent to the other security provider's rights against the debtor as acquired under IV. G. – 2:113 (Security provider's rights after performance) paragraphs (1) and (3), including proprietary security rights granted by the debtor. IV. G. – 2:110 (Reduction of creditor's rights) applies with appropriate adaptations.

(2) Where a security provider has recourse against the debtor by virtue of the rights acquired under IV. G. – 2:113 (Security provider's rights after

performance) paragraphs (1) and (3) or under the preceding paragraph, including proprietary security rights granted by the debtor, every security provider is entitled to a proportionate share, as defined in IV. G. – 1:108 (Several security providers: internal recourse) paragraph (2) and III. – 4:107 (Recourse between solidary debtors), of the benefits recovered from the debtor. IV. G. – 2:110 (Reduction of creditor's rights) applies with appropriate adaptations.

(3) Unless expressly stated to the contrary, the preceding rules do not apply to proprietary security provided by the debtor.

IV. G. – 1:110: Subsidiary application of rules on solidary debtors

If and in so far as the provisions of this Part do not apply, the rules on plurality of debtors in III. – 4:107 (Recourse between solidary debtors) to III. – 4:112 (Opposability of other defences in solidary obligations) are subsidiarily applicable.

Chapter 2:
Dependent personal security

IV. G. – 2:101: Presumption for dependent personal security

(1) Any undertaking to pay, to render any other performance or to pay damages to the creditor by way of security is presumed to give rise to a dependent personal security, unless the creditor shows that it was agreed otherwise.

(2) A binding comfort letter is presumed to give rise to a dependent personal security.

IV. G. – 2:102: Dependence of security provider's obligation

(1) Whether and to what extent performance of the obligation of the provider of a dependent personal security is due, depends upon whether and to what extent performance of the debtor's obligation to the creditor is due.

(2) The security provider's obligation does not exceed the secured obligation. This rule does not apply if the debtor's obligations are reduced or discharged:

(a) in an insolvency proceeding;

(b) in any other way caused by the debtor's inability to perform be-cause of insolvency; or

(c) by virtue of law due to events affecting the person of the debtor.

(3) Except in the case of a global security, if an amount has not been fixed for the security and cannot be determined from the agreement of the parties, the security provider's obligation is limited to the amount of the secured obligations at the time the security became effective.

(4) Except in the case of a global security, any agreement between the creditor and the debtor to make performance of the secured obligation due earlier, or to make the obligation more onerous by changing the conditions on which performance is due, or to increase its amount, does not affect the security provider's obligation if the agreement was concluded after the security provider's obligation became effective.

IV. G. – 2:103: Debtor's defences available to the security provider

(1) As against the creditor, the security provider may invoke any defence of the debtor with respect to the secured obligation, even if the defence is no longer available to the debtor due to acts or omissions of the debtor occurring after the security became effective.

(2) The security provider is entitled to refuse to perform the security ob-ligation if:

(a) the debtor is entitled to withdraw from the contract with the cred-itor under Book II, Chapter 5 (Right of Withdrawal).

(b) the debtor has a right to withhold performance under III. – 3:401 (Right to withhold performance of reciprocal obligation); or

(c) the debtor is entitled to terminate the debtor's contractual relation-ship with the creditor under Book III, Chapter 3, Section 5 (Termi-nation).

(3) The security provider may not invoke the lack of capacity of the debtor, whether a natural person or a legal entity, or the non-existence of the debtor, if a legal entity, if the relevant facts were known to the security provider at the time when the security became effective.

(4) As long as the debtor is entitled to avoid the contract from which the secured obligation arises on a ground other than those mentioned in the preceding paragraph and has not exercised that right, the security provider is entitled to refuse performance.

(5) The preceding paragraph applies with appropriate adaptations if the secured obligation is subject to set-off.

IV. G. – 2:104: Coverage of security

(1) The security covers, within its maximum amount, if any, not only the principal obligation secured, but also the debtor's ancillary obligations towards the creditor, especially:

   (a) contractual and default interest;

   (b) damages, a penalty or an agreed payment for non-performance by the debtor; and

   (c) the reasonable costs of extra-judicial recovery of those items.

(2) The costs of legal proceedings and enforcement proceedings against the debtor are covered, provided the security provider had been informed about the creditor's intention to undertake such proceedings in sufficient time to enable the security provider to avert those costs.

(3) A global security covers only obligations which originated in contracts between the debtor and the creditor.

IV. G. – 2:105: Solidary liability of security provider

Unless otherwise agreed, the liability of the debtor and the security provider is solidary and, accordingly, the creditor has the choice of claiming solidary performance from the debtor or, within the limits of the security, from the security provider.

IV. G. – 2:106: Subsidiary liability of security provider

(1) If so agreed, the security provider may invoke as against the creditor the subsidiary character of the security provider's liability. A binding comfort letter is presumed to establish only subsidiary liability.

(2) Subject to paragraph (3), before demanding performance from the security provider, the creditor must have undertaken appropriate attempts to obtain satisfaction from the debtor and other security providers, if any, securing the same obligation under a personal or proprietary security establishing solidary liability.

(3) The creditor is not required to attempt to obtain satisfaction from the debtor and any other security provider according to the preceding paragraph if and in so far as it is obviously impossible or exceedingly difficult to obtain satisfaction from the person concerned. This exception applies, in particular, if and in so far as an insolvency or equivalent proceeding has been opened against the person concerned or opening of such a proceeding has failed due to insufficient assets, unless a proprietary security provided by that person and for the same obligation is available.

IV. G. – 2:107: Requirement of notification by creditor

(1) The creditor is required to notify the security provider without undue delay in case of a non-performance by, or inability to pay of, the debtor as well as of an extension of maturity; this notification must include information about the secured amounts of the principal obligation, interest and other ancillary obligations owed by the debtor on the date of the notification. An additional notification of a new event of non-performance need not be given before three months have expired since the previous notification. No notification is required if an event of non-performance merely relates to ancillary obligations of the debtor, unless the total amount of all non-performed secured obligations has reached five percent of the outstanding amount of the secured obligation.

(2) In addition, in the case of a global security, the creditor is required to notify the security provider of any agreed increase:
   (a) whenever such increase, starting from the creation of the security, reaches 20 percent of the amount that was so secured at that time; and
   (b) whenever the secured amount is further increased by 20 percent compared with the secured amount at the date when the last information according to this paragraph was or should have been given.

(3) Paragraphs (1) and (2) do not apply, if and in so far as the security provider knows or could reasonably be expected to know the required information.

(4) If the creditor omits or delays any notification required by this Article the creditor's rights against the security provider are reduced by the extent necessary to prevent the latter from suffering any loss as a result of the omission or delay.

IV. G. – 2:108: Time limit for resort to security

(1) If a time limit has been agreed, directly or indirectly, for resort to a security establishing solidary liability for the security provider, the latter is no longer liable after expiration of the agreed time limit. However, the security provider remains liable if the creditor had requested performance from the security provider after maturity of the secured obligation but before expiration of the time limit for the security.

(2) If a time limit has been agreed, directly or indirectly, for resort to a security establishing subsidiary liability for the security provider, the

latter is no longer liable after the expiration of the agreed time limit.
However, the security provider remains liable if the creditor:

(a) after maturity of the secured obligation, but before expiration of
the time limit, has informed the security provider of an intention to
demand performance of the security and of the commencement of
appropriate attempts to obtain satisfaction as required according to
IV. G. – 2:106 (Subsidiary liability of security provider) paragraphs
(2) and (3); and

(b) informs the security provider every six months about the status of
these attempts, if so demanded by the security provider.

(3) If performance of the secured obligations falls due upon, or within 14
days before, expiration of the time limit of the security, the request for
performance or the information according to paragraphs (1) and (2)
may be given earlier than provided for in paragraphs (1) and (2), but no
more than 14 days before expiration of the time limit of the security.

(4) If the creditor has taken due measures according to the preceding paragraphs, the security provider's maximum liability is restricted to the
amount of the secured obligations as defined in IV. G. – 2:104 (Coverage of security) paragraphs (1) and (2). The relevant time is that at
which the agreed time limit expires.

IV. G. – 2:109: Limiting security without time limit

(1) Where the scope of a security is not limited to obligations arising, or
obligations performance of which falls due, within an agreed time limit, the scope of the security may be limited by any party giving notice of
at least three months to the other party. The preceding sentence does
not apply if the security is restricted to cover specific obligations or
obligations arising from specific contracts.

(2) By virtue of the notice, the scope of the security is limited to the secured principal obligations performance of which is due at the date at
which the limitation becomes effective and any secured ancillary obligations as defined in IV. G. – 2:104 (Coverage of security) paragraphs
(1) and (2).

IV. G. – 2:110: Reduction of creditor's rights

(1) If and in so far as due to the creditor's conduct the security provider
cannot be subrogated to the creditor's rights against the debtor and to
the creditor's personal and proprietary security rights granted by third

persons, or cannot be fully reimbursed from the debtor or from third party security providers, if any, the creditor's rights against the security provider are reduced by the extent necessary to prevent the latter from suffering any loss as a result of the creditor's conduct. The security provider has a corresponding right to recover from the creditor if the security provider has already performed.

(2) Paragraph (1) applies only if the creditor's conduct falls short of the standard of care which could be expected of persons managing their affairs with reasonable prudence.

IV. G. – 2:111: Debtor's relief for the security provider

(1) A security provider who has provided a security at the debtor's request or with the debtor's express or presumed consent may request relief by the debtor:

    (a) if the debtor has not performed the secured obligation when performance became due;

    (b) if the debtor is unable to pay or has suffered a substantial diminution of assets; or

    (c) if the creditor has brought an action on the security against the security provider.

(2) Relief may be granted by furnishing adequate security.

IV. G. – 2:112: Notification and request by security provider before performance

(1) Before performance to the creditor, the security provider is required to notify the debtor and request information about the outstanding amount of the secured obligation and any defences or counterclaims against it.

(2) If the security provider fails to comply with the requirements in paragraph (1) or neglects to raise defences communicated by the debtor or known to the security provider from other sources, the security provider's rights to recover from the debtor under IV. G. – 2:113 (Security provider's rights after performance) are reduced by the extent necessary to prevent loss to the debtor as a result of such failure or neglect.

(3) The security provider's rights against the creditor remain unaffected.

IV. G. – 2:113: Security provider's rights after performance

(1) The security provider has a right to reimbursement from the debtor if and in so far as the security provider has performed the security obligation. In addition the security provider is subrogated to the extent indicated in the preceding sentence to the creditor's rights against the debtor. The right to reimbursement and rights acquired by subrogation are concurrent.

(2) In case of part performance, the creditor's remaining partial rights against the debtor have priority over the rights to which the security provider has been subrogated.

(3) By virtue of the subrogation under paragraph (1), dependent and independent personal and proprietary security rights are transferred by operation of law to the security provider notwithstanding any contractual restriction or exclusion of transferability agreed by the debtor. Rights against other security providers can be exercised only within the limits of IV. G. – 1:108 (Several security providers: internal recourse).

(4) Where the debtor due to incapacity is not liable to the creditor but the security provider is nonetheless bound by, and performs, the security obligation, the security provider's right to reimbursement from the debtor is limited to the extent of the debtor's enrichment by the transaction with the creditor. This rule applies also if a debtor legal entity has not come into existence.

Chapter 3:
Independent personal security

IV. G. – 3:101: Scope

(1) The independence of a security is not prejudiced by a mere general reference to an underlying obligation (including a personal security).

(2) The provisions of this Chapter also apply to standby letters of credit.

IV. G. – 3:102: Notification to debtor by security provider

(1) The security provider is required:
(a) to notify the debtor immediately if a demand for performance is received and to state whether or not, in the view of the security provider, performance falls to be made;

(b) to notify the debtor immediately if performance has been made in accordance with a demand; and

(c) to notify the debtor immediately if performance has been refused notwithstanding a demand and to state the reasons for the refusal.

(2) If the security provider fails to comply with the requirements in paragraph (1) the security provider's rights against the debtor under IV. G. – 3:109 (Security provider's rights after performance) are reduced by the extent necessary to prevent loss to the debtor as a result of such failure.

IV. G. – 3:103: Performance by security provider

(1) The security provider is obliged to perform only if there is, in textual form, a demand for performance which complies exactly with the terms set out in the contract or other juridical act creating the security.

(2) Unless otherwise agreed, the security provider may invoke defences which the security provider has against the creditor.

(3) The security provider must without undue delay and at the latest within seven days of receipt, in textual form, of a demand for performance:
    (a) perform in accordance with the demand; or
    (b) inform the creditor of a refusal to perform, stating the reasons for the refusal.

IV. G. – 3:104: Independent personal security on first demand

(1) An independent personal security which is expressed as being due upon first demand or which is in such terms that this can unequivocally be inferred, is governed by the rules in the preceding Article, except as provided in the two following paragraphs.

(2) The security provider is obliged to perform only if the creditor's demand is supported by a declaration in textual form by the creditor which expressly confirms that any condition upon which performance of the security becomes due is fulfilled.

(3) Paragraph (2) of the preceding Article does not apply.

IV. G. – 3:105: Manifestly abusive or fraudulent demand

(1) A security provider is not obliged to comply with a demand for performance if it is proved by present evidence that the demand is manifestly abusive or fraudulent.

(2) If the requirements of the preceding paragraph are fulfilled, the debtor may prohibit:
   (a) performance by the security provider; and
   (b) issuance or utilisation of a demand for performance by the creditor.

IV. G. – 3:106: Security provider's right to reclaim
(I) The security provider has the right to reclaim the benefits received by the creditor if:
   (a) the conditions for the creditor's demand were not or subsequently ceased to be fulfilled; or
   (b) the creditor's demand was manifestly abusive or fraudulent.
(2) The security provider's right to reclaim benefits is subject to the rules in Book VII (Unjustified Enrichment).

IV. G. – 3:107: Security with or without time limits
(I) If a time limit has been agreed, directly or indirectly, for the resort to a security, the security provider exceptionally remains liable even after expiration of the time limit, provided the creditor had demanded performance according to IV. G. – 3:103 (Performance by security provider) paragraph (I) or IV. G. – 3:104 (Independent personal security on first demand) at a time when the creditor was entitled to do so and before expiration of the time limit for the security. IV. G. – 2:108 (Time limit for resort to security) paragraph (3) applies with appropriate adaptations. The security provider's maximum liability is restricted to the amount which the creditor could have demanded as of the date when the time limit expired.
(2) Where a security does not have an agreed time limit, the security provider may set such a time limit by giving notice of at least three months to the other party. The security provider's liability is restricted to the amount which the creditor could have demanded as of the date set by the security provider. The preceding sentences do not apply if the security is given for specific purposes.

IV. G. – 3:108: Transfer of security right
(I) The creditor's right to performance by the security provider can be assigned or otherwise transferred.
(2) However, in the case of an independent personal security on first demand, the right to performance cannot be assigned or otherwise trans-

ferred and the demand for performance can be made only by the original creditor, unless the security provides otherwise. This does not prevent transfer of the proceeds of the security.

IV. G. – 3:109: Security provider's rights after performance

IV.G. – 2:113 (Security provider's rights after performance) applies with appropriate adaptations to the rights which the security provider may exercise after performance.

Chapter 4:
Special rules for personal security of consumers

IV. G. – 4:101: Scope of application

(1) Subject to paragraph (2), this Chapter applies when a security is provided by a consumer.
(2) This Chapter is not applicable if:
  (a) the creditor is also a consumer; or
  (b) the consumer security provider is able to exercise substantial influence upon the debtor where the debtor is not a natural person.

IV. G. – 4:102: Applicable rules

(1) A personal security subject to this Chapter is governed by the rules of Chapters 1 and 2, except as otherwise provided in this Chapter.
(2) The parties may not, to the detriment of a security provider, exclude the application of the rules of this Chapter or derogate from or vary their effects.

IV. G. – 4:103: Creditor's pre-contractual duties

(1) Before a security is granted, the creditor has a duty to explain to the intending security provider:
  (a) the general effect of the intended security; and
  (b) the special risks to which the security provider may according to the information accessible to the creditor be exposed in view of the financial situation of the debtor.
(2) If the creditor knows or has reason to know that due to a relationship of trust and confidence between the debtor and the security provider there is a significant risk that the security provider is not acting freely

or with adequate information, the creditor has a duty to ascertain that the security provider has received independent advice.

(3) If the information or independent advice required by the preceding paragraphs is not given at least five days before the security provider signs the offer of security or the contract creating the security, the offer can be revoked or the contract avoided by the security provider within a reasonable time after receipt of the information or the independent advice. For this purpose five days is regarded as a reasonable time unless the circumstances suggest otherwise.

(4) If contrary to paragraph (1) or (2) no information or independent advice is given, the offer can be revoked or the contract avoided by the security provider at any time.

(5) If the security provider revokes the offer or avoids the contract according to the preceding paragraphs, the return of benefits received by the parties is governed by Book VII (Unjustified Enrichment).

IV. G. – 4:104: Form
The contract of security must be in textual form on a durable medium and must be signed by the security provider. A contract of security which does not comply with the requirements of the preceding sentence is void.

IV. G. – 4:105: Nature of security provider's liability
Where this Chapter applies:

(a) an agreement purporting to create a security without a maximum amount, whether a global security or not, is considered as creating a dependent security with a fixed amount to be determined according to IV. G. – 2:102 (Dependence of security provider's obligation) paragraph (3);

(b) the liability of a provider of dependent security is subsidiary within the meaning of IV. G. – 2:106 (Subsidiary liability of security provider), unless expressly agreed otherwise; and

(c) in an agreement purporting to create an independent security, the declaration that it does not depend upon another person's obligation owed to the creditor is disregarded, and accordingly a dependent security is considered as having been created, provided the other requirements of such a security are met.

IV. G. – 4:106: Creditor's obligations of annual information

(1) Subject to the debtor's consent, the creditor has to inform the security provider annually about the secured amounts of the principal obligation, interest and other ancillary obligations owed by the debtor on the date of the information. The debtor's consent, once given, is irrevocable.

(2) IV. G. – 2:107 (Requirement of notification by creditor) paragraphs (3) and (4) apply with appropriate adaptations.

IV. G. – 4:107: Limiting security with time limit

(1) A security provider who has provided a security whose scope is limited to obligations arising, or obligations performance of which falls due, within an agreed time limit may three years after the security became effective limit its effects by giving notice of at least three months to the creditor. The preceding sentence does not apply if the security is restricted to cover specific obligations or obligations arising from specific contracts. The creditor has to inform the debtor immediately on receipt of a notice of limitation of the security by the security provider.

(2) By virtue of the notice, the scope of the security is limited according to IV. G. – 2:109 (Limiting security without time limit) paragraph (2).

Book V
Benevolent intervention in another's affairs

Chapter 1:
Scope of application

V. – 1:101: Intervention to benefit another
(1) This Book applies where a person, the intervener, acts with the predominant intention of benefiting another, the principal, and:
    (a) the intervener has a reasonable ground for acting; or
    (b) the principal approves the act without such undue delay as would adversely affect the intervener.
(2) The intervener does not have a reasonable ground for acting if the intervener:
    (a) has a reasonable opportunity to discover the principal's wishes but does not do so; or
    (b) knows or can reasonably be expected to know that the intervention is against the principal's wishes.

V. – 1:102: Intervention to perform another's duty
Where an intervener acts to perform another person's duty, the performance of which is due and urgently required as a matter of overriding public interest, and the intervener acts with the predominant intention of benefiting the recipient of the performance, the person whose duty the intervener acts to perform is a principal to whom this Book applies.

V. – 1:103: Exclusions
This Book does not apply where the intervener:
(a) is authorised to act under a contractual or other obligation to the principal;
(b) is authorised, other than under this Book, to act independently of the principal's consent or
(c) is under an obligation to a third party to act.

Chapter 2:
Duties of intervener

V. – 2:101: Duties during intervention

(1) During the intervention, the intervener must:

    (a) act with reasonable care;

    (b) except in relation to a principal within V. – 1:102 (Intervention to perform another's duty), act in a manner which the intervener knows or can reasonably be expected to assume accords with the principal's wishes; and

    (c) so far as possible and reasonable, inform the principal about the intervention and seek the principal's consent to further acts.

(2) The intervention may not be discontinued without good reason.

V. – 2:102: Reparation for damage caused by breach of duty

(1) The intervener is liable to make reparation to the principal for damage caused by breach of a duty set out in this Chapter if the damage resulted from a risk which the intervener created, increased or intentionally perpetuated.

(2) The intervener's liability is reduced or excluded in so far as this is fair and reasonable, having regard to, among other things, the intervener's reasons for acting.

(3) An intervener who at the time of intervening lacks full legal capacity is liable to make reparation only in so far as that intervener is also liable to make reparation under Book VI (Non-contractual liability arising out of damage caused to another).

V. – 2:103: Obligations after intervention

(1) After intervening the intervener must without undue delay report and account to the principal and hand over anything obtained as a result of the intervention.

(2) If at the time of intervening the intervener lacks full legal capacity, the obligation to hand over is subject to the defence which would be available under VII. – 6:101 (Disenrichment).

(3) The remedies for non-performance in Book III, Chapter 3 apply but with the modification that any liability to pay damages or interest is subject to the qualifications in paragraphs (2) and (3) of the preceding Article.

Chapter 3:
Rights and authority of intervener

V. – 3:101: Right to indemnification or reimbursement
The intervener has a right against the principal for indemnification or, as the case may be, reimbursement in respect of an obligation or expenditure (whether of money or other assets) in so far as reasonably incurred for the purposes of the intervention.

V. – 3:102: Right to remuneration
(1) The intervener has a right to remuneration in so far as the intervention is reasonable and undertaken in the course of the intervener's profession or trade.
(2) The remuneration due is the amount, so far as reasonable, which is ordinarily paid at the time and place of intervention in order to obtain a performance of the kind undertaken. If there is no such amount a reasonable remuneration is due.

V. – 3:103: Right to reparation
An intervener who acts to protect the principal, or the principal's property or interests, against danger has a right against the principal for reparation for loss caused as a result of personal injury or property damage suffered in acting, if:
(a) the intervention created or significantly increased the risk of such injury or damage; and
(b) that risk, so far as foreseeable, was in reasonable proportion to the risk to the principal.

V. – 3:104: Reduction or exclusion of intervener's rights
(1) The intervener's rights are reduced or excluded in so far as the intervener at the time of acting did not want to demand indemnification, reimbursement, remuneration or reparation, as the case may be.

(2) These rights are also reduced or excluded in so far as this is fair and reasonable, having regard among other things to whether the intervener acted to protect the principal in a situation of joint danger, whether the liability of the principal would be excessive and whether the intervener could reasonably be expected to obtain appropriate redress from another.

V. – 3:105: Obligation of third person to indemnify or reimburse the principal

If the intervener acts to protect the principal from damage, a person who would be accountable under Book VI for the causation of such damage to the principal is obliged to indemnify or, as the case may be, reimburse the principal's liability to the intervener.

V. – 3:106: Authority of intervener to act as representative of the principal

(1) The intervener may conclude legal transactions or perform other juridical acts as a representative of the principal in so far as this may reasonably be expected to benefit the principal.

(2) However, a unilateral juridical act by the intervener as a representative of the principal has no effect if the person to whom it is addressed rejects the act without undue delay.

Book VI
Non-contractual liability arising out of damage caused to another

Chapter 1:
Fundamental provisions

VI. – 1:101: Basic rule
(1) A person who suffers legally relevant damage has a right to reparation from a person who caused the damage intentionally or negligently or is otherwise accountable for the causation of the damage.
(2) Where a person has not caused legally relevant damage intentionally or negligently that person is accountable for the causation of legally relevant damage only if Chapter 3 (Accountability) so provides.

VI. – 1:102: Prevention
Where legally relevant damage is impending, this Book confers on a person who would suffer the damage a right to prevent it. This right is against a person who would be accountable for the causation of the damage if it occurred.

VI. – 1:103: Scope of application
The provisions of VI. – 1:101 (Basic rule) and VI. – 1:102 (Prevention):
(a) apply only in accordance with the following provisions of this Book;
(b) apply to both legal and natural persons, unless otherwise stated;
(c) do not apply in so far as their application would contradict the purpose of other private law rules; and
(d) do not affect remedies available on other legal grounds.

Chapter 2:
Legally relevant damage
Section 1:
General

VI. – 2:101: Meaning of legally relevant damage

(1) Loss, whether economic or non-economic, or injury is legally relevant damage if:

  (a) one of the following rules of this Chapter so provides;

  (b) the loss or injury results from a violation of a right otherwise conferred by the law; or

  (c) the loss or injury results from a violation of an interest worthy of legal protection.

(2) In any case covered only by sub-paragraphs (b) or (c) of paragraph (1) loss or injury constitutes legally relevant damage only if it would be fair and reasonable for there to be a right to reparation or prevention, as the case may be, under VI. – 1:101 (Basic rule) or VI. – 1:102 (Prevention).

(3) In considering whether it would be fair and reasonable for there to be a right to reparation or prevention regard is to be had to the ground of accountability, to the nature and proximity of the damage or impending damage, to the reasonable expectations of the person who suffers or would suffer the damage, and to considerations of public policy.

(4) In this Book:

  (a) economic loss includes loss of income or profit, burdens incurred and a reduction in the value of property;

  (b) non-economic loss includes pain and suffering and impairment of the quality of life.

Section 2:
Particular instances of legally relevant damage

VI. – 2:201: Personal injury and consequential loss

(1) Loss caused to a natural person as a result of injury to his or her body or health and the injury as such are legally relevant damage.

(2) In this Book:
  (a) such loss includes the costs of health care including expenses reasonably incurred for the care of the injured person by those close to him or her; and
  (b) personal injury includes injury to mental health only if it amounts to a medical condition.

VI. – 2:202: Loss suffered by third persons as a result of another's personal injury or death

(1) Non-economic loss caused to a natural person as a result of another's personal injury or death is legally relevant damage if at the time of injury that person is in a particularly close personal relationship to the injured person.

(2) Where a person has been fatally injured:
  (a) legally relevant damage caused to the deceased on account of the injury to the time of death becomes legally relevant damage to the deceased's successors;
  (b) reasonable funeral expenses are legally relevant damage to the person incurring them; and
  (c) loss of maintenance is legally relevant damage to a natural person whom the deceased maintained or, had death not occurred, would have maintained under statutory provisions or to whom the deceased provided care and financial support.

VI. – 2:203: Infringement of dignity, liberty and privacy

(1) Loss caused to a natural person as a result of infringement of his or her right to respect for his or her dignity, such as the rights to liberty and privacy, and the injury as such are legally relevant damage.

(2) Loss caused to a person as a result of injury to that person's reputation and the injury as such are also legally relevant damage if national law so provides.

VI. – 2:204: Loss upon communication of incorrect information about another

Loss caused to a person as a result of the communication of information about that person which the person communicating the information knows or could reasonably be expected to know is incorrect is legally relevant damage.

VI. – 2:205: Loss upon breach of confidence

Loss caused to a person as a result of the communication of information which, either from its nature or the circumstances in which it was obtained, the person communicating the information knows or could reasonably be expected to know is confidential to the person suffering the loss is legally relevant damage.

VI. – 2:206: Loss upon infringement of property or lawful possession

(1) Loss caused to a person as a result of an infringement of that person's property right or lawful possession of a movable or immovable thing is legally relevant damage.
(2) In this Article:
  (a) loss includes being deprived of the use of property;
  (b) infringement of a property right includes destruction of or physical damage to the subject-matter of the right (property damage), disposition of the right, interference with its use and other disturbance of the exercise of the right.

VI. – 2:207: Loss upon reliance on incorrect advice or information

Loss caused to a person as a result of making a decision in reasonable reliance on incorrect advice or information is legally relevant damage if:
(a) the advice or information is provided by a person in pursuit of a profession or in the course of trade; and
(b) the provider knew or could reasonably be expected to have known that the recipient would rely on the advice or information in making a decision of the kind made.

VI. – 2:208: Loss upon unlawful impairment of business

(1) Loss caused to a person as a result of an unlawful impairment of that person's exercise of a profession or conduct of a trade is legally relevant damage.
(2) Loss caused to a consumer as a result of unfair competition is also legally relevant damage if Community or national law so provides.

VI. – 2:209: Burdens incurred by the State upon environmental impairment

Burdens incurred by the State or designated competent authorities in restoring substantially impaired natural elements constituting the environment, such as air, water, soil, flora and fauna, are legally relevant damage to the State or the authorities concerned.

VI. – 2:210: Loss upon fraudulent misrepresentation

(1) Without prejudice to the other provisions of this Section, loss caused to a person as a result of another's fraudulent misrepresentation, whether by words or conduct, is legally relevant damage.

(2) A misrepresentation is fraudulent if it is made with knowledge or belief that the representation is false and it is intended to induce the recipient to make a mistake.

VI. – 2:211: Loss upon inducement of non-performance of obligation

Without prejudice to the other provisions of this Section, loss caused to a person as a result of another's inducement of the non-performance of an obligation by a third person is legally relevant damage only if:

(a) the obligation was owed to the person sustaining the loss; and

(b) the person inducing the non-performance:

  (i) intended the third person to fail to perform the obligation; and

  (ii) did not act in legitimate protection of the inducing person's own interest.

Chapter 3:
Accountability
Section 1:
Intention and negligence

VI. – 3:101: Intention

A person causes legally relevant damage intentionally when that person causes such damage either:

(a) meaning to cause damage of the type caused; or

(b) by conduct which that person means to do, knowing that such damage, or damage of that type, will or will almost certainly be caused.

VI. – 3:102: Negligence

A person causes legally relevant damage negligently when that person causes the damage by conduct which either:

(a) does not meet the particular standard of care provided by a statutory provision whose purpose is the protection of the injured person from the damage suffered; or

(b) does not otherwise amount to such care as could be expected from a reasonably careful person in the circumstances of the case.

VI. – 3:103: Persons under eighteen

(1) A person under eighteen years of age is accountable for causing legally relevant damage according to VI. – 3:102 (Negligence) sub-paragraph (b) only in so far as that person does not exercise such care as could be expected from a reasonably careful person of the same age in the circumstances of the case.

(2) A person under seven years of age is not accountable for causing damage intentionally or negligently.

(3) However, paragraphs (1) and (2) do not apply to the extent that:

    (a) the injured person cannot obtain reparation under this Book from another; and

    (b) liability to make reparation would be equitable having regard to the financial means of the parties and all other circumstances of the case.

VI. – 3:104: Accountability for damage caused by children or supervised persons

(1) Parents or other persons obliged by law to provide parental care for a person under fourteen years of age are accountable for the causation of legally relevant damage where that person under age caused the damage by conduct that would constitute intentional or negligent conduct if it were the conduct of an adult.

(2) An institution or other body obliged to supervise a person is accountable for the causation of legally relevant damage suffered by a third party when:

    (a) the damage is personal injury, loss within VI. – 2:202 (Loss suffered by third persons as a result of another's personal injury or death) or property damage;

(b) the person whom the institution or other body is obliged to supervise caused that damage intentionally or negligently or, in the case
of a person under eighteen, by conduct that would constitute intention or negligence if it were the conduct of an adult; and

(c) the person whom the institution or other body is obliged to supervise is a person likely to cause damage of that type.

(3) However, a person is not accountable under this Article for the causation of damage if that person shows that there was no defective supervision of the person causing the damage.

Section 2:
Accountability without intention or negligence

VI. – 3:201: Accountability for damage caused by employees and representatives

(1) A person who employs or similarly engages another is accountable for
the causation of legally relevant damage suffered by a third person
when the person employed or engaged:

(a) caused the damage in the course of the employment or engage-
ment; and

(b) caused the damage intentionally or negligently, or is otherwise accountable for the causation of the damage.

(2) Paragraph (1) applies correspondingly to a legal person in relation to a
representative causing damage in the course of acting as such a representative. For the purposes of this paragraph, a representative is a person who is authorised to effect juridical acts on behalf of the legal
person by its constitution.

VI. – 3:202: Accountability for damage caused by the unsafe state of an immovable

(1) A person who independently exercises control over an immovable is
accountable for the causation of personal injury and consequential
loss, loss within VI. – 2:202 (Loss suffered by third persons as a result
of another's personal injury or death), and loss resulting from property
damage (other than to the immovable itself) by a state of the immo-

vable which does not ensure such safety as a person in or near the immovable is entitled to expect having regard to the circumstances including:

(a) the nature of the immovable;

(b) the access to the immovable; and

(c) the cost of avoiding the immovable being in that state.

(2) A person exercises independent control over an immovable if that person exercises such control that it is reasonable to impose a duty on that person to prevent legally relevant damage within the scope of this Article.

(3) The owner of the immovable is to be regarded as independently exercising control, unless the owner shows that another independently exercises control.

VI. – 3:203: Accountability for damage caused by animals

A keeper of an animal is accountable for the causation by the animal of personal injury and consequential loss, loss within VI. – 2:202 (Loss suffered by third persons as a result of another's personal injury or death), and loss resulting from property damage.

VI. – 3:204: Accountability for damage caused by defective products

(1) The producer of a product is accountable for the causation of personal injury and consequential loss, loss within VI. – 2:202 (Loss suffered by third persons as a result of another's personal injury or death), and, in relation to consumers, loss resulting from property damage (other than to the product itself) by a defect in the product.

(2) A person who imported the product into the European Economic Area for sale, hire, leasing or distribution in the course of that person's business is accountable correspondingly.

(3) A supplier of the product is accountable correspondingly if:

(a) the producer cannot be identified; or

(b) in the case of an imported product, the product does not indicate the identity of the importer (whether or not the producer's name is indicated), unless the supplier informs the injured person, within a reasonable time, of the identity of the producer or the person who supplied that supplier with the product.

(4) A person is not accountable under this Article for the causation of damage if that person shows that:
  (a) that person did not put the product into circulation;
  (b) it is probable that the defect which caused the damage did not exist at the time when that person put the product into circulation;
  (c) that person neither manufactured the product for sale or distribution for economic purpose nor manufactured or distributed it in the course of business;
  (d) the defect is due to the product's compliance with mandatory regulations issued by public authorities;
  (e) the state of scientific and technical knowledge at the time that person put the product into circulation did not enable the existence of the defect to be discovered; or
  (f) in the case of a manufacturer of a component, the defect is attributable to:
    (i) the design of the product into which the component has been fitted, or
    (ii) instructions given by the manufacturer of the product.

(5) "Producer" means:
  (a) in the case of a finished product or a component, the manufacturer;
  (b) in the case of raw material, the person who abstracts or wins it; and
  (c) any person who, by putting a name, trade mark or other distinguishing feature on the product, gives the impression of being its producer.

(6) "Product" means a movable, even if incorporated into another movable or an immovable, or electricity.

(7) A product is "defective" if it does not provide the safety which a person is entitled to expect, having regard to the circumstances including:
  (a) the presentation of the product;
  (b) the use to which it could reasonably be expected that the product would be put; and
  (c) the time when the product was put into circulation,
  but a product is not defective merely because a better product is subsequently put into circulation.

VI. – 3:205: Accountability for damage caused by motor vehicles

(1) A keeper of a motor vehicle is accountable for the causation of personal injury and consequential loss, loss within VI. – 2:202 (Loss suffered by third persons as a result of another's personal injury or death), and loss resulting from property damage (other than to the vehicle and its freight) in a traffic accident which results from the use of the vehicle.

(2) "Motor vehicle" means any vehicle intended for travel on land and propelled by mechanical power, but not running on rails, and any trailer, whether or not coupled.

VI. – 3:206: Accountability for damage caused by dangerous substances or emissions

(1) A keeper of a substance or an operator of an installation is accountable for the causation by that substance or by emissions from that installation of personal injury and consequential loss, loss within VI. – 2:202 (Loss suffered by third persons as a result of another's personal injury or death), loss resulting from property damage, and burdens within VI. – 2:209 (Burdens incurred by the State upon environmental impairment), if:

    (a) having regard to their quantity and attributes, at the time of the emission, or, failing an emission, at the time of contact with the substance it is very likely that the substance or emission will cause such damage unless adequately controlled; and

    (b) the damage results from the realisation of that danger.

(2) "Substance" includes chemicals (whether solid, liquid or gaseous). Microorganisms are to be treated like substances.

(3) "Emission" includes:

    (a) the release or escape of substances;

    (b) the conduction of electricity;

    (c) heat, light and other radiation;

    (d) noise and other vibrations; and

    (e) other incorporeal impact on the environment.

(4) "Installation" includes a mobile installation and an installation under construction or not in use.

(5) However, a person is not accountable for the causation of damage under this Article if that person:

    (a) does not keep the substance or operate the installation for purposes related to that person's trade, business or profession; or

(b) shows that there was no failure to comply with statutory standards of control of the substance or management of the installation.

VI. – 3:207: Other accountability for the causation of legally relevant damage

A person is also accountable for the causation of legally relevant damage if national law so provides where it:

(a) relates to a source of danger which is not within VI. – 3:104 (Account-ability for damage caused by children or supervised persons) to VI. – 3:205 (Accountability for damage caused by motor vehicles);
(b) relates to substances or emissions; or
(c) disapplies VI. – 3:204 (Accountability for damage caused by defective products) paragraph (4)(e).

VI. – 3:208: Abandonment

For the purposes of this Section, a person remains accountable for an im-movable, vehicle, substance or installation which that person abandons until another exercises independent control over it or becomes its keeper or operator. This applies correspondingly, so far as reasonable, in respect of a keeper of an animal.

Chapter 4:
Causation

VI. – 4:101: General rule

(1) A person causes legally relevant damage to another if the damage is to be regarded as a consequence of:
    (a) that person's conduct; or
    (b) a source of danger for which that person is responsible.
(2) In cases of personal injury or death the injured person's predisposition with respect to the type or extent of the injury sustained is to be dis-regarded.

VI. – 4:102: Collaboration

A person who participates with, instigates or materially assists another in causing legally relevant damage is to be regarded as causing that damage.

VI. – 4:103: Alternative causes

Where legally relevant damage may have been caused by any one or more of a number of occurrences for which different persons are accountable and it is established that the damage was caused by one of these occurrences but not which one, each person who is accountable for any of the occurrences is rebuttably presumed to have caused that damage.

Chapter 5:
Defences
Section 1:
Consent or conduct of the injured person

VI. – 5:101: Consent and acting at own risk

(1) A person has a defence if the injured person validly consented to the legally relevant damage and was aware or could reasonably be expected to have been aware of the consequences of that consent.

(2) The same applies if the injured person, knowing the risk of damage of the type caused, voluntarily incurred exposure to that risk and is to be regarded as having accepted it.

VI. – 5:102: Contributory fault and accountability

(1) Where the fault of the injured person contributed to the occurrence or extent of legally relevant damage, reparation is to be reduced according to the degree of such fault.

(2) However, no regard is to be had to:
    (a) an insubstantial fault of the injured person;
    (b) fault or accountability whose contribution to the causation of the damage was insubstantial; or
    (c) the injured person's want of care contributing to that person's personal injury caused by a motor vehicle in a traffic accident, unless that want of care constituted profound failure to take such care as was manifestly required in the circumstances.

(3) Paragraphs (1) and (2) apply correspondingly where the fault of a person for whom the injured person is responsible within the scope of VI. – 3:201 (Accountability for damage caused by employees and representatives) contributed to the occurrence or extent of the damage.

(4) Compensation is to be reduced likewise if and in so far as any other source of danger for which the injured person is responsible under Chapter 3 (Accountability) contributed to the occurrence or extent of the damage.

VI. – 5:103: Damage caused by a criminal to a collaborator

Legally relevant damage caused unintentionally in the course of committing a criminal offence to another person participating or otherwise collaborating in the offence does not give rise to a right to reparation if this would be contrary to public policy.

Section 2:
Interests of accountable persons or third parties

VI. – 5:201: Authority conferred by law

A person has a defence if legally relevant damage is caused with authority conferred by law.

VI. – 5:202: Self-defence, benevolent intervention and necessity

(1) A person has a defence if that person causes legally relevant damage in reasonable protection of a right or of an interest worthy of legal protection of that person or a third person if the person suffering the legally relevant damage is accountable for endangering the right or interest protected. For the purposes of this paragraph VI. – 3:103 (Persons under eighteen) is to be disregarded.

(2) The same applies to legally relevant damage caused by a benevolent intervener to a principal without breach of the intervener's duties.

(3) Where a person causes legally relevant damage to the patrimony of another in a situation of imminent danger to life, body, health or liberty in order to save the person causing the damage or a third person from that danger and the danger could not be eliminated without causing the damage, the person causing the damage is not liable to make reparation beyond providing reasonable recompense.

VI. – 5:203: Protection of public interest

A person has a defence if legally relevant damage is caused in necessary protection of values fundamental to a democratic society, in particular where damage is caused by dissemination of information in the media.

Section 3:
Inability to control

VI. – 5:301: Mental incompetence

(1) A person who is mentally incompetent at the time of conduct causing legally relevant damage is liable only if this is equitable, having regard to the mentally incompetent person's financial means and all the other circumstances of the case. Liability is limited to reasonable recompense.

(2) A person is to be regarded as mentally incompetent if that person lacks sufficient insight into the nature of his or her conduct, unless the lack of sufficient insight is the temporary result of his or her own misconduct.

VI. – 5:302: Event beyond control

A person has a defence if legally relevant damage is caused by an abnormal event which cannot be averted by any reasonable measure and which is not to be regarded as that person's risk.

Section 4:
Contractual exclusion and restriction of liability

VI. – 5:401: Contractual exclusion and restriction of liability

(1) Liability for causing legally relevant damage intentionally cannot be excluded or restricted.

(2) Liability for causing legally relevant damage as a result of a profound failure to take such care as is manifestly required in the circumstances cannot be excluded or restricted:
  (a) in respect of personal injury (including fatal injury); or
  (b) if the exclusion or restriction is otherwise illegal or contrary to good faith and fair dealing.

(3) Liability for damage for the causation of which a person is accountable under VI. – 3:204 (Accountability for damage caused by defective products) cannot be restricted or excluded.

(4) Other liability under this Book can be excluded or restricted unless statute provides otherwise.

Section 5:
Loss within VI. – 2:202 (Loss suffered by third persons as a result of another's personal injury or death)

VI. – 5:501: Extension of defences against the injured person to third persons

A defence which may be asserted against a person's right of reparation in respect of that person's personal injury or, if death had not occurred, could have been asserted, may also be asserted against a person suffering loss within VI. – 2:202 (Loss suffered by third persons as a result of another's personal injury or death).

Chapter 6:
Remedies
Section 1:
Reparation in general

VI. – 6:101: Aim and forms of reparation

(1) Reparation is to reinstate the person suffering the legally relevant damage in the position that person would have been in had the legally relevant damage not occurred.

(2) Reparation may be in money (compensation) or otherwise, as is most appropriate, having regard to the kind and extent of damage suffered and all the other circumstances of the case.

(3) Where a tangible object is damaged, compensation equal to its depreciation of value is to be awarded instead of the cost of its repair if the cost of repair unreasonably exceeds the depreciation of value. This rule applies to animals only if appropriate, having regard to the purpose for which the animal was kept.

(4) As an alternative to reinstatement under paragraph (1), but only where this is reasonable, reparation may take the form of recovery from the person accountable for the causation of the legally relevant damage of any advantage obtained by the latter in connection with causing the damage.

VI. – 6:102: De minimis rule
Trivial damage is to be disregarded.

VI. – 6:103: Equalisation of benefits
(1) Benefits arising to the person suffering legally relevant damage as a result of the damaging event are to be disregarded unless it would be fair and reasonable to take them into account.
(2) In deciding whether it would be fair and reasonable to take the benefits into account, regard shall be had to the kind of damage sustained, the nature of the accountability of the person causing the damage and, where the benefits are conferred by a third person, the purpose of conferring those benefits.

VI. – 6:104: Multiple injured persons
Where multiple persons suffer legally relevant damage and reparation to one person will also make reparation to another, the rules in Book III, Chapter 4, Section 2 (Plurality of creditors) apply with appropriate adaptations to their rights to reparation.

VI. – 6:105: Solidary liability
Where several persons are liable for the same legally relevant damage, they are liable solidarily.

VI. – 6:106: Assignment of right to reparation
The injured person may assign a right to reparation, including a right to reparation for non-economic loss.

Section 2:
Compensation

VI. – 6:201: Injured person's right of election

The injured person may choose whether or not to spend compensation on the reinstatement of the damaged interest.

VI. – 6:202: Reduction of liability

Where it is fair and reasonable to do so, a person may be relieved of liability to compensate, either wholly or in part, if, where the damage is not caused intentionally, liability in full would be disproportionate to the accountability of the person causing the damage or the extent of the damage or the means to prevent it.

VI. – 6:203: Capitalisation and quantification

(1) Compensation is to be awarded as a lump sum unless a good reason requires periodical payment.
(2) National law determines how compensation for personal injury and non-economic loss is to be quantified.

VI. – 6:204: Compensation for injury as such

Injury as such is to be compensated independent of compensation for economic or non-economic loss.

Section 3:
Prevention

VI. – 6:301: Right to prevention

(1) The right to prevention exists only in so far as:
    (a) reparation would not be an adequate alternative remedy; and
    (b) it is reasonable for the person who would be accountable for the causation of the damage to prevent it from occurring.
(2) Where the source of danger is an object or an animal and it is not reasonably possible for the endangered person to avoid the danger the right to prevention includes a right to have the source of danger removed.

VI. – 6:302: Liability for loss in preventing damage

A person who has reasonably incurred expenditure or sustained other loss in order to prevent that person from suffering an impending damage, or in order to limit the extent or severity of damage suffered, has a right to compensation from the person who would have been accountable for the causation of the damage.

Chapter 7:
Ancillary rules

VI. – 7:101: National constitutional laws

The provisions of this Book are to be interpreted and applied in a manner compatible with the constitutional law of the court.

VI. – 7:102: Statutory provisions

National law determines what legal provisions are statutory provisions.

VI. – 7:103: Public law functions and court proceedings

This Book does not govern the liability of a person or body arising from the exercise or omission to exercise public law functions or from performing duties during court proceedings.

VI. – 7:104: Liability of employees, employers, trade unions and employers' associations

This Book does not govern the liability of:

(a) employees (whether to co-employees, employers or third parties) arising in the course of employment;

(b) employers to employees arising in the course of employment; and

(c) trade unions and employers' associations arising in the course of industrial dispute.

VI. – 7:105: Reduction or exclusion of liability to indemnified persons

If a person is entitled from another source to reparation, whether in full or in part, for that person's damage, in particular from an insurer, fund or other body, national law determines whether or not by virtue of that entitlement liability under this Book is limited or excluded.

Book VII
Unjustified enrichment

Chapter 1:
General

VII. – 1:101: Basic rule
(1) A person who obtains an unjustified enrichment which is attributable to another's disadvantage is obliged to that other to reverse the enrichment.
(2) This rule applies only in accordance with the following provisions of this Book.

Chapter 2:
When enrichment unjustified

VII. – 2:101: Circumstances in which an enrichment
is unjustified
(1) An enrichment is unjustified unless:
    (a) the enriched person is entitled as against the disadvantaged person to the enrichment by virtue of a contract or other juridical act, a court order or a rule of law; or
    (b) the disadvantaged person consented freely and without error to the disadvantage.
(2) If the contract or other juridical act, court order or rule of law referred to in paragraph (1)(a) is void or avoided or otherwise rendered ineffective retrospectively, the enriched person is not entitled to the enrichment on that basis.
(3) However, the enriched person is to be regarded as entitled to an enrichment by virtue of a rule of law only if the policy of that rule is that the enriched person is to retain the value of the enrichment.
(4) An enrichment is also unjustified if:
    (a) the disadvantaged person conferred it:

      (i) for a purpose which is not achieved; or

      (ii) with an expectation which is not realised;

(b) the enriched person knew of, or could reasonably be expected to know of, the purpose or expectation; and

(c) the enriched person accepted or could reasonably be assumed to have accepted that the enrichment must be reversed in such circumstances.

VII. – 2:102: Performance of obligation to third person

Where the enriched person obtains the enrichment as a result of the disadvantaged person performing an obligation or a supposed obligation owed by the disadvantaged person to a third person, the enrichment is justified if:

(a) the disadvantaged person performed freely; or

(b) the enrichment was merely the incidental result of performance of the obligation.

VII. – 2:103: Consenting or performing freely

(1) If the disadvantaged person's consent is affected by incapacity, fraud, coercion, threats or unfair exploitation, the disadvantaged person does not consent freely.

(2) If the obligation which is performed is ineffective because of incapacity, fraud, coercion, threats or unfair exploitation, the disadvantaged person does not perform freely.

Chapter 3:
Enrichment and disadvantage

VII. – 3:101: Enrichment

(1) A person is enriched by:

    (a) an increase in assets or a decrease in liabilities;

    (b) receiving a service or having work done; or

    (c) use of another's assets.

(2) In determining whether and to what extent a person obtains an enrichment, no regard is to be had to any disadvantage which that person sustains in exchange for or after the enrichment.

VII. – 3:102: Disadvantage

(1) A person is disadvantaged by:
- (a) a decrease in assets or an increase in liabilities;
- (b) rendering a service or doing work; or
- (c) another's use of that person's assets.

(2) In determining whether and to what extent a person sustains a disadvantage, no regard is to be had to any enrichment which that person obtains in exchange for or after the disadvantage.

Chapter 4:
Attribution

VII. – 4:101: Instances of attribution

An enrichment is attributable to another's disadvantage in particular where:

- (a) an asset of that other is transferred to the enriched person by that other;
- (b) a service is rendered to or work is done for the enriched person by that other;
- (c) the enriched person uses that other's asset, especially where the enriched person infringes the disadvantaged person's rights or legally protected interests;
- (d) an asset of the enriched person is improved by that other; or
- (e) the enriched person is discharged from a liability by that other.

VII. – 4:102: Indirect representation

Where a representative does a juridical act on behalf of a principal but in such a way that the representative is, but the principal is not, a party to the juridical act, any enrichment or disadvantage of the principal which results from the juridical act, or from a performance of obligations under it, is to be regarded as an enrichment or disadvantage of the representative.

VII. – 4:103: Debtor's performance to a non-creditor; onward transfer in good faith

(1) An enrichment is also attributable to another's disadvantage where a debtor confers the enrichment on the enriched person and as a result the disadvantaged person loses a right against the debtor to the same or a like enrichment.

(2) Paragraph (1) applies in particular where a person who is obliged to the disadvantaged person to reverse an unjustified enrichment transfers it to a third person in circumstances in which the debtor has a defence under VII. – 6:101 (Disenrichment).

VII. – 4:104: Ratification of debtor's performance to a non-creditor

(1) Where a debtor purports to discharge a debt by paying a third person, the creditor may ratify that act.

(2) Ratification extinguishes the creditor's right against the debtor to the extent of the payment with the effect that the third person's enrichment is attributable to the creditor's loss of the right against the debtor.

(3) As between the creditor and the third person, ratification does not amount to consent to the loss of the creditor's right against the debtor.

(4) This Article applies correspondingly to performances of non-monetary obligations.

(5) Other rules may exclude the application of this Article if an insolvency or equivalent proceeding has been opened against the debtor before the creditor ratifies.

VII. – 4:105: Attribution resulting from an act of an intervener

(1) An enrichment is also attributable to another's disadvantage where a third person uses an asset of the disadvantaged person without authority so that the disadvantaged person is deprived of the asset and it accrues to the enriched person.

(2) Paragraph (1) applies in particular where, as a result of an intervener's interference with or disposition of goods, the disadvantaged person ceases to be owner of the goods and the enriched person becomes owner, whether by juridical act or rule of law.

VII. – 4:106: Ratification of intervener's acts

(1) A person entitled to an asset may ratify the act of an intervener who purports to dispose of or otherwise uses that asset in a juridical act with a third person.

(2) The ratified act has the same effect as a juridical act by an authorised representative. As between the person ratifying and the intervener, ratification does not amount to consent to the intervener's use of the asset.

VII. – 4:107: Where type or value not identical

An enrichment may be attributable to another's disadvantage even though the enrichment and disadvantage are not of the same type or value.

Chapter 5:
Reversal of enrichment

VII. – 5:101: Transferable enrichment

(1) Where the enrichment consists of a transferable asset, the enriched person reverses the enrichment by transferring the asset to the disadvantaged person.

(2) Instead of transferring the asset, the enriched person may choose to reverse the enrichment by paying its monetary value to the disadvantaged person if a transfer would cause the enriched person unreasonable effort or expense.

(3) If the enriched person is no longer able to transfer the asset, the enriched person reverses the enrichment by paying its monetary value to the disadvantaged person.

(4) However, to the extent that the enriched person has obtained a substitute in exchange, the substitute is the enrichment to be reversed if:
   (a) the enriched person is in good faith at the time of disposal or loss and the enriched person so chooses; or
   (b) the enriched person is not in good faith at the time of disposal or loss, the disadvantaged person so chooses and the choice is not inequitable.

(5) The enriched person is in good faith if that person neither knew nor could reasonably be expected to know that the enrichment was or was likely to become unjustified.

VII. – 5:102: Non-transferable enrichment

(1) Where the enrichment does not consist of a transferable asset, the enriched person reverses the enrichment by paying its monetary value to the disadvantaged person.

(2) The enriched person is not liable to pay more than any saving if the enriched person:

(a) did not consent to the enrichment; or

(b) was in good faith.

(3) However, where the enrichment was obtained under an agreement which fixed a price or value for the enrichment, the enriched person is at least liable to pay that sum if the agreement was void or voidable for reasons which were not material to the fixing of the price.

(4) Paragraph (3) does not apply so as to increase liability beyond the monetary value of the enrichment.

VII. – 5:103: Monetary value of an enrichment; saving

(1) The monetary value of an enrichment is the sum of money which a provider and a recipient with a real intention of reaching an agreement would lawfully have agreed as its price. Expenditure of a service provider which the agreement would require the recipient to reimburse is to be regarded as part of the price.

(2) A saving is the decrease in assets or increase in liabilities which the enriched person would have sustained if the enrichment had not been obtained.

VII. – 5:104: Fruits and use of an enrichment

(1) Reversal of the enrichment extends to the fruits and use of the enrichment or, if less, any saving resulting from the fruits or use.

(2) However, if the enriched person obtains the fruits or use in bad faith, reversal of the enrichment extends to the fruits and use even if the saving is less than the value of the fruits or use.

Chapter 6:
Defences

VII. – 6:101: Disenrichment

(1) The enriched person is not liable to reverse the enrichment to the extent that the enriched person has sustained a disadvantage by disposing of the enrichment or otherwise (disenrichment), unless the enriched person would have been disenriched even if the enrichment had not been obtained.

(2) However, a disenrichment is to be disregarded to the extent that:
  (a) the enriched person has obtained a substitute;
  (b) the enriched person was not in good faith at the time of disenrichment, unless:
    (i) the disadvantaged person would also have been disenriched even if the enrichment had been reversed; or
    (ii) the enriched person was in good faith at the time of enrichment, the disenrichment was sustained before performance of the obligation to reverse the enrichment was due and the disenrichment resulted from the realisation of a risk for which the enriched person is not to be regarded as responsible;

  or

  (c) VII. – 5:102 (Non-transferable enrichment) paragraph (3) applies.

(3) Where the enriched person has a defence under this Article as against the disadvantaged person as a result of a disposal to a third person, any right of the disadvantaged person against that third person is unaffected.

VII. – 6:102: Juridical acts in good faith with third parties

The enriched person is also not liable to reverse the enrichment if:

(a) in exchange for that enrichment the enriched person confers another enrichment on a third person; and

(b) the enriched person is still in good faith at that time.

VII. – 6:103: Illegality

Where a contract or other juridical act under which an enrichment is obtained is void or avoided because of an infringement of a fundamental principle (within the meaning of II – 7:301 (Contracts infringing fundamental principles)) or mandatory rule of law, the enriched person is not liable to reverse the enrichment to the extent that the reversal would contravene the policy underlying the principle or rule.

Chapter 7:
Relation to other legal rules

VII. – 7:101: Other private law rights to recover
(1) The legal consequences of an enrichment which is obtained by virtue of a contract or other juridical act are governed by other rules if those rules grant or exclude a right to reversal of an enrichment, whether on withdrawal, termination, price reduction or otherwise.
(2) This Book does not address the proprietary effect of a right to reversal of an enrichment.
(3) This Book does not affect any other right to recover arising under contractual or other rules of private law.

VII. – 7:102: Concurrent obligations
(1) Where the disadvantaged person has both:
(a) a right under this Book to the reversal of an unjustified enrichment; and
(b) (i) a right to reparation for the disadvantage (whether against the enriched person or a third party); or
(ii) a right to recover under other rules of private law as a result of the unjustified enrichment,
the satisfaction of one of the rights reduces the other right by the same amount.
(2) The same applies where a person uses an asset of the disadvantaged person so that it accrues to another and under this Book:
(a) the user is liable to the disadvantaged person in respect of the use of the asset; and
(b) the recipient is liable to the disadvantaged person in respect of the increase in assets.

VII. – 7:103: Public law claims
This Book does not determine whether it applies to enrichments which a person or body obtains or confers in the exercise of public law functions.

Advanced electronic signature
See under "electronic signature".

Arbitral tribunal
See "Court".

Assets
"Assets" means anything of economic value, including property; rights having a monetary value; and goodwill.

Assignment
"Assignment", in relation to a right, means the transfer of the right by one person, the "assignor", to another, "the assignee".

Authorisation
The "authorisation" of a representative is the granting or maintaining of the representative's authority.

Authority
"Authority", in relation to a representative acting for a principal, is the power to affect the principal's legal position.

Avoidance
"Avoidance" of a juridical act or legal relationship is the process whereby a party or, as the case may be, a court invokes a ground of invalidity so as to make the act or relationship, which has been valid until that point, retrospectively ineffective from the beginning.

Barter, contract for
A contract for the "barter" of goods is a contract under which each party undertakes to transfer the ownership of goods, either immedi-

ately on conclusion of the contract or at some future time, in return for the transfer of ownership of other goods. Each party is considered to be the buyer with respect to the goods to be received and the seller with respect to the goods or assets to be transferred.

Benevolent intervention in another's affairs
"Benevolent intervention in another's affairs" is the process (sometimes known as negotiorum gestio) whereby a person, the intervener, acts with the predominant intention of benefiting another, the principal, but without being authorised or bound to do so.

Business
"Business" means any natural or legal person, irrespective of whether publicly or privately owned, who is acting for purposes relating to the person's self-employed trade, work or profession, even if the person does not intend to make a profit in the course of the activity.

Capitalisation of interest
"Capitalisation of interest" is the process whereby accrued interest is added to capital.

Claim
A "claim" is a demand for something based on the assertion of a right.

Claimant
A "claimant" is a person who makes, or who has grounds for making, a claim.

Clause
"Clause" refers to a provision in a document. A clause, unlike a "term", is always in textual form.

Co-debtorship for security purposes
A "co-debtorship for security purposes" is an obligation owed by two or more debtors in which one of the debtors, the security provider, assumes the obligation primarily for purposes of security towards the creditor.

Commercial agency

A "commercial agency" is the legal relationship arising from a contract under which one party, the commercial agent, agrees to act on a continuing basis as a self-employed intermediary to negotiate or to conclude contracts on behalf of another party, the principal, and the principal agrees to remunerate the agent for those activities.

Compensation

"Compensation" means reparation in money.

Condition

A "condition" is a provision which makes a legal relationship or effect depend on the occurrence or non-occurrence of an uncertain future event. A condition may be suspensive or resolutive.

Conduct

"Conduct" means voluntary behaviour of any kind, verbal or non-verbal. It includes a single act or a number of acts, behaviour of a negative or passive nature (such as accepting something without protest or not doing something) and behaviour of a continuing or intermittent nature (such as exercising control over something).

Construction, contract for

A "contract for construction" is a contract under which one party, the constructor, undertakes to construct something for another party, the client, or to materially alter an existing building or other immovable structure for a client.

Consumer

A "consumer" means any natural person who is acting primarily for purposes which are not related to his or her trade, business or profession.

Consumer contract for sale

A "consumer contract for sale" is a contract under which a business sells goods to a consumer.

Contract

A "contract" is an agreement which gives rise to, or is intended to give rise to, a binding legal relationship or which has, or is intended to have, some other legal effect. It is a bilateral or multilateral juridical act.

Contractual obligation

A "contractual obligation" is an obligation which arises from a contract, whether from an express term or an implied term or by operation of a rule of law imposing an obligation on a contracting party as such.

Contractual relationship

A "contractual relationship" is a legal relationship resulting from a contract.

Corporeal

"Corporeal", in relation to property, means having a physical existence in solid, liquid or gaseous form.

Costs

"Costs" includes expenses.

Counter-performance

A "counter-performance" is a performance which is due in exchange for another performance.

Court

"Court" includes an arbitral tribunal.

Creditor

A "creditor" is a person who has a right to performance of an obligation, whether monetary or non-monetary, by another person, the debtor.

Damage

"Damage" means any type of detrimental effect. It includes loss and injury.

Damages

"Damages" means a sum of money to which a person may be entitled, or which a person may be awarded by a court, as compensation for some specified type of damage.

Debtor

A "debtor" is a person who has an obligation, whether monetary or non-monetary, to another person, the creditor.

Defence

A "defence" to a claim is a legal objection or a factual argument, other than a mere denial of an element which the claimant has to prove, which if asserted defeats the claim in whole or in part.

Delivery

"Delivery" to a person, for the purposes of any obligation to deliver corporeal movable property, means handing it over or otherwise transferring physical control over it to that person, or taking steps to ensure that that person can obtain physical control over it.

Dependent personal security

A "dependent personal security" is an obligation by a security provider which is assumed in favour of a creditor in order to secure a present or future obligation of the debtor owed to the creditor and performance of which is due only if, and to the extent that, performance of the latter obligation is due.

Design, contract for

A "contract for design" is a contract under which one party, the designer, undertakes to design for another party, the client, an immovable structure which is to be constructed by or on behalf of the client or a movable or incorporeal thing or service which is to be constructed or performed by or on behalf of the client.

Distribution contract

A "distribution contract" is a contract under which one party, the supplier, agrees to supply the other party, the distributor, with products on a continuing basis and the distributor agrees to purchase them, or to take and pay for them, and to supply them to others in the distributor's name and on the distributor's behalf.

Distributorship
A "distributorship" is the legal relationship arising from a distribution contract.

Divided obligation
An obligation owed by two or more debtors is a "divided obligation" when each debtor is bound to render only part of the performance and the creditor may require from each debtor only that debtor's part.

Divided right
A right to performance held by two or more creditors is a "divided right" when the debtor owes each creditor only that creditor's share and each creditor may require performance only of that creditor's share.

Durable medium
A "durable medium" means any material on which information is stored so that it is accessible for future reference for a period of time adequate to the purposes of the information, and which allows the unchanged reproduction of this information.

Duty
A person has a "duty" to do something if the person is bound to do it or expected to do it according to an applicable normative standard of conduct. A duty may or may not be owed to a specific creditor. A duty is not necessarily an aspect of a legal relationship. There is not necessarily a sanction for breach of a duty. All obligations are duties, but not all duties are obligations.

Economic loss
See "Loss".

Electronic

"Electronic" means relating to technology with electrical, digital, magnetic, wireless, optical, electromagnetic, or similar capabilities.

Electronic signature

An "electronic signature" means data in electronic form which are attached to, or logically associated with, other data and which serve as a method of authentication.

An "advanced electronic signature" means an electronic signature which is (a) uniquely linked to the signatory; (b) capable of identifying the signatory; (c) created using means which can be maintained under the signatory's sole control; and (d) linked to the data to which it relates in such a manner that any subsequent change of the data is detectable.

Franchise

A "franchise" is the legal relationship arising from a contract under which one party, the franchisor, grants the other party, the franchisee, in exchange for remuneration, the right to conduct a business (franchise business) within the franchisor's network for the purposes of supplying certain products on the franchisee's behalf and in the franchisee's name, and whereby the franchisee has the right and the obligation to use the franchisor's trade name or trade mark or other intellectual property rights, know-how and business method.

Fraudulent

A misrepresentation is "fraudulent" if it is made with knowledge or belief that it is false and is intended to induce the recipient to make a mistake to the recipient's prejudice. A non-disclosure is fraudulent if it is intended to induce the person from whom the information is withheld to make a mistake to that person's prejudice.

Fundamental non-performance

A non-performance of a contractual obligation is "fundamental" if (a) it substantially deprives the creditor of what the creditor was entitled to expect under the contract, as applied to the whole or relevant part of the performance, unless at the time of conclusion of the contract the debtor did not foresee and could not reasonably be expected to have foreseen that result; or (b) it is intentional or reckless and gives the creditor reason to believe that the debtor's future performance cannot be relied on.

Global security
A "global security" is a security which is assumed in order to secure all the debtor's obligations towards the creditor or the debit balance of a current account or a security of a similar extent.

Good faith and fair dealing
"Good faith and fair dealing" refers to an objective standard of conduct. "Good faith" on its own may refer to a subjective mental attitude, often characterised by an absence of knowledge of something which, if known, would adversely affect the morality of what is done.

Goods
"Goods" means corporeal movables. It includes ships, vessels, hovercraft or aircraft, space objects, animals, liquids and gases. See also "movables".

Gross negligence
There is "gross negligence" if a person is guilty of a profound failure to take such care as is manifestly required in the circumstances.

Handwritten signature
A "handwritten signature" means the name of, or sign representing, a person written by that person's own hand for the purpose of authentication.

Immovable property
"Immovable property" means land and anything so attached to land as not to be subject to change of place by usual human action.

Incorporeal
"Incorporeal", in relation to property, means not having a physical existence in solid, liquid or gaseous form.

Indemnify

"Indemnify" means make such payment to a person as will ensure that that person suffers no loss.

Independent personal security

An "independent personal security" is an obligation by a security provider which is assumed in favour of a creditor for the purposes of security and which is expressly or impliedly declared not to depend upon another person's obligation owed to the creditor.

Ineffective

"Ineffective" in relation to a contract or other juridical act means having no effect, whether that state of affairs is temporary or permanent, general or restricted.

Injured person

An "injured person" for the purposes of Book VI is a person who has suffered damage. The term is not, unless the context so requires, confined to a person who has suffered personal injury.

Insolvency administrator

An "insolvency administrator" is a person or body, including one appointed on an interim basis, authorised in an insolvency proceeding to administer the reorganisation or liquidation of the insolvent person's assets or affairs.

Insolvency proceeding

An "insolvency proceeding" means a collective judicial or administrative proceeding, including an interim proceeding, in which the assets and affairs of a person who is, or who is believed to be, insolvent are subject to control or supervision by a court or other competent authority for the purpose of reorganisation or liquidation.

Intangible

See "Incorporeal".

Interest
"Interest" means simple interest without any assumption that it will be capitalised from time to time.

Invalid
"Invalid" in relation to a juridical act or legal relationship means that the act or relationship is void or has been avoided.

Joint obligation
An obligation owed by two or more debtors is a "joint obligation" when all the debtors are bound to render the performance together and the creditor may require it only from all of them.

Joint right
A right to performance held by two or more creditors is a "joint right" when the debtor must perform to all the creditors and any creditor may require performance only for the benefit of all.

Juridical act
A "juridical act" is any statement or agreement or declaration of intention, whether express or implied from conduct, which has or is intended to have legal effect as such. It may be unilateral, bilateral or multilateral.

Keeper
A "keeper", in relation to an animal, vehicle or substance, is the person who has the beneficial use or physical control of it for that person's own benefit and who exercises the right to control it or its use.

Lease (of goods)
A "lease" of goods is the legal relationship arising from a contract under which one party, the lessor, undertakes to provide the other party, the lessee, with a temporary right of use of goods in exchange for rent. The rent may be in the form of money or other value.

Liable
A person is "liable" for damage if the person is under an obligation to make reparation for the damage.

Loss
"Loss" includes economic and non-economic loss. "Economic loss" includes loss of income or profit, burdens incurred and a reduction in the value of property. "Non-economic loss" includes pain and suffering and impairment of the quality of life.

Mandate
The "mandate" of a representative is the authorisation and instruction given by the principal, as modified by any subsequent direction.

Mandate contract
A "mandate" contract is a contract under which one party, the representative, has a mandate to conclude a contract between another party, the principal, and a third party or otherwise affect the legal position of the principal in relation to a third party.

Merger of debts
A "merger of debts" means that the attributes of debtor and creditor are united in the same person in the same capacity.

Merger clause
A "merger clause" is a clause in a contract document stating that the document embodies all the terms of the contract.

Movables
"Movables" means corporeal and incorporeal property other than immovable property.

Must
"Must", when used of a person (e. g. "the lessor must"), means that the person has an obligation unless otherwise indicated. "Must", when used of a thing (e. g. "the goods must"), indicates a requirement.

Negligence

There is "negligence" if a person does not meet the standard of care which could reasonably be expected in the circumstances.

Non-economic loss

See "Loss".

Non-performance

"Non-performance", in relation to an obligation, means any failure to perform the obligation, whether or not excused. It includes delayed performance and defective performance.

Notice

"Notice" includes the communication of a promise, offer, acceptance or other juridical act.

Obligation

An "obligation" is a duty to perform which one party to a legal relationship, the debtor, owes to another party, the creditor.

Ownership

"Ownership" is the most absolute right a person, the owner, can have over property, including the exclusive right, so far as consistent with applicable laws or rights granted by the owner, to use, enjoy, modify, destroy, dispose of and recover the property.

Performance

"Performance", in relation to an obligation, is the doing by the debtor of what is to be done under the obligation or the not doing by the debtor of what is not to be done.

Person

"Person" means a natural or legal person.

Prescription

"Prescription", in relation to the right to performance of an obligation, is the legal effect whereby the lapse of a prescribed period of time entitles the debtor to refuse performance.

Presumption
A "presumption" means that the existence of a known fact allows the deduction that an unknown fact should be held true, until the contrary is demonstrated.

Price
The "price" is what is due by the debtor under a monetary obligation, in exchange for something supplied or provided, expressed in a currency which the law recognises as such.

Processing, contract for
A "contract for processing" is a contract under which one party, the processor, undertakes to perform a service on an existing movable or incorporeal thing or to an immovable structure for another party, the client (except where the service is construction work on an existing building or other immovable structure).

Producer
"Producer" includes, in the case of something made, the maker or manufacturer and in the case of raw material, the person who abstracts or wins it.

Property
"Property" means anything which can be owned: it may be movable or immovable, corporeal or incorporeal.

Proprietary security
A "proprietary security" covers security rights in all kinds of property, whether movable or immovable, corporeal or incorporeal.

Ranking
"Ranking", in relation to claims, means putting the claims in an order of preference or subordination.

Ratify
"Ratify" means confirm with legal effect.

Reasonable
What is "reasonable" is to be objectively ascertained, having regard to the nature and purpose of what is being done, to the circumstances of the case and to any relevant usages and practices.

Recklessness
A person is "reckless" if the person knows of an obvious and serious risk of proceeding in a certain way but nonetheless voluntarily proceeds without caring whether or not the risk materialises.

Reparation
"Reparation" means compensation or another appropriate measure to reinstate the person suffering damage in the position that person would have been in had the damage not occurred.

Representative
A "representative" is a person who has authority to affect the legal position of another person, the principal, in relation to a third party by acting on behalf of the principal.

Requirement
A "requirement" is something which is needed before a particular result follows or a particular right can be exercised.

Resolutive
A condition is "resolutive" if it causes a legal relationship or effect to come to an end when the condition is satisfied.

Revocation
"Revocation", means (a) in relation to a juridical act, its recall by a person or persons having the power to recall it, so that it no longer has effect; and (b) in relation to something conferred or transferred, its recall, by a person or persons having power to recall it, so that it comes back or must be returned to the person who conferred it or transferred it.

Right

"Right", depending on the context, may mean (a) the correlative of an obligation or liability (as in "a significant imbalance in the parties' rights and obligations arising under the contract"); (b) a proprietary right (such as the right of ownership); (c) a personality right (as in a right to respect for dignity, or a right to liberty and privacy); (d) a legally conferred power to bring about a particular result (as in "the right to avoid" a contract); (e) an entitlement to a particular remedy (as in a right to have performance of a contractual obligation judicially ordered); or (f) an entitlement to do or not to do something affecting another person's legal position without exposure to adverse consequences (as in a "right to withhold performance of the reciprocal obligation").

Sale, contract for

A contract for the "sale" of goods is a contract under which one party, the seller, undertakes to another party, the buyer, to transfer the ownership of the goods to the buyer, or to a third person, either immediately on conclusion of the contract or at some future time, and the buyer undertakes to pay the price.

Services, contract for

A "contract for services" is a contract under which one party, the service provider, undertakes to supply a service to the other party, the client.

Set-off

"Set-off" is the process by which a debtor may reduce the amount owed to the creditor by an amount owed to the debtor by the creditor.

Signature

"Signature" includes a handwritten signature, an electronic signature or an advanced electronic signature.

Solidary obligation

An obligation owed by two or more debtors is a "solidary obligation" when all the debtors are bound to render one and the same performance and the creditor may require it from any one of them until there has been full performance.

Solidary right

A right to performance held by two or more creditors is a "solidary right" when any of the creditors may require full performance from the debtor and the debtor may render performance to any of the creditors.

Standard terms

"Standard terms" are terms which have been formulated in advance for several transactions involving different parties, and which have not been individually negotiated by the parties.

Storage, contract for

A "contract for storage" is a contract under which one party, the storer, undertakes to store a movable or incorporeal thing for another party, the client.

Subrogation

"Subrogation" is the process by which a person who has made a payment or performance to another person acquires by operation of law that person's rights against a third person.

Substitution

"Substitution" of a new debtor is the process whereby, with the agreement of the creditor, a third party is substituted for the debtor, the contract remaining in force.

Supply

To "supply" goods means to make them available to another person, whether by sale, gift, barter, lease or other means; to "supply" services means to provide them to another person, whether or not for a price. Unless otherwise stated, "supply" covers the supply of goods and services.

Suspensive
A condition is "suspensive" if it prevents a legal relationship or effect from coming into existence until the condition is satisfied.

Term
"Term" means any provision, express or implied, of a contract or other juridical act, of a law, of a court order or of a legally binding usage or practice; it includes a condition.

Termination
"Termination", in relation to an existing right, obligation or legal relationship, means bringing it to an end with prospective effect except in so far as otherwise provided.

Textual form
In "textual form", in relation to a statement, means expressed in alphabetical or other intelligible characters by means of any support which permits reading, recording of the information contained in the statement and its reproduction in tangible form.

Transfer of contractual position
"Transfer of contractual position" is the process whereby, with the agreement of all three parties, a new party replaces an existing party to a contract, taking over the rights, obligations and entire contractual position of that party.

Treatment, contract for
A "contract for treatment" is a contract under which one party, the treatment provider, undertakes to provide medical treatment for another party, the patient, or to provide any other service in order to change the physical or mental condition of a person.

Unjustified enrichment
An "unjustified enrichment" is an enrichment which is not legally justified, with the result that, if it is obtained by one person and is attributable to another's disadvantage, the first person may, subject to legal rules and restrictions, be obliged to that other to reverse the enrichment.

Valid

"Valid", in relation to a juridical act or legal relationship, means that the act or relationship is not void and has not been avoided.

Void

"Void", in relation to a juridical act or legal relationship, means that the act or relationship is automatically of no effect from the beginning.

Voidable

"Voidable", in relation to a juridical act or legal relationship, means that the act or relationship is subject to a defect which renders it liable to be avoided and hence rendered retrospectively of no effect.

Withdraw

A right to "withdraw" from a contract or other juridical act is a right to terminate the legal relationship arising from the contract or other juridical act, without having to give any reason for so doing and without incurring any liability for non-performance of the obligations arising from that contract or juridical act. The right is exercisable only within a limited period (in these rules, normally 14 days) and is designed to give the entitled party (normally a consumer) an additional time for reflection. The restitutionary and other effects of exercising the right are determined by the rules regulating it.

Withholding performance

"Withholding performance", as a remedy for non-performance of a contractual obligation, means that one party to a contract may decline to render due counter-performance until the other party has tendered performance or has performed.

Writing

In "writing" means in textual form, on paper or another durable medium and in directly legible characters.

Annex 2
Computation of time

(1) Subject to the following provisions of this Annex:

    (a) a period expressed in hours starts at the beginning of the first hour and ends with the expiry of the last hour of the period;

    (b) a period expressed in days starts at the beginning of the first hour of the first day and ends with the expiry of the last hour of the last day of the period;

    (c) a period expressed in weeks, months or years starts at the beginning of the first hour of the first day of the period, and ends with the expiry of the last hour of whichever day in the last week, month or year is the same day of the week, or falls on the same date, as the day from which the period runs. If, in a period expressed in months or in years, the day on which it should expire does not occur in the last month, the period ends with the expiry of the last hour of the last day of that month;

    (d) if a period includes part of a month, the month is considered to have thirty days for the purpose of calculating the length of the part.

(2) Where a period is to be calculated from a specified event or action, then:

    (a) if the period is expressed in hours, the hour during which the event occurs or the action takes place is not considered to fall within the period in question; and

    (b) if the period is expressed in days, weeks, months or years, the day during which the event occurs or the action takes place is not considered to fall within the period in question.

(3) Where a period is to be calculated from a specified time, then:
   (a) if the period is expressed in hours, the first hour of the period is considered to begin at the specified time; and
   (b) if the period is expressed in days, weeks, months or years, the day during which the specified time arrives is not considered to fall within the period in question.

(4) The periods concerned include Saturdays, Sundays and public holidays, save where these are expressly excepted or where the periods are expressed in working days.

(5) Where the last day of a period expressed otherwise than in hours is a Saturday, Sunday or public holiday at the place where a prescribed act is to be done, the period ends with the expiry of the last hour of the following working day. This provision does not apply to periods calculated retroactively from a given date or event.

(6) Any period of two days or more is regarded as including at least two working days.

(7) Where a person sends another person a document which sets a period of time within which the addressee has to reply or take other action but does not state when the period is to begin, then, in the absence of indications to the contrary, the period is calculated from the date stated as the date of the document or, if no date is stated, from the moment the document reaches the addressee.

(8) In this Annex:
"public holiday" with reference to a member state, or part of a member state, of the European Union means any day designated as such for that state or part in a list published in the official journal;
"working days" means all days other than Saturdays, Sundays and public holidays.

Index

sellier.
european law
publishers

EC Contract Law
made accessible

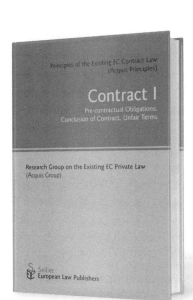

The Principles of the Existing EC Contract Law, commonly called the Acquis
Principles (ACQP), are a systematic
arrangement of the existing EC law in a
structure, which allows to identify com-
monalities, contradictions and gaps in
the Acquis Communautaire. The Acquis
Principles help to elucidate the common structures to be discovered within
the large and not throughout coherent
patchwork of existing EC private law.

Yes, I would like to order:

quantity

☐ **Contract I:**
Pre-contractual Obligations,
Conclusion of Contract, Unfair Terms
Principles of the Existing EC Contract Law
(Acquis Principles)
€ 120.- ISBN 978-3-86653-023-2

I'd like to stay informed about your publications
by email. Please send your email newsletter to:

My Address

....

....

....

....

Date, Signature

Free shipping for order value higher than 30 EUR. This order
can be cancelled within 2 weeks after reception of goods.

059

sellier.elp · Geibelstraße 8 · D–81679 München · Tel. + 49·89·451 084 58-0 · Fax + 49·89·451 084 58-9 · www.sellier.de

Steps towards a common European private law

The Study Group on a European Civil Code has taken upon itself the task of drafting common European principles for the most important aspects of the law of obligations and for certain parts of the law of property in movables. The results seek to advance the process of Europeanisation of private law. Among other topics the series covers

- sales,
- service contracts,
- distribution contracts,
- personal security,
- lease of goods,
- benevolent intervention in another's affairs,
- non-contractual liability arising out of damage caused to another,
- unjustified enrichment,
- acquisition and loss of ownership in movables,
- proprietary security rights in movable assets,
- and trust law.

These principles furnish each of the national jurisdictions a grid reference. They could be agreed upon by the parties within the framework of the rules of private international law. They may provide a stimulus to both the national and European legislator for moulding private law.

sellier.elp · Geibelstraße 8 · D–81679 München · Tel + 49 · 89 · 451 08 4 58-0 · Fax + 49 · 89 · 451 08 4 58-9 · www.sellier.de

sellier.
european law
publishers

Yes, I would like to order:

Complete Series
App. 14 volumes

Benevolent Intervention in Another's Affairs
Christian von Bar
March 2006. XXX, 417 pp.
€ 120.- (series price € 93.-)
ISBN 978-3-935808-40-8

Commercial Agency, Franchise and Distribution Contracts
Martijn Hesselink et al
March 2006. XLI, 371 pp.
€ 120.- (series price € 93.-)
ISBN 978-3-935808-43-9

Service Contracts
Maurits Barendrecht et al
November 2006. LX, 1034 pp.
€ 295.- (series price € 221.-)
ISBN 978-3-935808-41-5

Personal Security
Ulrich Drobnig
June 2007. XXXII, 567 pp.
€ 225.- (series price € 161.-)
ISBN 978-3-935808-42-2

Lease of Goods
Kåre Lilleholt et al
Dec. 2007. XXXVIII, 367 pp.
€ 120.- (series price € 93.-)
ISBN 978-3-935808-64-4

Sales
Ewoud Hondius et al
March 2008. App. 400 pp.
€ 120.- (series price € 93.-)
ISBN 978-3-935808-61-3

Non-Contractual Liability Arising out of Damage Caused to Another
Christian von Bar
2008. App. 650 pp.
€ 225.- (series price € 161.-)
ISBN 978-3-935808-63-7

Unjustified Enrichment
S. Swann/C. von Bar
2009. App. 450 pp.
€ 120.- (series price € 93.-)
ISBN 978-3-935808-62-0

Proprietary Security Rights in Movable Assets
Ulrich Drobnig
2009. App. 300 pp.
€ 120.- (series price € 93.-)
ISBN 978-3-935808-65-1

Loan Agreements
Edgar du Perron
2009. App. 400 pp.
€ 120.- (series price € 93.-)
ISBN 978-3-935808-67-5

Acquisition and Loss of Ownership in Movables
Brigitta Lurger/Wolfgang Faber
2009. App. 300 pp.
€ 120.- (series price € 93.-)
ISBN 978-3-935808-66-8

Donation
Martin Schmidt-Kessel
2009. App. 350 pp.
€ 120.- (series price € 93.-)
ISBN 978-3-86653-051-5

Mandate Contracts
Marco Loos/Odavia Bueno Diaz
2009. App. 300 pp.
€ 120.- (series price € 93.-)
ISBN 978-3-86653-052-2

Trust
Stephen Swann
2009. App. 600 pp.
€ 225.- (series price € 161.-)
ISBN 978-3-935808-68-2

My Address

....

....

....

....

Date, Signature

....

Prices are subject to change. Free shipping. This order can be cancelled within 2 weeks after reception of goods.

059

sellier.elp · Geibelstraße 8 · D–81679 München · Tel + 49·89·451 084 58-0 · Fax + 49·89·451 084 58-9 · www.sellier.de